Routledge Revivals

Behind the Poem

Published in 1988, this book is a teacher's eye view of how children come to write and rewrite poems, and of how they make aesthetic choices in their writing. Drawing on over twenty years' experience of teaching poetry in primary and secondary schools, Robert Hull presents a detailed account of the process of writing poetry in the classroom. The reader is invited, almost in confidence, to be witness to a skilled teacher's planning, recognition, and definition of children's emergent understanding and expertise. The author adopts a non-behaviourist model which stresses difficulty and uncertainty, rejecting a simplistic assumption of linear progression, predictability of outcome, and short-term results. The many examples of poems written by the children demonstrate in a very vivid and impressive way the value of this approach. All teachers, not just of poetry, will find this a fascinating and informed study, and an inspiration for their own work in the classroom.

Behind the Poem
A Teacher's View of Children Writing

Robert Hull

First published in 1988
by Routledge

This edition first published in 2018 by Routledge
2 Park Square, Milton Park, Abingdon, Oxon, OX14 4RN
and by Routledge
711 Third Avenue, New York, NY 10017

Routledge is an imprint of the Taylor & Francis Group, an informa business

© 1988 Robert Hull

All rights reserved. No part of this book may be reprinted or reproduced or utilised in any form or by any electronic, mechanical, or other means, now known or hereafter invented, including photocopying and recording, or in any information storage or retrieval system, without permission in writing from the publishers.

Publisher's Note
The publisher has gone to great lengths to ensure the quality of this reprint but points out that some imperfections in the original copies may be apparent.

Disclaimer
The publisher has made every effort to trace copyright holders and welcomes correspondence from those they have been unable to contact.

A Library of Congress record exists under LCCN: 87024775

ISBN 13: 978-1-138-54121-4 (hbk)
ISBN 13: 978-1-351-01105-1 (ebk)
ISBN 13: 978-1-138-54122-1 (pbk)

Behind the Poem
A teacher's view of children writing

ROBERT HULL

Routledge
London and New York

First published in 1988 by
Routledge
11 New Fetter Lane, London EC4P 4EE

Published in the USA by
Routledge
in association with Routledge, Chapman & Hall, Inc.
29 West 35th Street, New York NY 10001

© 1988 Robert Hull

Typeset by Times Graphics

All rights reserved. No part of this book may be reprinted or
reproduced or utilized in any form or by any electronic, mechanical or
other means, now known or hereafter invented, including photocopying
and recording, or in any information storage or retrieval system,
without permission in writing from the publishers.

British Library Cataloguing in Publication Data
Hull, Robert
    Behind the poem: a teacher's view of children writing.
    1. Poetics – Study and teaching –
    Great Britain 2. English literature – Study and teaching – Great Britain
    I. Title
    808.1   PN1101

    ISBN 0 415 00701 1

Library of Congress Cataloging-in-Publication Data
Hull, Robert.
    Behind the poem.
    Bibliography: p.
    Includes index.
    1. Children as authors. 2. Poetry – Study and teaching.
    3. Children's writings, English. I. Title.
    PN171.C5H85 1988   808.1'088054   87-24775
    ISBN 0 415 00701 1 (pbk.)

Contents

Preface	vii
Acknowledgements	xiii

Part 1 Introduction

1 'How do I get them to write poems?'	2

Part 2 Process

2 A new class	16
3 New subjects	51

Part 3 Dialogue

4 Children's 'autonomy'	88
5 Intervention	115

Part 4 Context

6 Literary models	140
7 The world out there	167
8 Other contexts	187

Part 5 Relations

9 Products and relations	222
10 'But is it poetry?'	243
Notes	259
Index	264

Preface

At the end of his *Prospect and Retrospect - Selected Essays,* James Britton says that he sees the 1980s as 'the decade of the teacher'; we have finally recognized that 'teaching consists of moment-by-moment interactive behaviour, behaviour that can only spring from inner conviction'.[1] Many teachers would find it odd that such a truism has had to wait more than a moment or two for recognition. But Britton is right, of course; teacher-trainers, writers on education, academics, and educationists have usually had their eyes on weightier issues than how to get the class settled down and listening properly. Britton believed, in the words of the Quaker Rufus Jones, in 'quiet processes and small circles, in which vital and transforming events will take place'.[2] Perhaps they are already taking place, as he believed, and perhaps the classroom is becoming as interesting intellectually as psychology of education, history of education, philosophy of education, sociology of education, curriculum development, philosophy and theory, research and evaluation, and contemporary sociology of the school (the current contents list of an education publisher's catalogue, with 'Classroom skills and methods' in ninth place).

Others would still be sceptical. In a *TES* article in October 1985, Mary Jane Drummond is quoted as saying that the authors of HMI, DES, and LEA documents degrade good practice by treating it as a thing, instantly recognisable by the *cognoscenti* (of a certain rank and above) instead of regarding it as a series of actions and incidents between live human beings in real schools with all the attendant messiness and hurly-burly of classroom life.[3]

In consequence, teachers' experiences are 'constantly devalued... Talking shop should be respected not ridiculed, and teachers' anecdotes about children and school life should be honoured.'[4] My own sense of it, out of twenty-odd years of teaching and conference-going and course-attending, is that she is right, and that there is still a deeply institutionalized reluctance to get down to exactly what does happen to ordinary people in dull rooms on cold mornings. What actually happens does not appear on agendas; it becomes insidiously defined as trivial and time-consuming. Our concerns are the curriculum, the course. What we talk about is GCSE, a new GRIST programme, a TVEI initiative.

I taught for eighteen months or so in a hut that finally appeared on regional television. Word had spread about the holes in the floor and the walls, the window catches that didn't work, the two doors that didn't close, and the ancient heater that often gave up. Apart from the bizarreness of its appearance and indeed its existence, it was a conspicuously difficult place to teach in. But what is interesting, in retrospect, is how difficult – or rather impossible – it was for our teachers' view of this grotesque workplace to be placed on any agenda, formal or informal. Not the agendas of department meetings, nor those of staff meetings, which were more to do with things like 'the guiding principle of the school in the last decade', new management styles, how to perform school visits, and so on. One felt that children could go on sitting around in their coats for years going numb with cold, watching the repair man wrestle the metal cage off the heater and set to for half an hour making so much noise they couldn't concentrate even if they hadn't been frozen, and that it would be bad form to mention it publicly too often. The mean spirit of the hut had to be placated by silence, it seemed, and there was a macho sense that you had to prove yourself as a teacher by surviving there, not bleating.

Perhaps the quasi-reverential neglect that the hut inspired in management was due to its being seen as not having quite as

Preface ix

much to do with education as had other truly urgent things. More essentially related to schooling were interviews with parents, governors' meetings and staff meetings, falling rolls, the new house system or the new year system, parents' evenings, visits from famous poets and television producers and politicians. By comparison the classroom was simply not visible enough; it lacked profile.

It is with the aim of making classrooms more visible that teachers have begun to write about them. Books by schoolteachers were a rarity on university and college bookshop shelves a decade ago. One reason for their appearance is the urgent need now felt by many teachers for accounts of the classroom to give some indication of what they actually do and intend, and how they feel. This book is written with the same concern in mind. The basic assumption I make is that the 'theory' of teaching starts with the practice of teachers as they know or recall their own work in the classroom; that the theory of teaching is the theory of teachers reflecting on their experiences, not the 'theory' that traditionally has been given to them from sociology, philosophy, psychology, and history of education. That is, it really is the theory of teaching, not of 'education'. The latter may be a necessary discipline in its own terms, refracting into teaching broader truths – about society, history, children's minds – of which teaching needs to take account. But the absorption of the study of teaching by 'education' has produced much literature that can only masquerade as literature about teaching; its true interests are elsewhere.

There are dangers in teachers' books too, of course. They may seem too personal and anecdotal, not theoretical or indeed thoughtful enough. But the pressing need for teachers and students to be afforded some glimpses into the actuality of classroom life means that these dangers – which are hardly unique to teachers' books – have to be risked. There is also the danger of writing in a self-regarding way about one's own work. Writing about what 'I' did and thought and said and believed is obviously fraught with problems, not just stylistic; but, just as obviously, it is unavoidable. If the 'I' grates occasionally here, it is not for want of awareness of the problem.

The accounts I have given of children writing are all from my own classrooms; all the poems that appear were written there at various times over twenty years or so. Some of the narratives go back twelve years; most are more recent. And they come from various kinds of school. The debt to Marjorie Hourd will be obvious,[5] and not just to her approach and method, clearly. Her sensitivity to the process of the developing poem, her respect for the seriousness children bring to writing, and her awareness of their motivations and needs as they write, were for me both educative and revelatory. It does seem puzzling that since she wrote relatively little seems to have been done, at the level of the classroom at any rate, to draw on the insights she developed.

This book is thus in a sense about one aspect of teaching, the teaching of the writing of poetry – and to some that may seem not especially important. But my intention was not to write with limited reference about a confined area, and certainly not to do so in the spirit of a specialist. Rather the opposite: by concentrating on an area I am familiar with I hoped to write about teaching in general. Such insights as there are here may seem to be more widely applicable, even across the curriculum. I would argue that the teaching that I describe is not just specifically an 'approach' for handling poetry but is rather a version of teaching alternative to that which is often implicit in discussions of schooling, and evident in practice. I am presuming, that is, that an account of one teacher's work with poetry has significance also for teaching maths or history or science, or anything else, at junior or secondary level; it would hardly have seemed worth writing otherwise.

Its provenance, though, is poetry, and that seems timely. Poetry is not high on some lists of current priorities. It will sink even lower if accountable achievement is what administrators start to look for any more zealously than they do now. James Britton spoke in a different essay of the danger of substituting 'a regime of surveillance for a regime of trust'.[6] He suggested that the 'evaluative function should be kept distinct from the teaching function', arguing that 'the evaluating procedure drives a wedge between a child's intention and its satisfaction'.[7] It seems to me clear that evaluation might at any time – had it been deployed – have driven a wedge between what children in my classrooms have set out to do and what they have finally accomplished. If teaching children to write depends ultimately – as I argue it does – on adopting a far less brisk and outcome-oriented approach than seems common, then the evaluative instinct has itself to be kept under greater surveillance, not let out to roam freely. Otherwise, young children may write less poetry than they do now, and with much less enjoyment.

The one thing that teachers can see more clearly than anyone about children writing in school is the pleasure they take in writing. That pleasure represents the thrust, the motive power that many teachers rely on to teach with – there is nothing for the potter's fingers to shape till the wheel is moving. The arresting force of evaluative judgements can bring that pleasure to a stop. The slowing towards inertia of children's natural driving interests is easily brought about; I recall the talk of 7-year-old twin sisters:

'I hate reading.'
'What's your favourite subject?'
'Reading by myself at home.'

The other side of the problem for the teacher is personal, in that the version I describe seems to be in conflict with the emphases that pragmatic accountability is already producing. It is not just that teaching will be difficult if there is a schizoid tension between a belief in one way of doing things and a desire or a need to accommodate another. The appraisal of teachers themselves is involved; appraisal is likely to be influenced by a conventional model of teaching, and the teacher wishing to substitute another model for his work is, to say the least, at a disadvantage.

These notes are sounded here rather than in the text, which is not intended to be polemical; they represent notions dwelt on since writing the book, notions which seem increasingly important, even worrying, and not just for the teacher of poetry.

One or two things need to be said about the poems themselves. The spelling and punctuation are the children's; with finished versions that have been worked on and shown to me, the spelling and punctuation have undergone the same kind of changes as the content of the poems; many others are first drafts, with content and spelling and punctuation exactly as first written. I generally describe in the text the stages poems are at. The children's names, and the two staff names, are fictitious; I arrived at these by using a dictionary of first names.

I shall add two unfictitious names. Ray Verrier's assiduous reading has been invaluable, and his own commitment to the outlook I try to articulate has been permanently encouraging. That is a large debt. Another is to John Fines, who read early drafts of several chapters. The largest debt, of course, is to the children themselves. Reproducing their words was pleasurable, even if the voices are lost in translation.

Acknowledgements

I am grateful to the following for permission to reproduce copyright material:

Faber and Faber for two extracts from 'The Coming of the Kings' by Ted Hughes.

John Cayley for his translation of a Chinese poem by Bing Xin.

Chatto & Windus for an extract from Norman MacCaig's 'An Ordinary Day', from *Surroundings*.

'Observation' from *Selected Poems 1936-1984* by William Hart-Smith is reprinted with permission of Angus & Robertson (UK).

The author and publisher have made every effort to obtain permission to reproduce copyright material throughout this book. If any proper acknowledgement has not been made, or permission not received, we would invite any copyright holder to inform us of this oversight.

Part 1
Introduction

1
How do I get them to write poems?

Whose question?

Teachers inevitably ask themselves, thinking about children's writing, 'How do poems get written?' This question is often taken to mean, 'How do I get them to write poems?' – with an implicit 'tell me' or at least 'advise me'. Just as often, an answer can be provided, either at the level of a 'this is what I do' chat in the staffroom, or in the form of conferences or in-service courses or books. In such contexts the response traditionally tends to be a matter of explaining how to do it, what stimulus to begin with, what resources to use as follow-up, what subjects are particularly good for asking children to write poems on, and so on. This is an answer, and there is no doubt that it is a kind of answer that can be helpful. But it is an answer to only one of two different interpretations of the question. That can also mean: what was in fact the story of the origin and development of those poems? what is in fact the nature of the process of their being written? These are different emphases, and the question itself becomes a different kind of question; it is a request not for advice, but for information about the sort of classroom in which poems seem often to be written.

The following poem was written about twenty years ago by a boy in one of the lower streams of a comprehensive first year.

How do I get them to write poems? 3

The Lone Ship 'Orm'

The lone ship 'Orm'
The Viking dragon
A sea-king's steed
Did ride the waves
Her figurehead drank
Deeply of the sea
And Thor's hammer sounded loudly
The Norsemen rowed
Horned men that did not fear
    The sea
But treated her as their Mother
From the Arctic North have I come
Stealing through the surf to
Lay waste to this
    Irish coast
I vomit my brothers on the shore
And wait
For my armoured cargo to return
Once more we head for home
To the land of snow and ice

I found it then, and do now, a remarkable poem. But I can only guess how it came to be written. I begin with it not because I do not know now how it came to be written, but because I did not know then either. I was asked, and recall being puzzled. I think I felt it had come 'from nowhere'. This, unfortunately, not only explains nothing, but could be taken to suggest that poems 'just happen'. I might have meant that it could have been drawn from some source I was unaware of, from reading, or another lesson, or a visit to Sutton Hoo, or from some other source; it was certainly not 'prepared' for in any way. And it was written by the kind of boy, more alive than clever, one might say, who might write one or two poems of that kind, and then disappear as a writer.

It seems to me important that the question of how such a poem can be written should be taken to imply the need, not for useful ideas on how to get writing on such a topic started, but for careful description of how particular poems did in fact come into existence. In respect of this poem, I could say nothing about that, not even as to whether the way of setting it out was his own or a piece of zealous intervention by the editors of the magazine where I rediscovered it. I believe it was his own, but cannot be

4 Behind the Poem

sure, I am equally unsure whether striking ideas like 'Her figurehead drank/Deeply of the sea' and 'I vomit my brothers on the shore' were unconsciously imported from his reading – or consciously borrowed even – or whether they were fresh with him. The tone of the poem is so even, the good moments so casually distributed, and the story so clear, that I feel it could hardly have been artificially assembled; but that is surmise. And other questions, such as whether it was written straight off, or revised, would have to be left unanswered.

This riddle, written by a girl of 11, appeared in the same school magazine the following year; in this case I do recall one or two things about how it was written:

> I have two waists
> and one noise in my life-time,
> I have a hat that I can't put on,
> And when I scatter
> I bring laughter.[1]

With this poem, I might seem to be able to give an answer of a kind to the question 'How did it come about?' I could say I 'concentrated' on certain features of Anglo-Saxon riddles: riddles disguise the object they refer to, but describe it in detail; they give neither too many clues nor too few; they cannot be ambiguously about more than the one object. I could say the class was encouraged to look at objects in such a way as to enable them to say something disguised and unexpected, yet descriptively accurate; that they had to do this by looking at things in as concentrated and unhurried a way as possible; that perhaps they were thus drawn into an empathizing closeness to what they described; that this seemed to lead towards metaphoric illumination of the kind the riddle exhibits, and that of course metaphor deepens the mystery. And so on.

But the recollection of having used some such formula is a long way from being able to describe the teacher's role in the kind of detail which would make its reconstruction persuasive. The memory can only offer a truncated form of it, like the one above, which might seem sufficiently suggestive to be plausible, and, ironically, sufficiently unrevealing of what actually took place as to make it almost ideally prescriptive. It can become useful *because* it oversimplifies, precisely because it is not a description of what the teacher actually does. What did I say or do to 'encourage' a class to observe in a certain way? How did I encourage and then recognize concentration, or empathizing involvement? How did the fertile metaphors emerge from this? Without looking much more closely into the dialogue between teacher and pupil, it is not possible to see what either the teacher or the pupil is doing to sustain it. I do not really know how the poem came to be written.

My assumption is, then, that the question 'How do poems come to be written?' is a question about what takes place in classrooms. That is, it can only be addressed through narratives which attempt to give to classroom theory (often a contradiction in terms) what it has too seldom had, namely a series of glimpses into the actuality of the classroom as a place where a legitimate craft is practised. This implies that accounts need to be presented as much in terms of the actor's – that is, the teacher's – perspectives as in terms of an observer's, since an understanding of what goes on depends on an awareness not just of the overt actions of teaching – like those recorded by means of schedules of observation – but of the teacher's intentions, hesitations, reflections, and so on. For the same reason, the teacher's interpretations of what children are doing also need to be understood, as part of the picture of the classroom.

The teacher can thus redress some of the imbalance in the tradition of writing about the classroom by taking his own work as the topic of the accounts that he writes himself. One result of the tradition that classroom teaching is written about largely by academic researchers, whose day-to-day concerns as practising teachers are at other levels of the educational system, is that reductive emphases have been much easier to come by than have perspectives which take for granted the general legitimacy of classroom teaching; yet presumably the research done on classrooms itself comes to be 'taught', and the general legitimacy of that teaching to be assumed so that it may. The researcher would presumably argue that his own subjectivity as a teacher could not be omitted from any account of his lectures and seminars, and that what happens there cannot be properly understood without reference to it. My contention is no more than that, applied to classrooms.

6 Behind the Poem

The teacher's intellectual disenfranchisement in consequence of the way schools have been written about in academic literature has resulted in her assuming that academic or serious knowledge about the classroom is produced by non-teachers. Knowledge about how poems come to be written, like knowledge about anything else important in the classroom, must be something one reads up in the right books. Another consequence of divorcing knowledge from practice seems inevitable: that the practitioner asks why she should trouble to know – that is, trouble about 'academic' knowledge – at all. Is it not enough that good poems do get written, and apparently in increasing numbers by more and more children in schools over the last fifteen to twenty years in particular? Why not devote one's energies to the encouragement of good practices, teaching strategies of the kind that produce good poems?

The problem with this is that 'good practices', 'imaginative teaching strategies', and so on, do not exist for other teachers until they have been observed or described in detail. Their summary forms acquire the character of prescriptions or booklets of advice, particularly when they are presented to teachers by those whose primary purpose is not to enlighten them intellectually, but to influence them administratively. Summary descriptions of practice tend to omit descriptions and become summaries. One way in which other teachers might be given access to good practice or strategy might be to observe them over a sufficiently long period. The accessibly discrete entities that constitute items of strategy and practice would then be seen as part of the more elusive whole of a particular teacher's craft; working alongside the teacher closely would be a way of revealing the informing purposes lying beneath the routine surface. But that way of seeing inside another teacher's classroom implies redistribution of teachers' time in a way that seems unforeseeable; one thus falls back on writing to convey a sense of the classroom.

Where do we start?

I have suggested that discovering something about how poems come to be written should send us back to actual classrooms. I have also noted how easy it is for the teacher to forget how poems

How do I get them to write poems? 7

came about. This point may seem too obvious to have needed making, were it not that many accounts given by teachers, as talks at conferences, as articles in journals, and so on, appear to address problems at a level at which the memory has to function as an adequate source of information, rather than the more detailed version arising from written notes, and including actual conversational interchanges between teacher and pupil, for instance. The memory plays tricks, tidies up, selects according to its own hidden criteria. On the other hand, even quick handwritten notes, made just after lessons, or at the start of breaks or free periods, or in the quieter moments of lessons when children are writing or reading, can preserve significant moments with some clarity; and the fragmentariness of such notes need not reflect the arbitrariness of opportunities for recording so much as the teacher's search for significance.

Before attempting any exploration or account based on a record of that kind, however, it seems useful to raise one or two more difficulties that illuminate the basic problem of not being able to infer a great deal from the poems themselves about how they came to be written. In this connection, it might seem that one way of gaining some initial purchase on the question of how poems come to be written, of pushing aside some of one's sense of unawareness of what happened, would be the kind that occurs when looking back at certain 'autobiographical' poems that carry the stamp of a personality with particular vividness. Their very individuality, the fact that they summon back a particular tone of voice, a particular situation, argues for their genuineness, for their having been written in some important sense autonomously. It may even seem as if one need then go no further, having seen an origin and explanation in the writer's personality. The following poem, which comes from a fifth-year CSE class of the late 1960s, recalls clearly for me the personality of the girl, and the friend she writes about; the fact that it is 'them', and expresses exactly the feel of their pleasant, half-remote, and whisperingly preoccupied presence, seems to suggest that it had little to do with any suggestion of mine – except for the title, '40 Minutes Behind a Shut Door':

Coming out of the French room,
I look forward to the next lesson,

8 Behind the Poem

'Ah', you say to yourselves,
'A girl who likes English',
But, I'm afraid to disillusion you,
I look forward to the next lesson
Where I sit, with friend Verona.
I look out the window and watch
The trees beckoning me to leave the room.
I wish I could,
Verona talking silently about 'Him',
The boy she likes and dislikes.
I, talking about my love problems,
Wondering if I'll get my needlework
Done by Wednesday afternoon and
Will I ever get my ...
'Oh, Elaine ...' (It's him.) 'Here is your work
I'm not sure I like this' – and that and
The other.
By the time I've finished taking this
And that and the other out,
I'm left with a blank piece of paper.
Back to dreaming ...
'Oh Elaine ...'
'Yes, sir?'
'Here is your work. Most beautifully written.
Touching in parts. A wonderful piece
Of work, nine and three quarters out of ten.
Excellent.' 'Thank you sir.'
Verona whispering on about 'him'.
'I like him, but I don't.'
A weird but likeable girl.
I don't care if I don't get
Nine and three quarters out of ten,
As long as I've got a friend
To look out of the window with,
To stand, warming our hands on the radiator.
'Worrying about English?' you ask.
'No, not us, we just worry about boys.'

On one level, this may have had nothing directly to do with my teaching at all; the poem visited my workplace, I might say. At most the English lesson was, perhaps, a place where she was able to pause and gather her thoughts. The fact that the thoughts were about English itself and not doing it, the nice note that what she

How do I get them to write poems?

wrote in or as part of English was about her remoteness from it, also suggests some essential independence of the teacher, at the same time as it nicely captures the amiable aimlessness, in some ways, of the time they spent 'doing English'.

It might be persuasive to say, then, that it was 'entirely hers'. There are two difficulties about this suggestion. First, it is intuitive, a presumption based on recollection. The 'autonomy' of such a poem needs to be demonstrated, by describing the background against which it appeared, and showing the absence of 'dependency'. The second difficulty is with the word 'autonomy' itself, and all those expressions, like 'writing on one's own', which, in saying in effect that a poem just happens, tend to overlook the pedagogic context in which writing takes place. But here, clearly, the poem itself issues from a context, and is in fact about that context. She was asked to write a poem; she says what she was 'really' doing in English. Nor is the piece really dismissive of the work she is doing; it is not that she doesn't care but that she doesn't care as long as she has a friend to look out of the window and lean on radiators with. She does care, but she cares more about what is more important.

But this seems to be as far as I can go in an attempt to explain the poem. There was a classroom, a course, a teacher, a known reader. It may be that something about the classroom allowed her – or influenced her – to be herself. But that classroom is inaccessible now, so that the initial feeling that it is enough to say that the poem was the girl herself is replaced by the feeling I had about the two poems already looked at, that there is a good deal more that needs to be said before I can understand how it might have been written.

There is a further problem to do with the activity of the writer, which can perhaps be illustrated by another poem in which the emotional resonance of a particular personal situation, in a context I recall, seems equally clear. I remember reading André Obey's play *Noah*[2] with a group of secondary-school first-years, after which, in the thematic way of the 1970s we had gone on to read extracts from the Penguin collection *Creatures Moving*.[3] The children were making their own collection of poems about animals. The writer of the poem below, a boy of 12, had been in tears after hearing Theodore Roethke's poem about a field mouse.[4] His own had just died. The loving knowledgeable detail of his Budgie poem, the solicitous concern audible in every line, make the tears only too comprehensible.

Budgie

Valuable to a budgie
is his seed in the dish,
and his water in a drinker
on the wire.

A home which is comfy,
and a nice warm temperature,
and roomy thick perches
away from the draught.

His welcomed little luxuries
are millet sprays in heaps,
and cuttle fish to nibble on
to sharpen up his beak.

But besides his mainseed
the most important thing
is a little bowl of grit
to digest his food.

The poem presents the same kind of difficulties as the previous one, and some extra ones to do with what seems to be the artistic – it is tempting to say unconsciously artistic – shaping of his experience. First, the poem feels to me as genuinely his as a poem can be. What persuades is not just the vocabulary and the tone of voice; it is the careful ritual that is enacted, the assembling of particulars in the poem that parallels the preparations made in actuality; the poem seems to mirror these, as if he were putting the things out again as words. It seems in one way such a skilful poem that a question arises for me here, to do with the degree of self-awareness that went into it.

I should like to know how he decided on the rhythms he deploys, which seem oddly right; whether he felt the shorter lines were different or right or out of place; whether any of it was a matter of 'conscious' decision. For a literary 'appreciation' of the poem as a poem, one need not know these things, but the teacher stands in a particular relation to children's writing; it is never enough to be a literary critic, or even simply a reader. As critic

How do I get them to write poems? 11

one might note certain successes about the poem: the strong inversion in the first line – 'Valuable to a budgie', and in the third verse the small collection of trochaic words – little, millet, cuttle, nibble – that almost half rhyme and create a sense of repeated tiny movement. As a teacher I also wonder what gift or perception or instinct or accident or deliberation led to the rhythms, the confident homely adjectives, the four one-statement verses with full stops, the lines agreeably end-stopped and over-run, the nice solidity of having the nouns at most line-ends. What does all this mean from an 'ordinary' lad of 12, taking an ordinary middle-of-the-road unambitious route through school?

The teacher, in other words, has to confront a question that a critic would generally leave to aesthetics, and ask how far those were conscious acts of shaping. For the critic the effects are 'good' (or not) whether or not they are consciously produced. But the teacher's concerns cannot stop there. Since even as I read my business is to understand the poem in a way that will help me to encourage the writing of more, I need to find out about the details of the process; I need some knowledge of the kind of activity it is that I encourage children to engage in, and initiate for them.

It seems necessary, then, amongst other things, to try to separate out on the one hand a power that is the pupil's own, and from which the poem is to an extent autonomously derived, and on the other a pedagogic context which includes specific things the teacher may do and say, and other factors in the particular milieu in which children write. This may seem obvious and indeed trite, but there is a need, perhaps, to stress the presence, and the importance, of the work both child and teacher do in the business of drawing out poems from the situation in which they face each other and work together. It is easy, as I have just now suggested, to intimate that many poems are written 'entirely unaided', or quite outside the dialogue between pupil and teacher. The autonomous activity of children, where it manifests itself, as it often does, as continuously vigorous and frequently remarkable, may be seen to exist not 'on its own', though, but as a reflection of the richness of possibilities in situations created by the teacher, and hence in some attenuated sense a 'result' of what the teacher actually does. And if 'result' is in quotes, it is because the actual connection between any specific action on the teacher's part and something the pupil subsequently does – such as write a particular poem – must always be elusive.

In the same way, the interventionist vigour of the teacher's work, providing it is an appropriate and not an intrusive or interfering intervention (a distinction the exemplification of which I shall leave to one side for the moment), should not be seen as somehow diminishing the chances for true creativity, true freedom to write 'what they please', and so on. The opposite is perhaps much nearer the truth. Rather than thinking of the relation between autonomy and intervention as exhibiting binary seesaw characteristics, whereby when the contribution of one rises, that of the other necessarily falls, it would be more accurate and more fruitful, I suggest, to see the richness of one as implicit in and dependent on the richness of the other. Potentially, when there is vigorous intervention, there is vigorous autonomy, and vice versa.

Issues

The issue of the relative 'contributions' of pupil and teacher (or the pedagogic contexts devised by the teacher) to the writing of children's poems is as crucial as it is fascinating. However, it might be best addressed not merely by direct confrontation, though I shall attempt that in Chapters 4 and 5, but by placing it also in contexts which seem for a number of reasons to be necessary ways of exploring the broader question of how children come to write poems.

There are a number of ways in which it seems possible to consider this, reflecting the different situations that teachers find themselves in. For example, new classes arrive, and the fact that teacher and pupil are, for a while at least, relative strangers to each other creates a particular situation with its own problems. Chapter 2 attempts to deal with the question of how, over the space of a term, my developing acquaintance with a new class created or set free certain possibilities. The time scale of the account of getting to know something about a class is large, and the treatment rather broad; it is not a lesson-by-lesson narrative account, rather a series of notes on individual children and their

How do I get them to write poems? 13

shifts forward, time-lapse pictures rather than film. I have dealt with this first because it seems basic to those other situations.

This first episodic narrative in Chapter 2 forms an introductory context for the other questions, all of which are alluded to or implicit in this first narrative. Chapter 3, which is also about process and hence also largely narrative, goes closer in, as it were, and deals with what happens at the level of the lesson or series of lessons. It describes two attempts at 'beginning' to write poems, and deals with certain things that may happen once one is 'under way', beyond what feels like beginning. For the sake of balance, I have tried to deal with moments when things go smoothly, and moments when they do not. The second section of Chapter 3, for instance, recounts a problematic episode that seemed to be produced by an inept decision about how to handle resources.

The second part of the book changes the focus from process, recounted in narratives, to the relationship of teacher and pupil. In Chapters 4 and 5 I have tried to separate out their distinct roles in bringing poems to fruition; but this is in order to argue that the 'autonomy' of the pupil and the 'interventions' of the teacher are, in a vigorous and fertile environment, interdependent and reciprocally vitalizing. Distinctions are made between the action of one and the action of the other, but only in order to describe the ways in which, paradoxically as it might seem, each is in reality implicated in the other.

Part 3 of the book deals with different overall 'contexts' for writing, such as literature, the 'real' world, film, and so on. It would be possible to discuss more, but I have preferred to give lengthy treatment to a few rather than try to pronounce on a greater number. Chapters 6–8 therefore deal with matters that are perhaps more often written about; in a sense they are about kinds of resource, so that the later part of the book is where sometimes consideration of writing seems to begin. But it is necessary to suggest that just as there are distinguishable situations or phases in teaching which need to be separately considered, as influences on writing or conditions of writing, so there are influences and conditions implicit in one kind of 'resource' or approach rather than another. Just as the new class creates a context which seems worth discussing, so – it seems to me – does the interdisciplinary project, for example, create a certain style of working, a certain set of possibilities of its own. Literature as a context for imitation – or a source of inspiration – is the subject of Chapter 6, and surrounding physical reality that of Chapter 7. These are both large issues in themselves. Four other contexts – film, myth, other subjects, and interdisciplinary projects – are handled in Chapter 8, though myth is treated very briefly, since writing on mythic subjects is described also in earlier chapters. What is sought through narration of the particular encounters which form the body of those chapters is some sense of what is intrinsic to and distinctive about each context, and some hint as to the particular possibilities opened up by means of them.

The final section has two chapters, which together constitute an attempt to say something about what children are essentially doing when they write poems. I suggest in Chapter 9 that they can be seen as taking up a certain relation to the writing of poems, and from time to time embodying this relation in material products – books, files, magazines, and so on. The last chapter returns to the poem itself, to the sceptical question that is often put, as to whether what the child writes is 'really a poem'. Here my suggestion is that teachers need worry less than they do about this, since the problem of what is or is not poetic language – what a poem really is – is also troublesome to philosophers of language looking at poetry in general. The teacher aware of philosophers' historic difficulties in trying to articulate some essential differences between poetry and prose will see the problem of when a child's poem is really a poem as part of the larger question, and as a shared or even relinquishable burden.

Part 2

Process

2
A new class

A sense of failure

Occasionally, a teacher may meet a new class, simply ask them to write a poem, and the same evening be reading impressive pieces of children's writing, without having done any 'teaching'; the request itself is a 'stimulus' of a kind, and it is sometimes effective. But a more common and depressingly recognizable experience is to work painstakingly towards the moment of asking children to write, time that moment carefully, and then find oneself reading a batch of nondescript pieces, in response to which it seems hard to say anything definite, either purposeful or in praise. The teacher comments, feeling not altogether comfortable debasing the coinage of true enthusiasm: 'Well tried', 'Some nice ideas here', 'An interesting subject to choose', and so on. The commonness, even the universality, of this experience amongst those who encourage children to write poems makes it a useful starting point.

An anxiety settles on teachers when their best efforts seem to run into the sand; it also seems tempting to try something less risky. And in general, one of the difficulties about encouraging children to write poems is the teacher's anxiety and diffidence; but it is not so much the anxiety and the diffidence *per se*, as the fact that for many teachers such words possess exclusively negative connotations, pointing to the wholly unhelpful burden such emotions are thought to place on the teacher's sense of what is possible. They can certainly amount to a disabling uncertainty which inhibits some teachers from ever asking children to write poems, and many more from doing so with any frequency; it is particularly dispiriting that there are others who are not thus disabled, who appear successful and confident about 'getting poems out of' children. But reflection might suggest that at times feelings of uncertainty, anxiety, and indecision are useful; they can stand for self-scrutiny, for the reflective pause, for listening, and they warn against whatever can harden into inflexible predictability – strait-jacket plans, unwavering attitudes, plodding tunnel vision.

I wish to put it more strongly, though, and suggest that for the teacher anxiety and diffidence, and other feelings of indeterminacy, are important, positive, and helpful teaching emotions. It would be surprising if good teachers of writing were without them, if good poems were not in some sense the outcome of work which is both less 'confident' than it sometimes appears, and certainly far less the result of a mystique than some teachers wish it to remain. It therefore seems to me crucial that teachers who have grown accustomed to the fact that children write well in their classrooms should place their own uncertainties – their own improvisatory diffidence, reappraising anxiety, and lack of any surefire system and prescient knowhow – at the centre of their version of 'teaching writing'. It is for this reason that I wish first to offer an account of work in which a central concern is a complex of feelings that might be considered 'negative', and which involve what might be described as a sense of failure.

A sense of having failed may of course be experienced against a background of recollections of successfully encouraging good writing. But there is enough of the uncertain and imponderable in all teaching, and enough puzzling discomfort in seeming not to succeed, to justify the attempt to place this situation in the foreground for teaching in general; teachers encounter failure so frequently that it is puzzling that it is little talked about. And if there are recollections of success to draw on, they tend not to point unambiguously to the way out, but to say that a way out is as likely to appear as another labyrinthine confusion.

18 *Behind the Poem*

A recent situation that for me clearly exemplifies this contention arose out of the experience of meeting a new class of 9-year-olds. The poems I shall look at first are not quite the first the class wrote for me; an anxiety that things are going wrong is not likely to develop until one has some degree of acquaintance with a class, and after some attempts at encouragement. In this case, after working for four weeks or so carefully towards writing poems (in a way I shall describe later) I received a batch that seemed dispiritingly lifeless. Claire and Lorraine for instance, both aged 10, seemed very uncertain what kind of thing to say:

Daddy

He loves you very much,
He cares for you,
He makes thinks right for
you, and helps you with things.

Nits and Lice

Nits
Nits crawl through your hair
Lice tickle your head
Lice come from nits.

Marina wrote a number of things with a similar shape, each seeming quick and trite:

Summer

Summer hot
Summer lazy
Makes you feel as lite as a daisy,
When the sun burns fizley,
Then hides behind a cloud.

Peter, aged 9, wrote a poem for each season, with each line beginning 'Look at':

An Autumn Poem

Look at the leaves, thier changing colour,
Look at the leaves, thier falling.
Look at the mist thats roling down the hill, it's very thick.
Look at the ivy, nothing happens.
Look at the holy, is growing berries.

In a similarly ponderous way he had earlier written his first poems about episodes in the Heracles story, in which the Hydra had 'a long beard and a big mustash', the Centaurs 'long beards and a mustash', and another giant 'a beard that's very long and also a mustash'; in each poem there were two or three lines of anatomical inventory: 'He has two eyes a nose and a mouth', 'he has four legs and two arms'.

James liked rhymes:

The Stable of Grime

Once their was a Fable,
about herclis and a staBle,
he cleaned out some of the muck,
But it got hard and he got stuck,
he got out pritty fast
this was all in the anchant past,
he finly got out all the muck
and then he said it Looked like yuk.

Nicholas tried to do without rhyme:

The Killer Whale

Blue and Black,
big and long,
Through the water it swam.
He saw a little boat,
Knocked it over,
and that was the end of the sailor.

These, and most of the other attempts, were, I felt, disappointing. The first group had been too, three weeks previously, but that had been so early in the term that I related it to the children's unfamiliarity with a new teacher, perhaps with some aspect of my approach to writing. While the first failure was comprehensible, the second came after a conscious effort not to repeat it. In such a situation, a teacher's responses are likely to be critical, directed either at self – where did I go wrong? have I tried too hard? are they bored? – or at the children – perhaps they're not very imaginative, or just not good at writing. It was difficult not to see this second rather barren outcome as a genuine kind of failure.

A number of strands of feeling were woven together in the aftermath. I shall summarize these now, and the bulk of the rest of the chapter will be devoted to examining them further. The predominant feeling was professional dissatisfaction – a kind of guilt. This was accompanied by an attempt to look back to see what had gone wrong, an informal appraisal of my own teaching. There followed, as there usually does, an urgency immediately to do something more interesting, to redeem things. At the same time, the children themselves must clearly 'try harder', particularly to realize that I believed them capable of writing interestingly. Another feeling was, in spite of that, that the possibilities of writing poetry with that class were perhaps somewhat limited; it was not going to be a good year. Few teachers perhaps would make a pessimistic judgement on that after one attempt, but there are likely to be more who respond in that fashion after a second batch of unexciting pieces, and fewer with enough confidence to go on waiting if children continue to disappoint them.

So far, the responses I describe were essentially those that many teachers are prey to at such moments. Memory of the transience of such feelings in the past may provide some psychological damage limitation but does not prevent them from shaping the teacher's basic mood. But other feelings derive more directly from past awareness, distancing the present to some extent and making it less oppressive. In this instance, the sense that some such impasse had often been reached before, and surmounted, helped to produce the precarious but clear sense that if I bided my time something would very likely turn up, that some good writing would somehow materialize despite the inadequate beginning. Related to this was the residual suspicion that despite this collective failure I vaguely recalled at least some touches of vitality in their writing. Here again, the sense that there might be possibilities in a generally featureless collection derived partly from previous experience of later finding valuable things that I had overlooked at first reading.

Looking back

Perhaps the expression 'looking back' implies more of a balanced review than is possible; but what for the moment I am calling failure does make likely some gathering-together of all the doubts and uneasy insights that come to anyone during the course of a few weeks' teaching; it is as if, once things have gone astray, doubts that were played down at the time return inquisitorially to subject one's teaching to more careful scrutiny. It was in this anxious way that I mulled over the first few weeks' work of the term, up to the point of asking the class to write this batch of poems. How might I have contributed towards the lack of inspiration I felt I noticed?

To try to answer that question retrospectively in writing is quite different from the floundering dissatisfaction of 'looking back' at the time; while sources of possible difficulty might have defined themselves then much as they do now, they did so much less clearly. None the less, from that rather shapeless picture the outlines of a kind of reappraisal began to emerge even at the time. I shall therefore describe in some detail what happened early in the term, focusing on certain emerging anxieties. This necessitates a rather extended narrative.

The first two lessons of the year were spent talking with the children about the kind of things they felt they could write, and write about. I had already decided that I should like to encourage them, if possible, to start with some story of the kind that they felt they could do, and if possible to let them choose a subject 'of their own'. I decided on a rather 'open' start, in other words, though I was aware that this might not be a way familiar to the children. They then wrote a story 'of their own'. Two or three children wrote long stories (500 words and more) that felt enthusiastic and natural. Most tales were to do with war, space travel, spying, fantasies of various kinds, and so on. Two of the most down-to-earth stories were about show-jumping. Several children tried stories involving magic, and I decided to read aloud to them Helen Cresswell's story 'Particle Goes Green'.[1] We had more talk, this time about witches, the Book of Spells that appears in the story, and the interesting science-against-magic idea we found there. This pleasant talk gave me the idea of suggesting they might like to make up another Particle adventure, or invent a 'scientific witch', or magic tales on similar lines.

Even at the time, I wondered about the wisdom of inviting them so early in the term to write on a subject 'of their own', though we had talked for some time, and interestingly, on subjects they had enjoyed writing about in previous years. Perhaps to some extent I forgot – or in the hurry to build a relationship chose not to remember – that the previous year's 'openness' had been the outcome of a whole year's work. Clearly openness cannot just be offered; it has to be worked towards.

Moreover, the zealous start I had made with the idea of the story was perhaps at the very beginning in danger of making the writing itself solemn or burdensome. I had hoped during that term to be a little more purposeful than 'simply' getting them to enjoy reading and writing stories. I had wanted some reflective concern about how stories work to infiltrate the pleasure they were likely to get from reading Bill Naughton or the collection *Stories for Tens and Over* by Sara and Stephen Corrin.[2] So that after their second piece of writing, which was started half-way through the second week of term, I went on to read with them the Orpheus and Eurydice story from the Corrins' book, and then three stories from Bill Naughton's collection *The Goalkeeper's Revenge*.[3] We noted the different ways stories began, with talk, or a description of a person, or with some action taking place, and the class tried three such beginnings of their own.

But what was intended as a way of focusing on one aspect of story-telling began even at the time to feel heavy, an exercise split off from writing itself. Looking back it seems to have been done only in dubious theoretical pursuit of some increment of literary awareness about the fabric of the short story. At the time of inflicting this particular task on my class (inventing the beginning of a story in different modes without necessarily thinking of finishing it) I was taken with the idea that children 'ought' to begin to 'study' the genres of literature as soon as they could. This kind of intellectual influence, from reading, or from courses and conferences, is likely to distort teaching away from what feels right in the direction of 'covering' the desirable new content. Another anxiety, then, was that I might be intellectualizing and deadening what we were doing, through trying to give the work a particular 'structure'.

I raised what seemed a more useful question next time, asking them how they knew whether a story was getting going, and what they did when they got stuck, and offered some advice that might have been potentially helpful, but was possibly also, given the uncertainties of the start, doubtful and double-edged. Writers, I said, sometimes put work to one side for a while, and when they come back to it they have new ideas for it; very occasionally they may abandon stories that don't seem to work at all. I asked three or four children what they would like to do with the stories they had begun; did they think they'd got going, or were they struggling? 'I haven't got any more ideas', Geoffrey wrote; Janet's written reply was, 'Sorry Mr H but I have no poem or story I want to write'. Nadine simply wrote 'Yes'. Here again, then, despite having already sensed that I was trying to go too quickly, I perhaps repeated the mistake.

The same reservation applied to the next move. I suggested to the class that they could turn the practice start into a complete tale, or work on something else, or read some other stories in the books we had already looked at. It was a 'choice' session – offering more freedom to opt out, perhaps, than to be positive. For such gestures to work they have to be interpreted correctly, and for many children the freedom to choose a subject or a way of writing – apart from being burdensome in other ways – may simply be an odd departure from previous teachers' practice, and may even look casual, as if the teacher can't be bothered to set a real piece of work.

In the midst of uncertainty, it is hard to anticipate that a self-critical insight that seems basically right will later seem to have been formulated too severely. My perception of what I was doing and of what the children were doing – achieving, even – was perhaps blurred by a preoccupation with what was already 'going wrong'. It is unlikely, after all, that a relationship develops without some difficulties. Like unstable terrain in which faults are bound to develop somewhere, it might matter less where they occur than that they are bound to. If too much openness had not been offered, too little might have been, in the attempt to avoid the opposite. An uncertainty about such uncertainties might have helped.

It may be, then, that the presence of a difficulty represents something more (or other) than the intrinsic problem of the difficulty itself; it may also fulfil the expressive function of articulating an awkward phase in a relationship. This possibility, which is also the possibility of seeing the difficulty less 'personally', is hidden from the teacher by various emotional reactions to not doing well, not least by increased tension. One looks round for any convincing way forward, or out. I thought of a withdrawal to more workable terrain, to being more 'definite'. Why not simply back-pedal? This thought occurred to me during the uncertain 'choice' lesson I referred to a moment earlier; but one girl inadvertently pushed my original enterprise, of trying to leave things somewhat more open, a little further along by asking if they could write poems. I said yes. Several children then did, in preference to the other activities. These were the first poems from the class, and they were all about 'nature'. Lorraine wrote 'Seasons':

> Sumer is going
> Winter is coming
> leaves are falling
> And flowers dieing
> Spring is drawing in
> And clouds of mist
> Snow is falling
> And blossom is here.

Reading this curious amalgam of impressions, I felt that I should have 'prepared' what I offered as a 'free choice'; I perhaps missed some of the value of the open way they arose as a result of concern with their 'quality'. Marina's was also about autumn:

> Autum is coming
> Cos winter has gone,
> the leaves are turning
> From green to bronze.
> The evenings get shorter
> As Autum comes on,
> Bulbs are waiting to suprise an eye,
> Autum what a wonderful thing it is.

There was a hint of the same incoherence here, and yet the lovely idea 'bulbs are waiting to surprise an eye' seemed personal, and a clear allusion to spring. The same idiosyncratic note occurred in another poem of hers, in the line 'Frost is weaving in and out of the trees': I wrote 'nice' opposite both of these.

I registered these as moments of poetic insight. They suggested a way in which to approach the idea of asking all the class to write a poem. I had talked about their writing, and read aloud several short extracts, most from the prose pieces, by way of encouragement. It had occurred to me that one way of beginning to write poems with them would be to work from forms of expression they used in prose. The cautious idea of working from prose reflected my judgement that up to this point, as I noted at the time, they had done only 'rather weak, unadventurous work'. Needless to say, that was not a comment made to the children themselves. Later in the lesson I wrote up several sentences from the extracts I had read aloud: 'Her granny was strict but nice, the secret way they are'; 'He is a genius at loafing'; 'Whenever he ran you could see his brown legs going like the wind and his tubby thighs looking as if there full of water'; 'Bulbs are waiting to surprise an eye'; 'Frost is weaving in and out of the trees'.

I wrote the extracts on the board, without line breaks in poems, and asked the children to guess whether they were from poems or stories, saying that I had lined them out differently just to make it harder to guess. They guessed, and instead of giving the 'answers' I said we would experiment by taking the lines in whichever way they wished to treat them, and using them to try a short poem or a piece of prose. My motive for this was that it seems important that children feel confident to treat language as plastic, a medium to be experimented with; but I felt immediately that it represented another ill-timed lurch towards openness.

I stressed that it was 'an experiment', and didn't give the children the 'answers', only asked them to use one or two of the sentences on the board for a short piece of their own, poem or prose. I felt the results were not very impressive. James wrote a quite neat short piece:

He is a genius at loafing,
he is a genius at boasting
he is a genius at skipping school
he is a genius for being a fool

Most efforts looked perfunctory, very likely, I thought, through puzzlement as to the purpose of the work. Lorraine wrote:

In the treetops see the birds singing and of course the little insects on flowers leaves and grass/flowers and leaves falling and dying.

Nicholas had nothing much to say:

> A genius he is at loafing,
> He loafs and loafs all day,
> He goes to sleep for an hour and starts loafing all over again.

I took these pieces as showing symptoms of boredom or even something like desperation, evidence perhaps of having set a futile exercise. This feeling was suggested also by some children writing down no more than one or two of the sentences on the board, and returning immediately to their more favoured piece of writing, which my lesson had evidently interrupted.

Apart from the several spontaneous 'nature' poems mentioned above, these then were the first poems they had written for me, and because of that, and my interpreting their lack of conviction as related to their unfamiliarity with a new teacher, they were not a source of real worry, as the later ones were. At this point I decided to work on other things for a while. I looked at some riddles with them, and they wrote two or three, and I then drew back through lack of conviction. It was an uncertain phase, of casting around and marking time. Many teachers will fall back, when thus cornered, on some old device, or trusty resource. I read to them the beginning of the Heracles story, in Ian Serraillier's version,[4] published in the New Windmill series, and they carried on reading it on their own, with every sign of being involved. Some Greek tales had been part of my informal forecast for the year, although not necessarily Heracles; but he had 'gone well' with a parallel class the previous year, and there seemed no reason not to try him again now.

Two weeks or so after this change of direction to Heracles, with the feeling of being on tried and true ground, I suggested that we would 'try out a poem together'. Using an approach similar to the one earlier, I asked the class to look for, and write out, some 'memorable sentences' – sentences they found especially dramatic or exiting. I took one of these, and wrote it on the board, lining out as if it were a short poem:

> Half stunned,
> The beast wagged its tail drunkenly,
> The flames in its eyes flickered,
> And they grew dim.

I suggested that the children should take four or five episodes in the Heracles story, start with a 'memorable line' of their own choice, line it out like a poem, and carry on writing. One or two children immediately asked whether they had to use a line from the book to start with. I said no, stressing that they were 'trying out' a way of writing, and suggested they made three or four attempts at different subjects, and we could see later which ones seemed to work. To familiarize them with how other children might be writing, I gave them *The Second Cadbury Book of Children's Poetry*.[5] They read a good deal on their own, and towards the end of the lesson I asked them to notice that some of the titles fitted the Heracles stories: Love, Madness, Joy, for instance. They could also, I said, try a poem like those on their own; they didn't have to stick to Heracles.

For a number of reasons, to do with having noticed some signs of life in their responses and one or two poems, and with the feeling that they found the Heracles material interesting, I felt confident that some livelier poems would emerge. The result, though, was the collection I described at the beginning of the chapter, which I had found depressingly nondescript. That was my response at the time. The review I have just now given of what I had done up to the point of asking them to write on Heracles derives from the self-critical perspective that I had when I looked back over the work, and from time to time in the midst of it.

But this is, perhaps, always the case with retrospective views that are still too immersed in what they are looking back on to be clear or dispassionate. They tend to apportion blame and find reasons for 'failure' in contexts where there is insufficient information for proceeding in that judgmental manner. A more detached viewpoint – the kind that is available only later – might well see in some of the confusion and apparent stalemate a difficult but perhaps inevitable phase in the business of finding out what one can do with a particular class that one met only a few weeks ago. But detachment is not available at the time. In other words, the casting around, the persistent uncertainty, the bouts of anxiety, the meagre glimpses of what seems workable, the stalling and experimenting, were what that 'teaching' was at that time; and I should argue that they are what much teaching is. The apparently negative appears almost to swamp the positive;

but realizing later how the positive is somehow latent in much that appears negative alters a teacher's perception of the process as a whole, and particularly of the relation between the two kinds of feeling.

What of the positive? I said that one strand of feeling was of recalling touches of vitality in their writing. It is interesting that a few days after I had written 'nice' in Marina's exercise book, twice on the same page, I forgot that I had. So that when I said that I noticed 'signs of life' in their writing, it was not quite accurate; what happened was that I saw afresh things I half-noticed before anxiety about other things induced me to forget them. I also looked again at the earlier work and saw things I had overlooked. It seems worrying that routine judgements can be wrong, or incomplete. But the reflective conviction that the judgements one makes will sooner or later be qualified or overturned never seems to turn into effective practical withdrawal from inadequate appraisal; the reflective caution never quite catches up with or cancels out the less reflective practice.

In the case of the poems I began this chapter with, my first impressions of certain children's work were modified within days. It may be that as crude disappointment recedes, a more reflective mood prepares the mind for a revision of perspectives. Such revision may also take place continuously and as a matter of course, because by being better acquainted with the children the teacher is better able to interpret their writing, seeing it against a ground of personal knowledge about them. The field in which I looked at these children's writings certainly seemed to widen in this way. For example, 'The Stable of Grime' looked different when it was typed out and when James had himself crossed out the last two lines. It seemed even witty, in the sardonic way of the clerihew. Misreading of personality contributed to misreading the poems; underneath the floundering of a pupil new to the school and seeming somewhat lost the humour was more positive and aware than I had at first thought. I then re-read the following first few lines of another of his poems, written a few days later, with the same feeling of not having done it justice initially.

Star Wars

In the year 2001,
some alins decided to have some fun,

one shot the moon down,
God gave an angry frown,
He said if you ever do that agin
I shall turn you outside from in,

It ended with a pointless rhyme – 'he saw a mole,/then he fell into a deep hole'; the idea that he generally wrote empty doggerel predisposed me to see this, when I had not noticed the '2001/fun' rhyme at all, and failed to appreciate the 'agin/in' lines ('agin' might be a deliberate misspelling, when 'alins' wasn't).

My judgement on Marina's poems (the one above was one of several she wrote) was that they looked 'dashed off'. In retrospect, this was harsh and inadequate. She did in fact write a lot and fast, and some of it worked. I had noticed this the previous week, with 'Night Fall':

As it comes slowly slowly,
As it comes swiffly swiffly,
Will it beat the lonly traveller
Will it beat him to his shelter.

But I had forgotten, or not noticed well enough. Instead of assuming that her rapid, untidy-looking, short pieces, which seemed at times almost nonsensical and banal, were this week further expressions of hurry and indifference, I might have registered headlong fluency as an integral part of her style.

These misreadings and misjudgements, while not in themselves unduly severe or alarming perhaps, seem worth mentioning because their occurrence seems probable in any similar context. Anxiety about generally 'getting moving', a concern that handwriting is indecipherable and misses the line by a millimetre or two, worry that a child seems not to be bothering or trying, and so on, all militate against seeing their work clearly enough to discern and value some of the thought-processes at work in it. Again and again, a less hurried re-reading weeks later allows the teacher to see virtues in writing that were missed first time. My own reading and listening was 'dashed off', not in the sense that it was personally casual, but in the sense that like every teacher I was immersed in routines which inhibit the kind of slower-paced reflectiveness needed for discrimination.

There is another view that could be taken of all this, of course. The effort to find 'signs of life' in the pieces discussed above might well be seen as the attempt to discover virtues where none exist. This view might have considerable appeal on several levels. Many classroom teachers would, I suspect, endorse such a bluff commonsense rebuttal on the ground that the claims of creativity are overstated and result in a precious and deferential response to what children do. In academic writing this would be echoed by attempts to dismantle what is seen as the myth of *The Child as Poet*;[6] Myra Cohn Livingstone's recent book has that title, and she argues essentially that for all the spontaneity and metaphoric vitality of children's talk and writing, the specifically poetic effort to concentrate, organize, and shape is for the most part beyond children. (This is precisely the contention I take issue with throughout, more directly in Chapters 4 and 10 than elsewhere, and because it is continuously confronted I shall do no more than refer to it here.)

There is often strong institutional pressure on the teacher to relinquish the standpoint I am taking towards these poems. The strongest pressure to take a more sharply pragmatic view, to achieve quickly, to judge prematurely, to misread, to distort a developing relationship, is likely to come from within school. If the head lays the emphasis primarily on 'neat, accurate writing', on 'good spelling', and so on, without setting that emphasis in the context of the whole process of writing, a tendency is set in motion to identify writing with the end point of writing. (By 'emphasis' I mean anything a head does or says which tends to settle for subordinates the rank order of competing values.) But if writing is reduced to its culmination in written products, the slow, valuable build-up to the achievement represented by such products is unacknowledged. For the teacher working in the way I describe, but under pressure to redistribute emphases (that is, to think differently), that can mean a refusal to acknowledge the crucial part of his craft, beginning in the patient search for 'signs of life' in the child's writing, and going on to the way those are drawn out into achievement. The identification, endorsement, and encouragement of those moments preclude any early emphasis on aspects of writing like tidiness and carefully checked spelling; these are not only not necessary at a sketching-out-of-ideas stage, but are dysfunctional when tactlessly introduced at the wrong time. A sharp conflict is then likely to emerge between the teacher–craftsman with a feel for the inner pace of achievement and the head or administrator sensitized to objective outcomes.

Doing better

It was hardly a regard for the inner pace of achievement that produced out of reappraisal another of these strands of feeling – the vigorous desire to do better. It seemed necessary to confront what had 'gone wrong' more directly. One way seemed to be for us all to look at their poems together, to see what could be improved. I typed out a number of complete poems and some extracts, some on Heracles and some not, and asked children to volunteer to let what they had written be discussed. Leo, after looking at his poem for a while when I asked him what he thought of the rhymes he had used, said 'they came out of the top of my head'; he was 'rhyming for the sake of rhyming', he said. Such a perception, illuminating and useful though it seemed at the time, evidently came in advance of practice; Leo went on writing rhymes that came off the top of his head:

The Old Man

The old man had a wooden leg,
He ripped his real one on a metal peg,
He was hanging up a sock,
And looking at a clock,
When a cat jogged him,
And caused him to rip his limb.

He remained keen on this, and used it in his selection of best pieces for the term. Even so, he had made a personal judgement about his own work, and if he did not follow it up immediately it may have remained in his mind as a way of looking at what he came to write later. (In fact his best piece later in the term had some rhyme.) Generally, though, the attempt to encourage awareness of their own practice by focusing on actual examples looked premature; nearly all the written comments reflected perspectives I had introduced on particular poems in the hope

32 Behind the Poem

that they would use them to develop their own views of other poems. Thus several wrote what I said I felt about the following piece by Marina, that it seemed 'complete':

> Don't cry little prisoner
> Don't weep so bitterly
> Don't drown yourself in sorrow
> Because little prisoner
> There'll be no tomorrow

And most asked of Claire's piece the question I had posed: 'But is it a poem?'

> Born with Zeus,
> The father of the gods
> His mother Alcmena
> His father Prince of Thebes
> But his real name Amphitryon.

In one or two instances judgements made on one poem were transferred to another. The 'rhymes for the sake of rhyme' notion was evidently a helpful way to express suspicions of many rhyming poems, though there was one thoughtful dissenting judgement on a piece by James which most had disliked; this was 'good and humeros', John wrote:

> Heracles got stone drunk
> then went to his bunk
> A cup-bearer told him the truth
> He said to himself, 'I've been a gouf.'

I felt that the attempt to review in midstream and pull things round by direct confrontation with issues had accomplished little, and perhaps even added yet another touch of unwanted solemnity to the business of writing. I was so much in danger of making the very idea of writing poems dull and unrewarding, that it seemed best, again, to retreat. If I bided my time, moreover, something would very likely turn up; that was the one feeling left undeployed, so to speak.

A change of atmosphere was due anyway, I felt. 'Atmosphere' is a notion teachers do seem to work with, though the word itself seems vague. For me it seems to indicate something more than a change of activity, and more than moving on to a different kind of resource. The work had been slipping towards heaviness, and my own posture towards the children felt rather insistent. I needed to be less demanding, and some relaxation and humour would not come amiss. I decided to show them a day or two later a 'Picture Box' film about a North American pig farm, a beautifully observed and undidactic piece. Having showed it I asked whether they wanted to see it a second time; they did.

On the second showing, not having intended to through wanting to keep things 'light', but tempted to because the children evidently found the film amusing, I used the pause button to arrest and isolate images that were visually appealing – a ruck of piglets, a close-up of the snout and huge ears of a sow asleep, and so on; the children made at least one quick drawing. I suggested – and this was also unpremeditated, even against the grain of the conscious attempt to lighten things – that they could (not should) make 'notes', with a sentence or a phrase per line, so that they could remember the interesting moments of the film, either the images or the equally graphic sounds. I stressed the need to record these observations in detail, and promoted their descriptions with one or two of my own; that one sounds like a motor bike, and so on. In the space of a few minutes, without expecting to and in response to the children's evident relish for the film, I had pulled back from the 'casual' offer of the film as straight experience, valid in its own right, to exploring the possibilities for writing that seemed to be emerging through it. If their recent 'unadventurous' writing seemed to necessitate some positive priming, this seemed an ideal way to accomplish that.

By this time I had it in mind that they might write something in a narrative or descriptive manner, avoiding the poem, and suggested a few titles with narrative implications: 'A Pig's Day' and so on. Even so, I was asked, 'Can I do a poem?' It seemed difficult to refuse outright, and I suggested they might do a prose piece with a poem in it – a pig describing the day, throwing a song in at a lyrical moment. They then wished to see it a third time. This was a surprise. More to the point, the fact that they did so made an immediate difference, I think, to the expectations I had of their writing. It suddenly seemed as if they were not reeling under the impact of an unduly heavy or even obsessional approach to writing. Their resilience and powers of recovery – or their tolerance – were greater than mine.

This wish to see the film a third time, in a context where yet more writing was in the offing, made it seem as if the motivation or set of attitudes I had presumed needed creating was in fact present. It may be that teachers discover where they are in a teaching relationship at about the same time that pupils do; this would hardly be surprising, since the relaxation of any tensions felt by either, such as might arise through the teacher's uncertainty about what might be achieved, or the pupils' worry about not doing well enough, must be conveyed to the other. The teacher's tension, in particular, is bound to hold the frame of his work with children, however they might be feeling. Walking round the class looking at the notes they were jotting down endorsed this optimism. There was much vitality in them.

What I noticed might well have been partly a product of beginning to think that things were improving. The writing that they then did, using their notes as a basis for a continuous piece, was confirmation of this 'improvement'. The list of phrases I jotted down, mainly from their finished long pieces, contained several that seemed to be 'imaginative' in a way that their earlier work had not been, or had not seemed to be at the time:

> they slumber along
> radar snouts
> wobbling stomachs
> asleep and breathing softly
> snoring like the sound of construction equipment
> bombarding their mother
> sparkly piglets
> lost in the grass
> scratching time on posts

And so on. I felt it was opportune to go further, since the notes seemed so positive. None the less, a suspicion inherited from the previous failures combined with the optimism accruing from these notes to generate a cautious compromise. I asked the class to write the notes out, then photocopied them, chopped them up, and gave each child a copy of the bits, which I asked them to link together in any way they wanted to, adding words and missing out words.

This itself may again have been unduly 'purposeful', and yet – and this is the central point, it seems to me – because I had in some sense broken through to a point where both my actions and theirs were clearer and more interpretable, the presumed fatuity or wisdom of a particular action became less important than the fact that a context for interpretation had come into existence and made such interpretation in general both more plausible and less precarious; which is a way of saying that a relationship was, or felt as if it was, in the process of being formed, in which events do not have to be handled as isolates, with more or less enigmatic and frequently overstated significances deriving from their isolate character, but as moments in that relationship. In this regard, clearly, the relationship of teacher and pupil – in its pedagogic as in its social aspect – is like any other close relationship; the meanings it embodies become clearer as the protagonists understand each other better.

Waiting

Another way of putting this would be to say that a crucial part of teaching is the willingness not just to defer judgement but to wait for a relationship to develop to the point where interpretations of children's writing and their 'worth' are made in a context with a history. Having been compelled to wait by a series of misfires, as they seemed to be, I began to feel that waiting was what I might have devoted myself to from the beginning. That is, I did not know what was going to happen, and could not make things happen; a lack of assurance – a diffidence about proposing outcomes – was simply realistic. I should not have expected 'results' from work done early in the term with children new to me. That was not because there were no results, but because their interpretation as such, when I was still unaware of the 'capacities' of children producing them, limited the possibility of responding openly to what followed.

Hence the slight shock of pleasure noticing what Marina had written and herself revised without intervention:

> Get up
> Get fed
> Go back to bed
> Untill youve woken up
> Go to the troff
> look for left overs
> Scrach
> Your ichey patch
> Go back to bed.

Her revised version:

> Get up
> Get fed
> Go back to bed
> Untill you've woken up,
> Go to the trough
> And really scoff
> Yourslef,
> Scratch, scratch, scratch,
> Scratch your itchy patch,
> And go to doze again.

Noticing these autonomous improvements involved acknowledging that her writing was not the naive outpouring I had assumed, but reflected – or could at times reflect – a shaping intelligence, a capacity for reworking.

At about this point in the term, then, in a way that many teachers will recognize, a cluster of 'difficulties' began, without seeming entirely illusory, to recede into the background. An altered set of expectations about these pupils' writing set in like a change in the weather. Nor is this to say that actual 'improvements' were not discernible, only that expectation and performance seemed to affect each other reciprocally. Expectation functions like an intuitive forecasting device, and is responsive to signals that are not clearly available to a sharp but local perception of the immediate present. At any rate, beyond this point, as over a watershed, the landscape changed.

For example, when Janet had done her Heracles poems, she had written down sentences almost word for word from the book, lining them out beautifully, but changing virtually nothing; she added 'bright morning' to the sentence 'their eyes sparkled like rock pools in the sun'. In other ways she seemed extremely concerned not to risk mistakes. And yet there was a second version, written at the same time, where she added 'big, open' before 'rock pools', as if making a tentative move towards experiment. Then after the pigs film, for the first time in the term, she wrote a more relaxed-sounding poem (as well as a prose piece) on the pigs, colloquial in tone and less nervy:

> Running black and white pigs
> Running to their food disier [desire]
> Eager to get there before the birds do,
> Queue-barging,
> Toppling over
> Head-banging
> And then suddenly colapsing!

Leo had accused himself of rhyming for the sake of rhyming and had then gone on to produce trite rhyming poems. Yet just after rewriting the one quoted earlier, on p. 31, he wrote this, after looking at some slides of dragons, in this case a painting by Uccello:

> *St George and the Dragon*
>
> T'was glorious day
> When George killed the dragon
> The blood was kept in a see-through box,
> On the temple wall,
> To be seen by all,
>
> The scean was dark,
> the leaves of the trees
> had been burned,
> by the dragon's firy-breath,
> And there were parts of animals' flesh
> lying around.

There are five more lines of description, then he repeated the lines at the beginning, ending with capitals and exclamation marks:

> ... on the temple wall/ TO BE SEEN BY ALL!!!

He combined the free-verse manner of the Heracles work with his own inclination to rhyme, here confined to the single rhyme, used in dramatic fashion as a refrain with a variation in tone which points the meaning perfectly. He had found a use for rhyme, then, and the earlier 'practice' was not wasted effort if it contributed to this small breakthrough. In one sense it is small, of course, and it might seem that there is some absurdity involved in reading significance into such minutiae. Leo's next effort was as trite as the earlier ones, moreover. Why focus on it at all?

For one thing, any such achievement is an accomplishment which is valuable in itself, whether it is repeated or not. Second, it stands as a kind of marker of what is possible for that child, defining him in terms of his furthest throw, so to speak. Third, it immediately becomes slightly enigmatic, in that it poses for the teacher the problem of how to gain renewed access to what is evidently 'there'. Leo's poem is significant in relation to what he might come to do, in the near future and eventually.

What the teacher notices, though, is not simply the writing itself. After a few weeks with a class it seems possible to interpret small bits of what would earlier have been indecipherable behaviour as signs of commitment, increasing confidence, willingness to take risks, and so on. Nicholas, for instance, had earlier tried the piece quoted on p. 19 about a killer whale; I had written underneath, 'Have you seen a killer whale?', thinking he might not have:

> White and black,
> Big and long
> Through the water it swam.

And so on in the same vein. He had in fact seen one, and the fact that a month later he returned to the same subject, treating it quite differently, suggested some need to put the experience into words:

> It was the afternoon we went whale-watching,
> On a big boat,
> We didn't see anything,
> but a dolfin and a shark.
> But then we saw something
> that was black and white,
> big and long.

This second attempt ends unrealistically, with the whale eating Nick 'for its afternoon snack'. But his wanting to try again, in quite different terms, signals something about his relation with writing; I recall thinking that, when there was a moment, he could look at a video of whales that we had – which he did. With him, as with Marina, Leo, Janet, and others, my clearer sense of what I could suggest for their writing, my firmer grip on teaching, came about through increased awareness of the situations of individual children; this in turn was a consequence of having waited for a while, or rather having had to.

Waiting may seem an oddly passive and unpromising attitude of mind to take up when, here as in other areas of the curriculum, there is so much 'to do'. It may seem that what is needed is not primarily patience but a sense of urgency, a brisk commitment to explicit teaching aimed at sensitizing the class to the possibilities of poetic techniques and ways of speaking; one decides that the children need 'teaching', that they need to 'learn something about' metaphor, how to listen to the rhythms of what they write, how even, as Ted Hughes suggests,[7] to think. There are many inducements to embark on such a remedial programme, and many ways of doing so. But the danger implicit in pursuing this course seems to be that without being aware of doing so one begins again to assume the simple consequentiality of what one does, making the same mistake as at first, this time with 'putting it right' instead of with 'getting them going'. One finds a different short cut, but a short cut none the less.

Clearly, waiting does not imply not teaching in this direct fashion; but it does imply that the teacher looks less for results, for prompt, overt signs of remediation, than for something else. The teacher has expectations, that is, but they are not immediately for 'good poems'. Then what are they for? Clearly waiting must be for something. What it seems appropriate to look for, in the absence of achievement, is any trace of the possibility of achievement. Trite or obvious though that may sound, it is a difficult programme for a number of reasons.

First, looking for the fragment of utterance that is evidence of the possibility of growth is intellectually more strenuous than receiving writing as evidence of growth not yet achieved. Second, the teacher of writing, who is traditionally efficient in that latter skill, has been socialized into far greater awareness of recognizing shortfall from stated standards than into recognition of what may be waiting to come into being. Third, valuing the hint of what might emerge is apt to seem like finding portent and significance where there is none, clutching at straws, and pretending they're in the wind. Finally, it is likely to seem like a betrayal of the child, a relative inattentiveness shown to those things the child 'cannot do' and needs to do. For these reasons, which all relate to involvement in school practices which are socially constructed, one imposes on oneself habits of mind which continuously work against more serious intentions. In short, it remains difficult to wait, even with a commitment to doing so.

Perhaps part of the difficulty is that waiting seems less an activity in itself than a mood that settles on other activities – properly so called. For teachers the activities are syllabuses, strategies, methods, and so on. And yet they are not themselves a mode of attention paid to the child, they are social objects that need to be attended to, through which attentiveness to the child flows. The recognition of the child expressed through what I am calling waiting does not exclude from consideration those very solid social objects, but is perhaps a way of revaluing them, of seeing them neither as efficacious instruments of learning *per se*, nor as peripheral bits of the classroom landscape through which, with the children, we pass, but as something in between, at the same time consequential and inconsequential.

Another obvious consideration argues for patience. Children arrive in one's class with words, and ways of arranging words. The poems they write derive from earlier encounters with the idea of the poem, an idea which may be fertile in its recognition of what children do through poems, but which also can often be reduced in various ways – for instance, and typically, to a set of intrinsically 'poetic' subjects, a heightened vocabulary and emotive stance, and a preoccupation with rhyme. From the impoverished idea of the poem emerges, inevitably, the impoverished poem, the poem that fails to discern its own possibilities. Much of what children write, when they seem to fail, may be seen as issuing more from a lack of sustenance, a lack of awareness of possibilities, than from a lack of the 'poetic' impulse in them. Starting to encourage children to write therefore seems to be less to do with pulling interesting levers than with slowly finding out what their ways of writing are, and what may be done through them, with them, and beyond them; and with what the teacher may do and say.

Early work with children is thus likely to be confusing; and particularly to mean bouts of uncertainty about what can realistically be asked of them. A brilliant demonstration lesson on how to start a fire in a dustbin may leave behind it a great darkness as to how to get out of the dustbin and into the poem, and the uncertainty is a result of not knowing, because the children are new to the teacher, what this classroom event has meant for them. It seems clear that this uncertainty will extend into the responses that the teacher makes to what they write, especially when it appears unimpressive, flat, and so on. In respect of the pieces with which I began the chapter, anxiety to 'get them moving', concern with indecipherable handwriting, awareness of real spelling problems, a judgement that one child was unhappy, and so on, all militated against seeing their work clearly.

Even if my basic assumption was that everyone was going to write something sooner or later that would give pleasure to both writer and reader, and even if I had settled down prepared, as it were, to wait all term for this to happen, actual immersion in the term's work tends to thin this patience very quickly. It always seems particularly hard, and it did with this class, to keep in mind that the point of departure is not the idea for writing, not the resource itself, the book or film or poem that I decide to 'start the term with' or carry on or change direction with. It is somewhere in the bewildering confusion of voices that surrounds me as it surrounds all teachers – bewildering until I start to hear something that tells me where I am.

Finding one's place

With this class a sense of the location of individual children, particularly a few about whom I had been concerned, emerged towards the end of November. Again, some narrative is needed even for a cursory view of how this sense of finding one's place developed. With some children, it came in conversations about the files of writing they were putting together, to take home at the end of term. Two such conversations, with Claire and Geoffrey, were about the notes they had jotted down while making a brief piece of video film; this had been prompted by a lesson about avoiding cliché and the obvious, during which I had asked the class how we might make this impromptu and deliberately empty 'poem' 'less boring':

> The branches are bare,
> Snow is falling,
> The robin is chirping,
> It is cold.

Could they remember anything personal and private to add to any line? When Geoffrey suggested 'To complete the white blanket', I said we could perhaps look at how Ted Hughes wrote about winter, and we read a few poems from *Season Songs*,[8] pausing on 'The Seven Sorrows' and then 'Sheep'. I said I thought that 'Sheep' couldn't have been written if he hadn't been there himself, and that perhaps we can't really write about robins either just from vague memories of them. It was at this point that Marina suggested going outside to look, and I mentioned the video camera. We might see things about branches that would let us say something less boring than 'The branches are bare'. We wouldn't try anything else, just that one line, as an experiment, to see if going out and looking helped us. Nor would we start a new piece of writing – unless anyone specially wanted to; we'd done a good deal of writing and we were just looking at a way of improving rough ideas. Even here, though, someone said, 'Can I write a poem?'

We spent forty minutes taking bits of film, all involving trees, and when we watched it I asked them to jot down notes, including things people said, like 'If you lick your finger you'll die' after touching something fungal. They read out their improvements to 'the branch is bare', and it was striking that Claire, who volunteered, said things that sounded much more free than the stiff little pieces she had written before. A few minutes later I read her lines over with her, and said I thought they were 'good', and the best she'd done so far, but I couldn't follow one or two bits, which I pointed to, and I asked her to go over the following notes herself and see if there was anything she could make easier to understand:

A new class 43

> The branches are bare with no leaves to keep it warm,
> The ivy climing to kill the bark.
> A poinse log waiting to kill,
> A small white bud waiting to come for summer,
> Dead trees, dead leaves going pass,
> Snow is falling with a small laire to the ground,
> The robin is chirpping with cheeful song,
> It is cold with the day gone bye,
> You tough the cold wet leaves.

She brought her book back a few minutes later, and I asked if she liked what she'd done? Yes. I said I thought she had really made it sound clearer, but that in a couple of places I still couldn't quite see what she meant:

> The branches are bare with no leaves to keep it warm,
> The Ivy climing to kill the bark,
> A posinous log waiting to kill,
> A small white bulb waiting to come for summer,
> Dead trees, Dead leaves going pass as time comes,
> Snow is falling with a small layer to the ground,
> The robin is chirping with cheeful song,
> It is cold with the day gone,
> You touch the cold wet leaves in the winter wind.

I asked if she felt like trying one more time, perhaps? I put a pencil line under the awkward bits in lines 1, 4, 5, and 6, and she made a second attempt at revision, but made only one further alteration, and a spelling correction. Again she said she liked it. Then, I said, it would be nice to have in her file. I didn't push her any further towards a completely grammatical, clear version; the gain she had made seemed solid enough.

With Claire, I had been concerned that what little she did had been featureless and dull; I now had a clear sense, read off from her demeanour, that she could do all this without loss of momentum and enthusiasm. Evidently she could write far more expansively than the cramped and inert pieces from early in the term implied. My concern about Geoffrey had been of a quite different order; I feared that his natural enthusiasm might have been driven underground somewhat, perhaps through my asking for too much writing, or by the over-serious or 'heavy' emphases

I mentioned earlier. This meant that when I looked at his, though I was pleased at how impressive they were. I was also chary of suggesting anything that involved reworking. But in fact he had, I then noticed, already taken two further steps without having been asked to do so, converting his notes immediately into a poem, and then revising and rewriting it for his file. He was already engaged on what I had worried about asking him to try. His eight-line piece ended:

> The larch trees wilting,
> The maple leaves claw their way to the top of the path,
> As all the tree die and droop into winter.

Was the fear of submerging his enthusiasm misplaced? Partly, perhaps, but at the same time it presumably worked against the possibility of taking that enthusiasm for granted – or continuing to do so. Without such anxiety the teacher is likely to keep a less sharp weather-eye than usual on children whose talents are 'obvious'. If they are thought special, it is easy to assume either that they will write interesting things as a matter of course and can be left alone to do so, or that they can 'take' much more than others, and need less protection from coercive styles of attempting to stimulate their talents. It seems clear that a casually tolerant neglect disqualifies itself as teaching. What is less clear is that while the teacher needs positively to draw talent out towards expression and fulfilment, the pressure which an intent drive to 'get children to write' can inflict on children is a form of classic classroom un-freedom no less than any other.

In a different way, Marina, who had suggested going outside to find less boring things to say, was beginning to show me that my fears about her 'dashing things off' were misplaced:

> As little children laugh
> Chattering about the place
> craciling leaves
> where they tread
> Danger looms of [off?] uncertain plants
> Death is possible even here.
> Moss shows through as green as grass
> Leaves are shinning like sparkling brass.

One or two other children were less inhibited than earlier, and this relaxation into expressiveness was illuminating. Janet, for instance, had done two or three pieces which were derivative, and which plagiarized here and there (in the way that children unsure of their identities as writers seem to do). I made suggestions for freeing the poems of echoes, and for writing something fresh, on her own. She then did a piece she called 'Secrets', of which this is the first section:

> Knowbody knows of my den
> In the garden,
> The hen that had chicks
> The thisel bush that's dead
> And the golden apple tree
> Know body knows of my den
> In the garden
> And knowbody will ever know.

Peter had earlier written four seasons poems with every line beginning 'Look at': 'Look at the snow, it's very white,/Look at the ice, it's very slippery.' and: 'Look at the grass so green so green,/Look at the sky so blue, really.' His writing had gradually seemed to loosen up, and on 24 November he produced this:

Poem of the Sky

> The thunerclouds come, all is still,
> The roaring thunder, the shaking earth,
> The clashing rocks, the ruff sea,
> The bumpy waters of the ocean.
> The rocks are falling, the rocks are crumbling
> and the sea can't keep still.
> The sharks came up and started to look about the sea,
> The thunder clouds go, the damage
> is there, the wether is normall the wether is nice and evryone
> comes out to play.

He wrote underneath it: 'I thought I would make a change. Its realy what I see from my boat when its bad whether.' So that it was not just the freedom and enthusiasm of the piece itself that changed my view of what he was doing, but his personal decision to 'make a change', to write in a way that he chose to himself.

The sense that a number of children were gradually un-stifling themselves, if I can put it that way, was unambiguous, and gave me a clear idea of where we were, and a confidence about later outcomes. Of course there were still children who seemed to be stranded or relatively inert. Some of the personal suggestions I made to individuals were either listened to with enthusiasm but then not taken up, or received with apparent discomfort. I said to James that he might like to try a group of short, funny poems in his rhyming style on each of Heracles' adventures if possible, so that he would tell the whole story; his smile was full of amusement and keenness, but at that point nothing else was written. (When the same suggestion was made three months later he took it up actively.) Lorraine reacted in the same way when I suggested she might try to rewrite her original 'Nits' piece and improve it. George's best bit was a line or two about the pigs film; I said he should try to develop them, but nothing came of this. Edward, who had started the term writing keenly, had apparently quite lost his enthusiasm, though not his confidence. I was still waiting for this small group of children, but having waited successfully for the rest, I ended the term feeling that the general thaw into willingness that I had felt in a number of children was likely to affect the rest.

'How do I get them to write poems?'

Perhaps some clearing of the ground has been done when the teacher has begun to discard the exploitative stance and set of expectations connoted by expressions like 'get them' to write. One purpose of this chapter, though, has been to describe the way in which these impinge despite and even during the attempt to discard them. It would be helpful if the phrase itself, and the other mechanistic terms used to formulate the process of encouraging children to write, were to fade into disuse. A more useful language would still hint at the possibility of giving shape to the process as a whole, but would also recognize its messy and formless side, its arbitrariness and digressive uncertainty, and its occasional apparent pointlessness. It would acknowledge the shifting emotionality of teaching, and the structure of intentionality that underlies the apparent formlessness.

A new class

Behind mechanistic forms of expression survives a misleading model of the classroom, a way of looking at teaching which seriously distorts any complex versions of it, such as, and in particular, that which seeks to describe 'creative' processes like those under discussion. For example, in Larson's collection, *Children and Writing in the Elementary School*,[9] Beatrice Furner suggests that 'through pre-planned experiences, perceptions can be heightened, and the need to explore and express feeling created'. She proposes 'methodological steps in a creative writing experience', which are: first, a 'motivation period in which children's attention is fixed on a broad topic in order to generate interest, develop a mood or create a need to write'; second, an 'exchange of ideas to crystallize each other's thinking'; third, a 'writing period'; fourth, 'sharing of ideas'; and last, 'follow-up activities, if appropriate'. Seen from a distance, something like this may seem to be part of the practice of many teachers of writing (not entirely owing to the influence of the model). But the model hardly encapsulates what teaching feels like to a teacher. Indeed its inadequacy as a formalization of processes such as those described here is so blatant that its survival is puzzling; it simply omits most of what is crucial about what teachers and children do.

Yet it does appear to survive, in the literature on creativity, in the training course seminar, and not least in teachers' minds in the classroom. Teachers themselves draw on it; it is still readily assumed that purposeful movement takes place in a methodical progression, and that the causal certitudes of the language (helped in the example above by using the passive to skim past what the teacher might actually be doing) express self-evident and predictable relations between activities and outcomes. It characteristically conceives first of an initiating move, such as the presentation of a 'stimulus' – a film, say – followed by a task which 'arises' from it; or the task may be introduced at one stroke by the peremptory 'setting of a sensate problem', to use Witkin's oddly bleak phrase.[10] A move to 'related', or 'connected' activities may then take place; the film becomes dance, discussion, improvised drama, and so on, in imaginative waves out from the centre.

Causal words like 'arise', and 'connected' sustain the illusion that some energy in the stimulus transfers as a matter of course to the task 'arising', and charges with purposefulness the disparate activities beyond that which have become 'related' to it. The 'logic' of the model disregards the fact that these shifts and developments do not just happen. The relating of a story to the film, the drawing out of an idea for writing from consideration of the film, are the achievements of teaching. They are teaching, they are what makes teaching difficult. To accomplish a move from the film to the task 'arising' is precarious not just because of the problems of control that can develop when changing direction. Every such move raises questions, about the legitimacy and worthwhileness of the path taken, about possible outcomes, about neglected alternatives, and so on. While the causal terms suggest smooth unproblematic transition, the stages they refer to – or rather the stages they omit to refer to – are often drawn-out phases of particular uncertainty.

In short, the model does not even conceive of the continuously pressing question of movement as a problem for the teacher: how to go, for instance, from the enjoyment of a film to the different experience of writing, or drawing, and so on, without undercutting either. One aesthetic experience tends to drive out another; the teacher has to ensure that neither the experience of the film, nor any subsequent experience, is driven out by urgent 'follow-up'. Drawing up lists of useful resources and follow-up activities can leave the teacher without inspiration as to the actual things he intends to do and say or not do and not say when the film finishes. The notes that accompany the fine 'Picture Box' series exemplify the way in which this model confronted me at one point during the term. Looking at the notes for the lovely pigs film I mentioned (Spring 1985), I found a wealth of suggestions about what to do next, but nothing about how to look at the film itself, how to 'respond' to the 'stimulus' – for instance by staying with it. Similarly, the booklet suggests a descriptive poem, but the teacher in need of advice on either how to introduce the idea of the descriptive poem, or how to start writing one with a class, confronts the omission of such problematic stages from the model. The advice which the booklet has for pupils – 'keep the words and phrases of your "sow" verse sleepy, heavy' – is similarly offered as if it were non-problematic. The mystery (just how do we keep words and phrases sleepy) is hidden by the simplicity of the instruction.

Despite the inadequacy of such approaches, children may none the less, as I suggested at the beginning, write interesting things without apparent difficulty. But it is just as likely that careful preparation will produce little of the good writing that is hoped for, and a great deal that is featureless. The teacher has 'failed'. But the idea of failing in this sense is no more than the counterpart of the mechanistically conceived version of 'success'. Both ideas derive from the model, and assume implausible connections between teaching and what the children do. The teacher-centredness of this outlook, whether it punishes or flatters the self, might easily be tempered by the obvious consideration: that with children the teacher hasn't met before, the events that take place for the first weeks – or perhaps months – may have much more to do with what happened last year and the year before than with one's own current 'influence'. This is obvious, perhaps, as a proposition put before the mind, but the involvement and seesawing emotionality of teaching, in which the children's first efforts are felt as manifest reflections of one's own skill, will have little of this detachment.

Perhaps the child saying 'I can't write poems', and the teacher saying 'I can't get poems from my class' may both be giving expression to a sense of failure which is bound up with proceeding in the way I have described. It is failure not in fact with writing or the eliciting of writing, but with those inadequate procedures of setting and performing tasks that are often defined in practice as 'writing'. If eliciting or writing poems means working in the manner sanctioned by the model, then failure is inevitably far more frequent than success. But the failure then is not a failure of a child or teacher, but an expression of the inadequacy of an idea.

The idea we need to formulate to describe how we may elicit writing from all children needs first to recognize the real complexity – and apparent messiness – of what is being attempted. This frees the teacher from the most burdensome expectations, and in so doing allows him to place at the centre of his concerns not the programme for writing or the course or the slab of curriculum, but the child as writer, and the personal meaning for children of what, often very slowly, they eventually achieve. There is more to children's achievement in writing than 'language development'. It seems simply more realistic, certainly more in tune with the satisfactions they appear to take from writing, to see the writing they are pleased with as existentially important, as an increment to the sense of being. It is possible to handle their writing simply as a task-like and peripheral something they have 'done', which incidentally (but for some more importantly) also shows how well they can construct sentences, spell, and so on. The poem may be that, but it is more significantly part of what the child is. If there is one activity, therefore, for the overstretched word 'creative' still to perform, it is to acknowledge this central complexity, to cry 'hands off' to any demand to have the writing of poems conform to the briskly assembled intellectual tidiness that still seems visitable on many writing tasks in school.

The fabric of school life is continuously expressive of ways of thinking that see the 'results' of teachers' actions in children's behaviour. Their consequence for writing is the belief, which has truth in it but far less than is implied in routine thinking, that the teacher wields some power over children analogous to that of a conductor over an orchestra; good teachers get good performances out of children. The truth that there may be in this is buried by the failure to note how much the children themselves are doing, how much depends on them, how totally the writing that may emerge belongs to the child and originates with the child. There is a more balanced view of the respective work of child and teacher which pays sufficient attention to both. The task is to recognize that when children write well it may not be in direct response to the *kapellmeister* teacher's good preparation, interesting lessons, and so on. It is perhaps more oblique altogether, more to do with the nebulous matter of trying to make it possible for the divergent and multifarious impulses towards writing that may exist in children to surface into actuality. Time, patience, and much else are needed for that. To attempt to offer autonomy, an authentic relation to writing, freedom to find their own subjects, and so on, at a stroke, is itself a sign of thinking in that deterministic way I am suggesting the teacher should escape.

One can know something like this, and yet make the kind of errors I described above. Looking out for direct consequences, not finding them, and being concerned, may mean not noticing other things taking place which derive from elsewhere. The fundamental mistake is disappointment, which is here a form of impatience.

3
New subjects

Starting – a lesson

I have tried to describe the slow and uncertain way the teacher comes to terms with a new class, stressing the anxieties and doubts that surround the effort of encouraging their writing. I wish now to describe some attempts to initiate writing when the teacher is more familiar with the children, and works with a sense of individual possibilities defined enough to function as a rough map of what the class might do. It might be thought that a greater straightforwardness now enters the picture, and to an extent it does. But given an overall basic awareness of what a class is 'capable' of, the process is still by no means without that disconcerting unpredictability I drew attention to in the last chapter. In particular, there is the problem now not so much of establishing a general environment for writing, as of initiating writing on particular topics. In its way, this can be as numbing as meeting a new class; like any fresh start, it can involve anxieties and procrastinations; what to write about, when exactly to start, and how, what approach to take – these issues produce their minutes or more of hesitancy, and imply decisions that can be put off or muffed.

I want therefore to look at children 'beginning to write' in response to particular ideas for writing, in the context of the lesson itself and immediately beyond. I shall describe first the process of embarking on a piece of writing with a group of 8- and 9-year-olds. The narrative begins, for reasons that will be clear, before the actual collaborative construction of a poem.

I was again using *The Labours of Heracles* with the class. I had read aloud two chapters to start with, and the children had read a good deal on their own once they became captivated, as children of that age readily seem to be, by the drama of Heracles' adventures. Having begun with a clear notion both of what we should read together and of one topic I thought it would be appropriate for them to attempt writing about, I stalled at the moment of beginning to work towards what I had intended to be a longish piece of prose writing. Someone mentioned the amazing number of things Heracles had to learn at the hands of his tutor, Chiron; he had counted thirteen. We talked about what he would find easy to learn, or more difficult. Someone else wondered how he would get on doing ballet.

This appealing idea, and one or two others thrown up in pure burlesque spirit, diverted me from the original idea I had of starting with a piece about the strangling of the two snakes. To gain time to think, I asked them to read for half an hour, and after some deliberation over alternatives suggested they should describe one of Heracles' lessons in some detail; they could devise their own 'subject' for him to learn, and it could be funny. I also said, almost inadvertently and certainly without quite having intended to at that point, that we might write some poems about Heracles. Who likes writing poems? 'Not serious poems', someone said, 'About the Middle Ages', James said, evidently referring to one of his that had appeared in the school magazine of writing the previous year.

Two days after this I read to them Heracles' encounter with Cerberus, 'The Hound of Hell', still dithering about the appropriate moment to write a poem with them. Despite their absorption in the story, I lacked any sense of what they might find especially powerful in it, where for them were the moments of drama that might be starting points for working fragments of original text into poems. I had decided that a way in to writing Heracles poems was by thus drawing on the condensed poetry of such a story. The intensely compacted drama of the tale makes it compelling as poetic raw material, and the spare manner of Ian

Serraillier's version[1] seemed to make it particularly suitable for reworking. Recasting and elaboration do not seem to compromise the imaginative power of such stories, or to resemble paraphrase. In some way, indeed, retelling and re-creating seem to add to the fictive hold of myth; and focusing on one part of the tale may become a way of penetrating it more deeply.

At any rate, to deal with this indecision, I asked the class to write down from any one place in the story so far, (comprising by now several of Heracles' exploits) two or three sentences which they thought they would remember for some reason, or which were particularly exciting. (This was roughly the idea I fell back on, a few months later, with the class I wrote about in the previous chapter.) The next day, they read several of these out aloud, and to get some clue as to their feelings about the extracts they had chosen, I asked why we remembered certain things in stories, certain sentences.

> Rachel: Because they impress us.
> Self: I wonder why?
> Rachel: Because they are imaginative.

I wrote this word on the board, and then there was a kind of hiatus, not prefigured in my idea for a lesson. I still was not sure whether to say baldly, 'Right, we're going to write a poem', or to leave the sentences they had read hanging about, so to speak, for a moment or two, partly to see if something else was going to be said, partly to see if some fresh perception of their poetic or dramatic power struck any of the children without further intervention, I remember saying, somewhat lamely, 'What shall we do with these sentences, I wonder?' After a second or two Karen said, 'Write a poem? In our own phrases?' Perhaps she was being 'helpful', even a shade ingratiating, guessing my thinly disguised intentions, but she may also genuinely have sensed an opportunity to write about something appealing – and in fact she subsequently tried six Heracles poems that evening.

Her words 'In our own phrases' might suggest how she looked on poems; as her own, and as a group of phrases, or short lines, or statements without verbs. The expression made me think again of James's 'medieval' poem in the magazine; it had been written after similar 'preparation', though in fact it was constructed out of complete sentence statements. I gave out the classroom set of magazines, and we read this fine heroic-sounding piece:

The Black Knights

When the Black Knights arrive at your castle
You'd better start packing
Their arrows swoop on you like an eagle at its prey
They won't let you get away.
Their bows stretch like the sun rising at dawn.
Their arrows are faster than a leopard.
Their armour is black and magical.
When you see them in the distance, it's a message of death!
Then, when there's a wind of arrows, it's like a thousand deadly drops.
People say, 'They come from the stars!'
Others say, 'They come from the Devil!'
No-one knows, nothing knows,
Anything about the Black Knights.

I suggested that to write about Heracles we might need bows and arrows and similar heroic things, and praised James for having found a dramatic and different way of using these frequently mentioned objects. The class also thought the poem was splendid. 'Brilliant', one or two said. I asked James, with the class listening, how he got the idea about bows stretching like the sun at dawn. It seemed that it was a remarkable allusion to a visual similarity between the sun lifting above the horizon and the increasing fullness of the bending bow. That image, I felt, came from a very alert sensibility. The very interestingness of the idea, and his own relish for the poem, must have acted to some extent as an incentive to the class, so that part of the later success of the work may well have derived from the lucky chance of striking not just on James's poem, which was always available, but on his very positive relation to it. His pointing out to me that I should have read it more dramatically made this even clearer.

By this stage, then, we had a version of what poems are – things 'in our own phrases' – a model of a fine poem, and an area of genuine interest, though no clear subject. I asked where we might start, to attempt a poem together, 'for practice' – a tactic which might have been no more than further procrastination. David suggested Heracles in the Underworld, and I mentioned the river, and Heracles crossing it. I began a brief oral description, which was completed, or continued, by Kim saying, 'And the ghosts screaming away', which I wrote on the board, without the 'and', as the first line – 'phrase' – of our poem. Stella said, 'I have a phrase', and gave us 'in the misty darkness', so that the poem began with the two phrases:

The ghosts screaming away
in the misty darkness.

I hadn't asked whether we should take the phrases as lines, simply written them like that. Not surprisingly, Rachel asked, 'Are these lines a poem?' 'Yes – we can change them about.' Despite this limply enigmatic reply – the kind one can produce confronted by a large aesthetic question in the midst of a small artistic struggle – Rachel said, 'Can I miss the first one out?' Already, five minutes or so into the communal beginning intended as 'practice', there is someone who is eager to break away, to write 'her own' poem.

I asked where Heracles was at this point, which side of the river? Several voices decided he was on 'this' side. How could we show, then, that he was listening from a distance? Mark suggested 'On the other side of death', which Anna promptly amended to 'On the other side of life'. I wrote up this second phrase, perhaps because Anna hadn't contributed so far. We now had:

Ghosts screaming away
in the misty darkness
on the other side of life   (or death)

How about Acheron's boat, I asked? 'A netty mess', Stella said. Others suggested that it would have dead fish in it, and that the oars would squeak. Someone offered 'squealing' instead. This crowding in of ideas implied that there were several who might prefer to construct their own poem from that point on, and I suggested this. There was some discussion of how to continue, and I said they could carry on writing in shortish lines the way we had begun, as in phrases like 'the oars squealing like ghosts', and not necessarily in complete sentences. Jane pointed out that 'You can guess what's in between.' That perception suggested how aware some of them might be about what they were doing.

I also suggested that they might try one or two short poems from other parts of the Heracles story that interested them. This was about half-way through the double lesson. As the others were writing Anna, who was recently new to the school, came up and said she couldn't really do poems, only stories, and showed me this attempt at a poem about Heracles and Atlas; she wasn't pleased with it.

> Heracles looked up at the great giant.
> His hands were holding up the great sky of stars and planets, all looking like tons of little glow worms.

I asked her, not very helpfully perhaps, whether there was anything she could miss out to make it sound more like a poem and less like a story. This is one example of how I must have shaped their sense of the poem through implying a particular way of 'defining' it. I found myself slipping into this 'like a story/like a poem' way of speaking quite often with this group; they took hold of it themselves, not surprisingly perhaps, frequently coming up to say, in criticism of what they had written, that 'it sounds like a story'. Without being quite clear myself as to why, I felt it was valuable that they were making a distinction of this kind. This of course is what one means by saying that notions like the idea of the poem are 'socially constructed'. Teachers can hardly teach children what poetry 'is' in any universal sense; it is rather that through their speech and in social interaction with particular pupils in a particular place they set up a quite local and provisional working sense of the poem.

Anna 'didn't know what to miss out'; she hadn't done poems at her other school, and she couldn't really do them. They didn't sound like English. I underlined one or two phrases for her and asked her to think whether she could miss them out, and I wrote in her book her own phrase 'holding up the great sky'; that way of isolating phrases and 'making it sound less like a story' was, I said, one she could try out. She came back a few minutes later with a new version, lined out differently, having added a satisfying last line and kept in two of the three phrases I had underlined as expendable. It now read:

> Looking up at the great giant
> Holding up the mighty sky
> All the stars and planets
> Like lots of little glow worms
> Glitter over the whole world

She had made two autonomous changes, missing out 'all looking like tons of' and changing the second 'great' to 'mighty'. The following day she wrote some more verses, most of which were in the earlier, 'story-like' manner; one, though, was a clear verse with a strong and appropriate metaphor for Heracles' footsteps:

> He knelt over with this weight
> And gave the sky to Heracles
> Then he went to get the apples
> And trudged back making earthquakes.

She also tried a short version of the Augean Stables story, in her more story-telling manner for the most part, with a strong metaphor to finish with: 'A string of excitement ran through his body.'

The poems written by the class at this stage, in response to my suggestion that they should 'write one or two more', and finish the poem started communally if they wanted to, seem to show, at the least, a willingness to believe in themselves as poem-writers, and at best a remarkable capacity to create something of worth out of such help as had been offered. Several were done without any further intervention. After further work on them the next day, Marion came up and said 'I've written six!' Jane wrote four poems. This is her first:

> The deadly poison dripping
> from the snakes' open fangs,
> Then lifelessly they drop to the ground.
> Heracles smiling
> sitting up in his cradle,
> Iphicles screaming
> on the floor,
> The women shrieking
> in terror,
> and the men frozen
> to the ground.

58 Behind the Poem

Paul did three poems, one two sides long called 'The Underworld – Part 2', which rhymes in a rather original fashion:

> Sisyphus, always pushing his rock uphill,
> Always moving, never still

And:

> the warrior Meleager
> clad in shining armour

And:

> There began a furious battle
> Jumping and thrashing
> All their teeth a rattle

He mentions Heracles' friend Theseus, and the trip he and Pirithous made:

> Who had wanted the Queen of the Underworld
> For his bride.
> Without her, he said he would have died.

It seemed evident that for several members of the class at least the stage of 'beginning' to write poems about Heracles was over. Moreover, Anna's willingness to work at her piece and revise it thoughtfully meant that her initial inhibitions were no longer a problem. The feeling of coherence that this work with the class had was in fact not compromised by this or any other particular uncertainty. As with the other dithering and indecisiveness I have mentioned, the fact that difficulties emerged against a background of general familiarity seemed to make even the least positive lessons comprehensible. This was in marked contrast to my feelings about the work with the group in Chapter 2, where little sense of meaning and design developed at the level of the lesson until I saw it emerging over a longer period.

This contrast suggests more to me than that interpretation depends on acquaintance. Certainly classroom events need antecedents before they become meaningful. But this is not to say that familiarity 'takes' a particular length of time. Part of my

New subjects 59

difficulties with the first class lay in trying to read the detailed pattern of learning before seeing any of its overall shape, but part also lay in assuming that the overall shape ought to be discernible sooner than it was.

The robust commonsense view would be that what one is really talking about is the difference between a dull class and a clever class, and no more than that. This seems to me dubious. On the face of it, and leaving aside the absurdity of the expressions themselves, there seems no reason to expect a clearer sense of the coherence of work with a quicker group than of the work of a slower group. It may be that teachers are sensitized to the pace at which quicker children learn, and recognize more readily the achievements that happen at that pace. The temporal unit of a short series of lessons may be assumed to be the length of time which begins to reveal the shape of all learning because it is that length of time which makes plain the learning contours of certain kinds of children. If the teacher's awareness is focused on the fastest-ripening process, the other slower processes will be left somewhat mistily out of focus. And if familiarity is built up out of numerous fleeting recognitions of the process of learning, that familiarity will build up more efficiently with those 'quicker' groups whose pace of achievement the teacher is sensitized to notice.

Another start

I shall describe one more starting point, with a third class. The unpredictability of these beginnings calls for more narratives than there is space for, but something may be achieved by pointing up differences of treatment in an approach basically similar to that just attempted. It illustrates further the implausibility of contending that launching into – or loitering or moving crab-wise towards – writing can be adequately described as a series of phases. Narratives of lessons or series of lessons resemble much more the quirky and arbitrary twists and turns of real life – and real fiction – than they do textbook models; exemplifying that thoroughly calls for an anthology of such starting points.

I had read to this class of 10- and 11-year-olds the tales of

Proserpine and Ceres, and Glaucus and Scylla, from Rex Warner's *Men and Gods*.[2] When they had read one or two more on their own I returned to the Proserpine story, to focus on the plight of Cyane, the river-nymph who attempts to impede Pluto in his abduction, and whose pool is struck open and destroyed by him as he forces his way down to the underworld carrying off Proserpine. Her plight seemed poignant; also, the fact of her not being one of the three central protagonists seemed to make it a usefully oblique way of re-reading the story. The choice of this starting point was my own; there was no consultation about what might make an interesting focal point, and no attempt to search round for what they found moving or powerful in the story.

We would write a poem about Cyane, I said, imagining the horrifying event from her point of view, and writing it in the first person, as if she herself were re-creating the experience, from the moment of seeing the chariot bearing down on her. I intended, as with the other group, to start 'communally' and then encourage them to finish on their own. Here there was a difference, in that there was no pause to accommodate diffidence, no hesitation about plunging straight in; it was a week or so after the lesson just described, and it may be that once such tentativeness had led successfully into a lesson, like stepping carefully in the dark, it felt unnecessary, even with a different class. So, what would she see that would frighten her? 'Black horses', someone said, and I wrote that on the board. 'What else would be black?' 'Black flaring nostrils', came one reply, and others offered reins, eyes, manes, and so on.

At this point I was reminded of the Green Knight, and described him as well as I could remember, suggesting that we should write one or two more 'black' lines. Did we need another colour? There were suggestions about 'red eyes' and so on, and they coloured the developing picture as they wished to. It then seemed appropriate to relinquish colour, and I asked what we should have 'in the next section'. There were several suggestions about the horses' movement, and I wrote up one – 'the horses beat down on me' – because, I said, I found it frightening. It is difficult to make choices for a communal line or verse without seeming to reject those that are not incorporated in the developing poem; the danger is avoided if it is clear that the teacher is making a personal, off-the-cuff choice between alternatives that

New subjects

might be equally good, and clear also that they need not follow the communal version themselves. I said that the idea was to provide them with a means of making their own way into the poem, not to write it for them. Two other lines were called out at the same time – 'broke the silence', 'broke the surface' – and since they were syntactically parallel but different in degree of literalness they made an interesting vibration against each other. We now had:

Black horse
black flaring nostrils
red eyes

The horses beat down on me
and broke the silence
and broke the surface

Other phrases that were offered were incorporated in the version on the board, and the lines below were added:

They smashed the pool
and drowned the peace.

The pace of all this was quite brisk; the only role for the teacher at such moments, where there has been a rush of ideas, seems to be to guide the flow by encouragement and approval, and to resist the tendency to slow up into critical 'appreciation' of what is being said. Even so, the appearance of a metaphor like 'drowned the peace' seemed to demand acknowledgement; and I said this was a 'different' kind of idea, involving violence done to something abstract – could anyone think of some other abstract ideas that might 'suffer' at this point? I asked the class to note them down if they could. I said we ought perhaps to have a section on Cyane's own body, since that itself disintegrated. Perhaps we could mention part of her body not referred to in the story, such as her eyes. Her hearing would be blurred, someone said; then two more lines were suggested in quick succession:

My feelings collapsed
my blood froze

As soon as this pair had been written on the board, Catherine said 'Swop them around'. I did this, with a comment of endorsement of the value of experimenting in such ways.

The collaborative construction of a poem about Cyane had gone on for about twenty minutes or so, and it then seemed appropriate to 'leave them to it', to finish individually what had begun communally. More important than the amount of time itself, though, is the teacher's awareness of the moment to relinquish the role of pilot, in the recognition that the pupils wish to be on their own way, and that they can navigate themselves. This is an imponderable of timing that seems hard to talk about except in terms of intuitive awareness. I suggested that they should carry on on their own by finishing the section about the dissolution of Cyane, and then rounding off the poem in whatever way seemed right. Below are some of the lines written in this part of the lesson – lasting for about fifteen minutes – when the poem became their own poems, and no longer communally assembled.

> Dominic: I hear the birds for the last time
>
> Chloe: The song of life was getting faint.
>
> Lorna: My fingers started melting away
>
> William: My heart melted
> It was adream
> that froze
> into water.
>
> Catherine: The sacredness of the pool
> was lost forever.

At the same time, in this short period, others started rewriting the early part of the poem:

> Rory: Black rider
> black reins
> black tossing mane
> red eyes
> red rider's cloak
>
> Catherine: Pluto
> turned the ripples
> into great breakers

I selected these lines, and others, and read them aloud to the class at the beginning of the next lesson. My 'criticism' amounted to little more than saying I liked them, and they made me imagine feeling the kind of things that Cyane was experiencing. I now wanted them, I said, to do a second version of their own, including the good bits they had thought up, but altering or missing out anything they wanted to (including the communal beginning, I stressed), and adding anything else they wanted to. This set off a brisk conversation or two, and some questions. 'I'm going to do that' (miss out the beginning), 'Does it have to rhyme?' 'Does it have to be a poem?' These last are two questions that any teacher of writing will recognize, and my replies, I'm sure, vary with the class and the occasion. I said in answer to the second: 'Let's have phrases and words on separate lines, the way we have done already.' And to the first, 'No, unless you want it to, and we haven't been rhyming so far.'

It is difficult, it seems to me, to do this part of one's teaching well, because the hard preparatory part seems to be over, and the children have shown some awareness of what they are being asked to do, and are starting to write well. It is easy to become impatient, and hope they'll 'settle down and get on with it', rather than recomplicate what seemed to be coming clear. You now want to see results, not go back to the uncertainty of a discussion of what the basic properties of the poem are, or what the outline of the task – which they 'clearly understand' – really is. Even so, the questions will come, and they did: 'Can you do two verses?' 'As many as you like, in separate bits, the way we did.' And: 'Did the pool actually vanish?' 'Look at the story again.' And: 'Do we have to have black horses in?' 'It's your poem, do what you like.'

Towards the end of the first session, I suggested that, once they had finished a second version of Cyane that satisfied them, they could try another poem from the *Men and Gods* stories about the metamorphic change (such as Scylla's) that we had read several examples of. As with the other class, I had dithered for several minutes in silence as they wrote, wondering if it might be the right moment to suggest more writing. There is always the danger of pushing an idea too hard (especially if it seems to be working), but there is also the danger of caution inhibiting the development of what has been begun. Moreover, there was enough time left – three-quarters of an hour – to talk individually to anyone in difficulties, and to remind anyone who might have forgotten about which stories we had read. Even so, several wanted to spend as much time as they could reading other stores in *Men and Gods*.

The questions that emerged during this latter part of the session point to the value for the children of having time to pause and reflect in mid-task, in that these questions seem to touch on deeper issues than did the earlier ones. (Again, their unexpectedness can seem digressive.) A boy asked, 'How can we call her "I" if she's disappeared?' I had no answer to this, as far as I can remember, beyond saying unilluminatingly that he might keep on saying "I" as long as he could. 'Can we do changes from another point of view, like the person doing it?' I thought this was a good idea, and mentioned Circe, envisaging a poem in which she expresses satisfaction at accomplishing the transformation of human visitors into beasts.

In this and other ways the range of possibilities for writing seemed to broaden during a session that had begun with an anxiety lest writing dry up prematurely. From seeming cautious, their questions became adventurous and expansive. One or two asked if they could move on to other mythologies, through the stories in the collection of non-Greek myths on the classroom shelves. Other questions related to the folder I had mentioned: 'Can I call mine "Metamorphoses?"' And to other kinds of writing: 'Can we make up our own changes?' My own response to such questions is that their adventurousness represents, in dramatic form, the endorsement through the pupils' own enthusiasm and interest of a subject which starts by belonging to the teacher, and in that sense representing the world of established knowledge. Any taking up of personal relations with 'knowledge' seems significant, and it is a question I wish to return to later. Here I shall only note in passing that this phase of the work, when I had paused for breath somewhat, provided time for several children to reveal a commitment to what they were doing which had been hidden during the busy, collaborative phase. That the relation between pupil and knowledge should change in this way seems as desirable a product of the work as the quality of the writing itself. The point here is also, of course, that neither the pause nor of course the consequences of it had been in my mind at the start of the session.

A final question, called out aloud by someone, was: 'Was Cyane born in the pool?' Promptly, from his next-door-neighbour, came the reply: 'She was born in the pool in the beginning of the world.' The unselfconscious Syngean lilt of that seemed to legitimate what we were doing with the tales. As the questions were asked, children were beginning to come to the desk to talk about what they were trying to write, or just to ask for an opinion. There were also problems. Nicholas came with his second version. I had earlier read part of the first attempt aloud to the class, saying I liked the lines:

> The song of time was getting faint
> My body became lifeless, then water

He corrected me at the time, saying that he had written 'song of life', and that I had misread it. He had then altered it and followed my misreading, and now had;

> The tick of time was getting faint

He had done this in response to my saying the song of time had seemed a good idea; I suggested that 'tick of time' sounded like 'nick of time', and he might use those two in a different poem about a watch or a metronome. He had also dropped the communal idea about 'the sacredness of the pool' and written his own three-line section:

> It drained the peace.
> My bath went down the plug-hole.
> I saw my birth-place melt away.

I was puzzled at this. I asked him what part of his poem he liked, and he chose 'I saw my birth-place melt away'. A less good part, he said, was the line 'With tremendous might', which came after 'It came tearing towards me/and broke the silence.' Why? It didn't really say much. Were there any other less good lines? He chose the line about the bath, but seemed unsure about why. I asked whether Cyane would be likely to say that? He wasn't sure, but did say he could see a 'clash' between that line and the one after it. He hadn't, as I had thought, put it in because it sounded funny, and in fact he didn't find it funny. His final version, which he wrote immediately after this talk at my desk, was:

> Black horses
> with black lips.
> And a black rider
> with black eyes.
>
> It came tearing towards me,
> and smashed the silence.
> Then shattered my pool.
>
> It drained the peace,
> My world became nothing,
> I saw my birth-place melt away.
>
> My feelings collapsed.
> The song of time was getting faint.
> My body became lifeless,
> then water.

Without prompting, he had added a line – 'My world became nothing' – which provided a lead in to the third line in the section, and made it a better unit rhythmically. The other changes were retained, so that the third version was the result of some conscious shaping and some conscious choices, made partly but not wholly in response to my questions and suggestions.

One more example might be given to show pupils moving away from reliance on the residual collaborative version to their own original Cyane poems. This again was a version brought to the desk for discussion during the session. Catherine showed me her second version, and alongside it some pencilled additions to the first version, done during the first collaborative lesson. These contained some shifts away from the communal start; for 'flaring nostrils' she substituted 'smokey nostrils', and she deleted 'fiery' for the eyes, preferring 'staring'. The last few lines of the collaborative version were altered, and four new lines inserted (in different places), so that the last part now read:

> evaporated into thin air

then new lines:

> I heard the last bird,
> saw the last tree
>
> my blood collapsed
> my feelings froze
>
> then silence fell again.
>
> My fingers went numb
> My body felt weak and shrivelled

then two more new lines:

> felt the last feeling
> then vanished into the mist.

Then, as the pencilled arrows in her book show, she moved the four new lines in a group to the end, so that it would now read:

> My body felt weak and shrivelled.
> I heard the last bird,
> saw the last tree,
> felt the last feeling,
>
> then vanished into the mist,
>
> then silence fell again.

I wrote in the margin, by her last line about silence, 'Would she say this?' Her pencilled reply was 'Yes!' Her confidence seemed justified. She made one further remarkable but simple alteration when she wrote her fair copy, substituting 'searing' for 'staring' (which she had at first altered from 'fiery') at the beginning.

The earlier reading aloud of first versions, and the approval of other children and myself, seemed to encourage the taking up and reworking – not in a plagiaristic way – of others' ideas. Alex took hold of Catherine's notion of hearing the last bird, developing it to:

> My fire in life was dimming,
> The last bird was singing.

Dominic developed the 'drained' idea:

> They drained the peace,
> They drained the light,
> Water was my only sight.

One or two others adapted the communal beginning; Jackie, for instance:

> Green eyes flaring down on me,
> The reins were burning with heat.

There is an adage that the strength of a poem, unlike that of a chain, is the strength of its strongest link. Looking at the reworked versions of poems that were written close to the beginning of the attempt to write about Cyane, I find strength of that kind, moments of real power, lines that are faithful to the spirit of savage invasion, and a loss of self consequent on loss of place.

> The silence fell
> and the cool water
> turned into burning water
>
> And then with a crack of terror
> they vanished, and my pool
> was flowing away.

I also see the poems as having emerged from 'teaching' in a way that seems, as a narrative, unique to those three or four lessons. In that respect such uniqueness might be compared with that of other narratives – the short story, say. Whatever resemblances one story may share with others, in terms of characterization, incident, development, pace, and so on, the story is encountered and readable only as that story. The account just offered is a gathering together of particulars which may resemble other accounts – and at the level of 'narratology' even be 'the same story' – but which is unique at the level of experience. One can no more draw from schematized accounts of teaching the truth that lies in any one coherent assemblage of narrative particulars than one could read, somehow, 'the short story' itself, the genre apart from its examples.

Under way?

I have given two examples of the process of 'beginning' poems. I want next to describe some of the situations that arise once writing seems to be under way. The expression could be misleading; some children take responsibility for their own work very early, even during a collaborative start, as we have seen. There have been glimpses of children confronting obstacles by themselves. Terms such as beginning, getting under way, revising, finishing, can distort by implication, in attempting to superimpose a convenient conceptual stability on a very fluid, even chaotic, state of affairs.

However, there is a point beyond which the sense that something is happening is strong enough for the teacher to feel what has been aimed at is, indeed, under way. The children are 'caught up' in what they are doing. This is not to say that teaching then becomes less difficult. It could only be thought less problematic and uncertain if the feeling were that the children are now 'on their own'. Because it sometimes seems to be assumed (by teachers of writing as well as by other teachers watching from a distance) that indeed they are, it seems worth commenting on such a view. It perhaps derives from two sources. The first is a notion of creativity which sees most intervention as interference, or as soon modulating into interference; artistic endeavour should be 'free'. This seems a simplified ideological stance rather than a pedagogic objection, but it can enter the classroom as undue respect for the freedom of 'their own unaided work', and a loss of the sense of the teacher as an active artistic collaborator.

The second source is a pedagogic resistance to the notion that teaching writing is a matter of relating to – and coping with the practical difficulty of helping – 'individual children'. Here the rhetoric of 'individual attention' is badly out of step with the actuality; a genuinely operational belief in the need to understand and work with individual imaginations undercuts the legitimacy of many group practices that are hard for many teachers to give up without inflicting on themselves the feeling that they are 'not teaching'. A dash of popular sentiment about creativity added to pedagogic resistance is strong support for the idea that encouraging writing means leaving children to 'get on with it'. Perhaps one reason why children write fewer poems than they might is that scrupulous teachers sometimes associate 'creative writing' in general, and the writing of poems in particular, with their own provisional withdrawal from that direct engagement which they feel children have a right to. In that case nothing much else would need to be said about the teacher's work. I am here of course making quite different assumptions, one of which is that the teacher's work – with individual children and their imaginations – becomes no less crucial once the children have started to write.

It is in this light that I wish to look at how the Cyane work developed. As I said above, the other part of the work that I had asked the class to do was to find another metamorphic change of physical identity from the *Men and Gods* collection and try to turn this into a poem on the lines of their attempts with Cyane. They had no further help with this, and were even more 'on their own', therefore, although of course by this time we had read a number of stories together; several children spent a good deal of the lesson reading to find other changes.

In a sense, the scaffolding of the teacher's support was being removed at this point. They would now be writing poems as somewhat more autonomous agents, without the prop of the communal beginning, and the shared subject. They were now moving from that rather public situation to something relatively private, more intense, and riskier. One might expect, perhaps, that they would be rather less assured, or less fresh, or that they would exhibit signs of the tedium they might well be expected to feel after focusing on the writing of a 'change poem' for three lessons or so. The poems themselves belie this fear, and perhaps even suggest that immersion over a period of ten days or so in stories of metamorphosis was what made possible the poetry that emerged from this second freer attempt.

Simon came up and said he didn't know what to read, and I suggested the Cadmus story. He wrote the following poem later in the lesson:

As I sowed the dragon's teeth,
great men flared up like an arrow just fired,
they rose from the ground
like a sword coming out of paper,
their shiny helmets glistening in the sunlight.

That was his second version, with one line added to the first and one line altered; I saw only the second version, so that his revisions were quite autonomous – though of course the idea of revisions had been stressed in the earlier lessons on the shared Cyane poem.

Two pupils wrote about Ascalaphus, who was turned into a screech owl:

> I saw a woman standing in front of me
> She looked enraged with anger in her eyes
> Yet in her body she was gentle and meaning
>
> Suddenly she dashed water in my face
> and then she cursed me with her mouth and fists.
> (Rory)

> A flash of anger come over her face
> She dashes water in my face
> I scream in pain
> My eyes feel like they're going to split
> My fingernails grow long and sharp
> My mouth goes numb then hard
> And all over my body grow feathers.
> (Catherine)

Catherine also found a subject of her own, Atalanta's race. The drama of part of her account is inescapable:

> I plunged my head into a book,
> muttered a few words
> and watched.

Towards the end:

> I looked at them...
> their sharp claws,
> their savage teeth.
> Somewhere I felt pity,
> but there's no stopping now.

There is drama also in Dominic's account of Midas fulfilling himself:

72 Behind the Poem

> First I took the twig off a tree,
> And there I held gold in my fingers.
> Then I took a stone from the ground,
> 'Zing!' it sparkled into precious metal.

In this, 'fingers' was substituted for 'hand' – a nice shift towards sharper realization.

William writes about Atlas as transformed by Perseus:

> A ghostly figure
> poissonous
> to the naked eye
> my features
> are hard
> my hand
> does not
> react to my brain
> and then
> I'm stone.

The short line is interesting, since it marries with a kind of stifled syntax, intuitively arrived at to convey the restricted movement of the story. The same device – again used with intuitive appropriateness, I suggest – is apparent in a rough draft poem about Actaeon:

> My head bursts
> horns instead of air
> hooves instead of feet
> a leathery hide
> a speed
> nimble and quick
> I try to shout
> no sound.

John, using the same method he did in the Cyane poem, of building up a picture by accumulating statements syntactically in parallel, writes about the Great Flood:

> The stones began to lose their hardness,
> And they became soft like cotton wool,
> And they wobbled like jelly
> And they changed shape,
> And the mud covered the stones.

And so on; it ends:

> And the eyes blinked,
> And then a person stood up,
> And then there were more and more.

These, and others, were written without further preparation or intervention. They seemed to represent an achievement, a completion in some sense of their initial efforts. I made a note to the effect that 'they'd come to the end of this push' and needed a change. I read all their poems aloud to them, with a good deal of praise because I genuinely felt that they had worked hard and that the results were impressive. We would give it a rest, change over to mainly reading and try one or two non-Greek myths, then move on to a quite new area.

It seems important at such moments to convey what one is, in fact, attempting to do in apparently moving on. I had not 'finished', for all the completedness, and completeness, of some writing; it was not a 'topic' that had been satisfactorily 'done'. Some writing had been left in a less completed state than some other writing; certain awarenesses of the drama of myth and the possibilities of writing poems had been raised, and somehow needed to be returned to. In particular, the poems might well need to be preserved, or exhibited, in a more satisfying context than that offered by the exercise book. It is more appropriate here, then, to speak of putting things to one side, taking a breather. In short, a decision about 'ending' this piece of work was also a decision about how to return to it.

Nor is such a decision necessarily best left to the teacher alone. I did not know, except intuitively, how children felt about what they were doing from day to day. It is easy to read enthusiasm into a display of conformist willingness, and to infer tedium when one senses a certain protractedness setting in. I had already offered to them the suggestion that the best pieces from their work on myth might be gathered together in a loose-leaf file, done individually or in small groups. They wouldn't simply copy their best pieces and leave it at that; it would be an opportunity to improve what they felt they could improve, and even to write anything they hadn't had the time or opportunity to write at the time. Should we do this now, or go on to something else and come back to the file later in the term? Later in the term, they said, more or less unanimously.

This might just have suggested tedium, but equally it might have meant that they felt their motivation would survive a period of doing something else. Either way, a decision of this kind means that children are afforded a period of gestation for their work, an interval of non-activity in respect of this work of the kind that seems valuable for any writer, and for any 'creative' work. Once the children had taken up some kind of serious relation to their writing – and to themselves as writers – it became more credible that they should be able to put their poems in a drawer for a while and then return to them, in the way that 'real writers' do. And clearly I could 'teach' or encourage the taking up of such an authentic relation to their work by endorsing such inclination to deferral as was felt here. What they would experience was the usefulness of letting go of an idea without giving it up.

I suggested it might be a good time to try reading some of the non-Greek myths from the collection of forty or so titles in the classroom. To give the work a different slant I proposed that they should find a story that they particularly liked, and write their own version of it, with a view to later retelling some of them in front of the video camera, to show to another class. They read for two lessons with apparent enthusiasm; I recall hearing a spontaneous 'that's good' at one moment from a girl reading a Japanese legend. The recording of several stories from memory in front of the camera was somewhat laboured, but one or two were successful enough to raise strong favourable comment; and all of these attempts were on non-Greek myth. They then suggested recording some of the poems they had written. This was done without any further work on the poems themselves, but it was a way, clearly, not only of keeping them in mind, but of altering their relation to what they had written, objectifying it in a different form from writing, and making of it a sophisticated 'product' and a performance to be listened to.

I shall sum up what I was doing at that point in a metaphor which might seem apt – or trite – for many moments in teaching. I was juggling with several purposes, as teachers very often are. There was the 'abstract' but central matter of the relation between the child and what had been done, which was positive enough, I hoped, to be resumed later; there was the work that felt completed, and the need somehow to register that achievement; there was the first-draft writing that could be returned to later, if a fresh access of zeal made that possible; there was the need to make clear the kind of shift to something else that was to take place, and the reasons for it, as to whether it was a genuine 'link', felt as such, or a quite new thing, felt as such. And always, of course, the basic dynamic that infiltrates and articulates all this, there was the need to observe and interpret moment-by-moment happenings in the classroom, and the need for continuous intervention in support of these aims.

The obviousness of all this might seem too tedious to spend a word on. Surely, if one understands 'teaching', one simply has to use the word, not pull out a series of empty tautologies from it. It might well be redundant thus to expand the word 'teaching' phrase by phrase; it would be so if such considerations could easily be dug out from the basic term – if the word 'teaching' commonly meant all that, or at least implied most of it. It seems to me that it does not, and that the essential reason for this is that the perspectives of the teacher have not commonly informed writing about the classroom. The complexities that are present to the teacher moment by moment (as purposes in need of expression or protection) have not found their way into the routine picture of the classroom as it is painted in literature 'on education', in administrators' minds, and in the minds of those who speak about and have power over the classroom without spending enough time in it to begin to understand it. The pluralism of purpose that is actually felt and acted on is not in the routine picture. That image reduces by disavowing 'nebulous' matters like the relation of child to work, and by undervaluing crucial questions like the nature of the product that issues from it.

The routine images are severely reductive and have room for 'content', 'work', 'product', and little else. Even in college seminars, the teacher is often still the one who 'introduces' a 'topic' which children 'work on', in the course of which the teacher 'provides follow-up' for the children and 'gets writing out of' them. What is difficult to grasp, perhaps, is that images which seem at first sight, so thin are they, to be parody or contemptuous short-hand, continue to function, in the absence of an adequate language for teaching, as a means of communication, even amongst practitioners. It is within such a semantic and conceptual framework that teachers articulate the often elaborate philosophical and ethical aspirations of teaching; and high-minded aspirations have had at some point to be translated into and filtered through an intellectual pidgin.

In other words, the problem of talking about the classroom is often, disguisedly, the problem of not having a language adequate to, or conceptually or semantically in harmony with, or fruitful for, the way practitioners categorize their experiences of it. An attempt to discuss 'moving on', whether it be from writing poems about Greek myth to reading a novel, or from one experiment in physics to another experiment in physics, runs up against the absence of a professional tradition of writing and reflecting about such moments; hence the sense of starting *ab initio*, of trying to haul oneself up with one's own bootstraps. One falls back, necessarily, on commonsense terminology, and tries to modify and extend what amounts to a crude 'phenomenological' schema, and adapt it to more sophisticated purposes. It was in such terms that I tried to describe the phases of feeling 'under way', and 'moving on', and suggested that several problems presented themselves, even in that optimistic period.

An obstacle

Problems can be disguised, of course, by optimism. I wish to describe now how a confident start that the same class made on a different topic became difficult because of a problem latent in my handling of it. The account stresses another unforeseen element, therefore. There is another typically problematic feature in the situation, in that I was confronted by an initial fertility of ideas which it seemed difficult to develop further. The question of 'knowing what to do with' ideas recurs frequently. It may be even more of a problem in some ways than initiating writing. I have described above what seems a purposeful continuation of such a beginning. I should like now to try to describe a phase of frustration.

A vital and even exciting beginning does sometimes seem to lose its impetus. Sensing that this is happening, a teacher's feeling may well be that she has done her work well enough, and after that they 'lost interest'; she may even think that the children she is teaching are less imaginative or less clever than she had thought. That might be so; equally, and more to the point here, is the fact that obstacles can be produced by the way in which an idea is developed, by something inherently problematic about what the teacher attempts.

With the same class as had written about Cyane, I tried to encourage the writing of poems that related to mathematical shapes; this involved the use of various photocopied images with a geometrical emphasis, some video of snow shapes, and eventually some professionally produced slides on mathematical shapes and some more video I had made, of Japanese prints in close-up. Initially, however, there were only the photocopied pictures, and the videoed snow picture. The fertility of the first 'notes' was encouraging. For example, writing about a picture of the Buddha, striking metaphoric images were frequent: 'archways in the eyelid', 'seagull's wings like lips', 'a boat on the sea of the eyes'. There were 'waves in the eyelashes'. Someone even wrote, impressively but obscurely for anyone trying to see a relation to the Buddha image, 'a massive burst of light falling/ or the peak of a mountain'. Others were purely visual; the ears were like 'canoes', 'iron doors', for instance. Similarly with shapes in snow: a number of arresting images were noted down; icicles like thermometers, the 'plough-lines' left by toboggans; and 'icicles with the spear-point/falling on heads'.

These promising and inventive phrases were called 'notes', as the first jottings for the Cyane poems had been. It seemed reasonable to think that the move from fertile notes to good poems might be no more problematic than with the earlier work. But one of the reasons for trying notes twice, on the Buddha image and then on snow, was the uncertainty of how to develop the first attempt; the same operation was repeated, perhaps rather tediously, because (for reasons I shall try to describe) I didn't know how to proceed. Twice in three or four days my notes refer to this: 'How to turn shape-expressions into poems?' 'How to USE these things?' I noted down possible solutions: give them a starter idea, like a verb that would introduce and help to assemble their discrete phrases. For a Buddha poem, it might be 'take' a seagull's wing for the lips ('seagull's wings like lips'), and so on, and construct a Buddha. This I didn't do; for one thing, the syntactic device for linking the phrases into a poem, hence a basic feature of the poem, would be mine, not theirs. I took my own notes on the snow and the thaw, thinking to draw those together publicly, as a model, but again failed to use this notion; the phrases were purely visual – snow like untrimmed pastry, and so on – and there was no emotional reason for trying to shape them into a poem. (It sank in later, of course, that this was also the children's situation.)

I also considered a session on 'how to change phrases into poems'. The expression has a rather doomed ring to it, and the ideas I jotted down felt cumbersome: to write a title first; to decide on a point of view (who is 'I', for instance – the icicle itself, the observer, the day?); to save some phrases, drop others, and add some if one could or needed to; to rearrange the order of ideas; to leave it for a few days and then reread it. There didn't seem enough movement even to use this shaping device.

Essentially what I am trying to describe is a form of attempted rescue; the attempt to keep afloat an idea that I believed in and which had started well but which, for reasons I was not clear about, seemed stranded. In such situations one legitimate procedure involves putting ideas to one side and turning one's attention to other things for a while. In this case, the shapes notion having been introduced on 5 February, and by the 10th or so still proving difficult, other things could be done that fitted in perfectly well, not just with the immediate 'topic' but with other broader purposes as well. We read one or two snow poems (by Hardy and Edward Thomas) in this dry period, and started to watch the video of a novel read the previous term.

The obvious is perhaps worth saying, that this was not an abandoning of the idea. Putting things to one side is likely to be interpreted, in a social context where the dynamic of work is continuously forward in the pull of clock time, as a kind of evasion. But if the teacher assumes in children, and tries to cultivate in them, a willingness to be serious as writers, they must be granted some awareness of the characteristic difficulties of writing, and some sight of the benefits of stepping away from the immediate task, so as to confront it better later. The conflation of work-time and clock-time is itself an obstacle to creative work in schools, particularly in the extent to which it carries over to

New subjects 79

children; in trying to break away from it, the teacher has to explain, justify, and – when work is accomplished after a 'delay' – point to the value of having handled time differently.

It is equally valuable and necessary for the teacher, whose influence needs to be 'creative' and who therefore needs to be able to allow ideas to ferment. The 'block' in the work is often, after all, the teacher's own creative block. As it happened, the putting to one side of the work did not seem to produce the helpful perception that occurred later. This was the awareness that there was far less similarity than I had assumed between the Cyane notes and the later ones, and that this difference was related to the presence in the former of a story – an integral whole gathering together and helping to order the parts, an emotional reason for ranking events; these things were all absent in the later work.

In retrospect it was clear that there was an obdurate discreteness about the 'ideas', and an exclusive focus on metaphor. This issued partly from the way I began, a 'clever' start; I had asked the children to fit together a dismembered dark Buddha image, consisting mainly of different curved lines. The (perhaps obscure) reason for this was not just to have an unusual game-like way in to writing, but also to try to see the geometric simplicities that made up the image. This was followed by a further nervous error, which involved describing each of the distinct lines (too distinct) in metaphorical terms, writing down 'what it made them think of', and so on. This was done in a rather analytic spirit, so that the result, in their notes, was a taking apart and then a 'poetic' labelling of parts: an operation of the mind somewhat removed from the synthesizing work of the imagination. The poetry, I soon came to feel, had been subverted by working in this analytical way.

An any rate, the shapes idea was left – for a second time, in effect – for a week or so, with both the initial sets of notes (on the Buddha image and on snow shapes) undeveloped. When I returned to it, it was from a new angle, by means of a photograph of a wrecked house, and then the video mentioned earlier, consisting of close-up pictures of Japanese prints: in other words, I used yet more 'resources'. Towards the end of a double lesson spent watching and talking about what we had seen, I asked them to write, one at the top of each page, the titles I had chosen from the video: Snow, Wave, Head, and Bridge, and to invent one of their own for the mysterious house; they wrote 'notes' in a similar way to previously.

Selections from one boy's notes suggest some similarity with the rather sterile earlier attempts:

> Snow: New York streets, criss-cross, chessboards. Fingers reflecting in the light and bleeding water. Chandeliers.
>
> Wave: Tree with snow, Volcano in the distance. Hands reaching to catch people. Boat race people leaning over to be sick. Lamb-chop with mountains and cliffs in the sea. (Someone had suggested the wave looked like spare-ribs, and several used this idea.)
>
> Bridge: Blue mountains. People making their way home. Purple flowers on banches of tree, maybe type of fruit.

On these three pages, then, Nicholas tried out interesting visual ideas, empathized with the people in the boat, or simply described rather neutrally what the picture contained. This is in contrast, it seems to me, to the kind of thing he then wrote about 'The Ship-Wrecked House' (his own title).

> A ghost of a chair sits in the doorway, waiting for someone to sit in it. Long poles groan as they try to keep the rest of the shambles up. Large logs stick out from the ground. The house is afraid to put its legs down in case it might find it cannot hold its own weight. The house wonders if the bomb which hit it is still intact.

The contrast appears to be between the discrete 'ideas' of the first three examples and the much more integral whole of the last. It seems that the last 'title' has become a felt subject rather than an exercise. There is psychological continuity, and an evenness of tone, reaching from 'A ghost of a chair sits' through 'the house is afraid' and down to the remarkable last sentence. It is continuous narrative, not a list, even though it was written as quick notes or ideas.

A similar contrast is discernible in the work of others, though the moments where exercises seemed to become subjects varied with the writer, and though there were some who did not escape – at this stage – the inhibiting inheritance of the earlier attempts. Despite some obscurely felt restlessness with my own efforts, no sufficiently clear reason presented itself at the time, indicating that there was a problem not at the level of the children's capacity to be 'imaginative', but with the whole idea of collecting particulars when no overarching sense of any context into which they might be placed – in which they might have 'meaning', that is – was available to the children. In this respect this work seems to be in interesting contrast to that described in Chapter 7, where the apparently isolated particulars of the children's observation are somehow more significantly framed, and where some later context and function for them is apparent at the time.

One might say, then, that the extent to which this work became successful, as I think it soon did, was related to the discovery (their discovery) of a more human context than the abstract idea of 'shape', or perhaps rather to the placing of the 'shape' theme in such a context. This was unintentionally encouraged by the use of the prints, through which (however I might wish to point, legitimately to some extent, to the 'shape' features of the picture) the children were brought up against the human significance of the situations they depicted. And perhaps there was a moment or two of fruitful tension, between my still earnestly labouring the original shapes idea, and the children's wishing to approach the pictures more directly. In some writing done later there are signs of an attempt at resolving such tension. Corin wrote:

Lady With a Mirror

The curves in her hair swaying gently,
A ridge of hair leans over her ear.
Pure shining white bone balancing in a mass of hair.
The reflection of her face shines in the mirror.
A hill of hair ready to topple on her shoulder,
The birds singing flattened on her dress.

Here, the curves, the ridge, the hill all seem to derive from an emphasis on shapes, and in so far as such pictures are in fact structured in a 'geometrical' way, such a way of seeing them seems exploratory rather than a nugatory interference. Even so, most writing done on the prints goes directly to the central human issues, such as the simple precariousness of the bridge we had looked at. This precariousness had become very evident when the bridge was seen in close-up (by means of pictures taken with the macro lens) so that the image was presented, and discussed, with its human significance to some extent already foregrounded, and the more geometrical or analytical way of looking set to one side. This is Jackie's poem:

Bridge

Rickety and old,
planks like piano keys.
A blue mountain
stretches up into the sky.
Falling you land in a bed of clouds.
Goats stare down, safe on the rocks.
Cliffs on either side,
a beige mist lies far below,
with birds high above not afraid.
Ivy stretches up to the forbidden rocks.
It looks as if it never ends.
Trees grow up and look into the looming blue.
The men look inexperienced and scared,
their bodies look unsteady and unsure.
A small net lies underneath,
but not enough to hold two men's weight.

The vertiginous feel of this might or might not have have derived to some degree from the accident of looking at the image in close-up; but certainly the shapes influence seems absent.

It seems as if this block to further development of their writing at this point in the term had begun to be removed, more or less fortuitously, by the partial abandonment, not of the cluster of subjects and images we had begun with, but of that way of seeing them which I had stressed. Several other children wrote straightforwardly and well in a 'human' way about the prints. But the description of this awkward stage in the process of children's writing is not quite ended with the observation that a number of them had perhaps begun to break out of the sterility I had encountered. For while they had begun to 'get under way' – as it seems in retrospect – my teacher's sense of the situation was that we were still becalmed, and in need of a push of air.

For that reason I resorted to a more 'methodical' approach. This was on the 24th, the work having begun on the 2nd and been intermittently pursued since then. With Trevor's permission, I photocopied his notes for 'Snow' and for 'Wave' and posed the problem of how we might 'turn notes into a poem', suggesting several 'methods' as ways of experimenting: we could add ideas, remove them, change the order in which they were written, see if there were more subjects than we wanted (snow and icicle, for instance), think about the metaphors we had used, and – after we had made one attempt to turn notes into a poem – 'leave it for a bit'.

Such a lesson might have been useful critically, as a way of suggesting that writing is to do with the conscious shaping of language into satisfying forms that are not necessarily available at first draft. It might well have been valuable to convey the notion that the teacher can respect 'unfinished' writing. Even so, to lay a generalized template of method over their writing at this point was, as it seems in retrospect, a piece of erroneous timing. I had assumed we were still becalmed when in fact the children, having found something to write about, had begun to write, not just assemble ideas.

In other words, beyond a certain point, the sense of being at an impasse was partly illusory, and perhaps derived from a slightly inflexible commitment to the original 'shapes' idea. The genuine impasse earlier was produced by my failing to appreciate the extent to which the shapes idea had implications for children's approach to the images we looked at. It tended to coerce them into an analytical approach to their subjects of the kind which is at a remove from what one thinks of as the imagination's synthesizing power. The examples I gave of children writing well – in Jackie's 'Bridge' and Nicholas's 'Shipwrecked House', for instance – convey a sense of subjects seized as wholes and written about with an evenness of tone and an emotional fidelity to responses which cannot be constructed methodically.

If this was interference rather than fruitful intervention, it was perhaps slowness of reaction that produced it, and my perceptions did eventually catch up with what the children were doing. Moreover, the temporary shelving of the earlier notes had left them still available for use, and some of the poems that later began to emerge used them successfully. I have tried to describe the middle, rather difficult phase of this particular writing project, and tried to locate the problem not in children's 'lack of imagination', but as something implicit in the teacher's decision about how to proceed. The work eventually (in the following term) issued in a short booklet of poems which contained successful work based on the earlier notes, and poems drawn from some professionally-produced slides about mathematical shapes (I had intended the earlier things to 'work up' to this). When the children returned to the shapes idea in that guise, and after an interval, it was clear that they had been working in a less fragmented way than I had thought. Examples might help to show this, drawn from the writing of children not yet represented here.

Two examples first from the early work, which perhaps show the over-analytic preparation already being overlaid or shaped in response to the writer's 'subject' rather than the teacher's 'theme'.

Face of a Buddha

Palm-tree eye-brows,
Waves in the eye-lash,
Lips like sea-gull wings,
Sinister cheeks.
Eyes closed as if dead.
Hair like jewels.
        (Thomas)

The pencil starts writing

and out the words come,
written on paper,
about:

rotten shells and
clockwork brains,
a computer screen or
a solitary car,
a peaceful pond
or a fiery mountain.
It goes on in time
till your hand feels weary,
then you get tired
and you stop.
        (Chloe)

Without being particularly remarkable, both these impose some kind of order on the disparate images offered to them, one by seeing the Buddha as sinister and deathly (in the penultimate lines at least), the other by frankly confronting them as a miscellany in a way which implies separate poems might be written about each image.

Of the following three poems from the next term, the first two (I believe) were developed from earlier ideas, and the third done at the time after looking at slides illustrating mathemetical shapes. They are by children not represented so far:

Waterfall

The water falls slowly,
like the moon's streaks of light streaming through the universe,
like long icicles reaching out for something,
like the icy cold blood streaming out of a vein.
(Andrew)

Geometry

Geometry is geometrical shapes like
intersecting cicles forming a pattern,
bridges, symmetrically parallel,
a knot of symmetrical marble entwined with gold,
and a pond covered with parallel lily-pads.
(Jeremy)

Dandelion

A golf ball like a creature,
furry but different from others,
a brain with a spiky hairstyle,
isolated like a flower,
destructed by people
wanting to know the time.
(Oliver)

It is a salutary note to end this chapter on, to acknowledge that the way round this particular obstacle was found by the children themselves while their teacher was still sizing it up; it also sums up a truism that I have been at pains to illustrate, that 'teaching' children how to write poems is often less about what the teacher 'does' than about what he is able to notice that the children themselves are doing. The extended narratives of process have been an attempt to see the classroom in these terms, as a place where the teacher continuously 'does' things, certainly, but in a context in which he watches and listens perhaps more.

Part 3

Dialogue

4
Children's 'autonomy'

A private struggle

In the last chapter I looked at some attempts to encourage children to begin to write poems, and at two situations which can arise thereafter, one in which writing seems to get under way, and one in which it does not, or does so far less readily. At the same time, it has also been evident, I think, that divisions into starting and any phases that occur beyond that are schematic; they are made largely for the convenience of talking about writing, and because they correspond to categories that teachers employ. In reality, I have tried at the same time to suggest, any close description of process is much more elusive than such a step-by-step commonsense model implies.

I wish to look directly now at a question which might have been asked at a number of points already, about the relative contributions of teacher and children to this whole process. In order to approach the fundamental question 'How do we get them to write?' the first three chapters have been concerned with the question 'What happens?' The next two chapters will consider the 'autonomous' activity of the child in all this, and the 'interventions' of the teacher – 'What does the child do?' and 'What does the teacher do?' Glimpses of these have been observed already, but some closer focus is called for. Here again, there is a danger of being schematic, for the autonomy of the child is elicited often by what looks like 'intervention' on the teacher's part, while the teacher's interventions are futile – and are better called interference – without some 'autonomous' response from the child.

Although this dialogic relation between teacher and pupil is, in most successful work, clearly discernible, and although the pupil's autonomy is a matter of degree, there are times when the child's contribution seems particularly clear. The desire to write can seem to occur spontaneously, for instance; or redrafting can incorporate the child's thoughtful amendments and additions in a way that reflects a markedly personal intent to make the best of an idea; and so on. At such times we are close to seeing the child as an 'authentic' writer who, for the moment at any rate, has risen above the relation of dependency that binds the young writer to the teacher. The pupil briefly becomes a 'real' writer and, however transitory this moment is, its significance is immense, since it marks the evanescent success that the teacher wishes to become permanent. What one is aiming at is not so much 'good poems' as the writing of good poems by children who see themselves as writers.

And of course such moments have a further significance for the teacher's own reflective attempts to see how far it is actually possible for the child to be a 'real' writer. Whether it is within their capacities spontaneously to want to write, and whether they can make reflective improvements in their work, are problems which have a crucial bearing on the question of what it is the teacher believes children are doing when they 'write poems'. And why is this important? Quite simply because all teachers, by virtue not just of asking children to write but through the various ways they do it, are giving expression to beliefs they hold as to children's capacities as writers; if these beliefs fail to correspond with the actuality of what children are capable of, either by being too ambitious or by being too narrow, then the children will not be enabled to function as 'writers', even if they are, in one sense of the word, writing.

I want to look first at some children making autonomous alterations in their poems. The first is a girl of 9, Lucy, making a series of efforts to write about some piglets she had seen in a short 'Picture Box' film. She made several attempts, on six separate

90 Behind the Poem

sheets of paper. The class was diversely engaged for several sessions, though all the work bore on a particular project. Groups and individuals chose to write, read, look at slides, or decorate their writing. Lucy's work was self-chosen, therefore. She had no contact with me about it; nor did she show her friends or ask for their help. Her first verson, abandoned after the fourth line, is:

> glorius great gratitude
> lovely lumpcius little and loved
> often optionall of course
> red rumbius and super
>   inglee

Her second, shown below, seems to have been begun – to judge from the appearance of the two sheets of paper – the moment after the first was abandoned, so that she had begun to revise the first version before she had finished writing it; she already drops a line, and adds more. The coinage 'lumpcius' and the mysterious word 'inglee' are used in both, and indeed in all her versions:

> Little pigs are
> glorius great gratitude
> lovely lumpcius little and loved
> ingenius inglee intelegent
> sweet snorting and sick!

Two crossed out lines follow: 'piglets and [indecipherable]/guilty and great'. Then:

> pick piglets playful
> inocent impy
> guilty and great giggling and giddy
> all ready all out alteration about

This is all written out again – a third version – minus the first line 'Little pigs are'. The next version, her fourth, which seems to have been done the next day or the day after, omits 'glorius great gratitude' from the first section, and alters 'sick' to 'slopy', transposing 'pink pigs playful' to the first half and trying various alternatives to the last two lines. The poem in this fourth draft begins:

lovely lumpcius little and loved
ingenius inglee intelegent
pink pigs playful
sweet snorting and slopy

inocent impy
giggling giddy

Then 'guilty and great' is missed out, and the rest of the last two lines of version three are crossed out. 'Jumpy jiggy/waging wadling' are substituted, and then a final pair of lines is added: 'radiant runty/sloshy and scum'. What is striking, perhaps, is not just the experimental relish in the alliterative collection of adjectives, playful to the point of nonsense, but also the immediate critical pulling back from the nonsensical 'alteration about' line. She also drops at this point the 'glorius great gratitude' line, leaving herself with a much neater collection of descriptive words.

The fifth version, the first I saw, and seen as far as I recall when going round the class, is reduced by the removal of 'radiant runty/sloshy and scum' from the end of the fourth, and reads:

lovely lumpcius little and loved
ingenius inglee inteligent
pink pigs playful
sweet snorting and slopy

inocent impy
giggling giddy
jumpy jigy
wigling wadling

The final alteration in a sixth version – with most spellings corrected at my prompting – was to add 'along' after 'wadling'. She only put her name to this sixth page.

There are several interesting, even remarkable, features in all this. There is the sheer drive of the enterprise, the determination, sustained across successive versions, to get the poem feeling right. There is the fact that the various alterations work to fine the poem down to a clean artistic whole. In particular, all the ideas that are not quite assimilable to the short alliterative-descriptive-adjectival version are discarded: the 'glorius great' phrase, the 'all ready' line, and the other tempting alliterations. At one point she alters the basic syntactical arrangement by adding a verb: 'little pigs are'; this is immediately dropped. She also invents ideas as she redrafts; it is not a matter simply of getting rid of what doesn't appeal, but of reshaping and re-creating. There are words that will 'do' but aren't good enough, such as 'sick', to which 'slopy' is preferred, as, presumably, more descriptively appropriate, and 'piglets', which she changes in one line to 'pigs'. The word order is changed around. The line 'pink pigs playful' is first line 7, then line 5, then line 3 for the last versions. She carries on reorganizing and tidying to the finish, adding 'along' at the end, in a way that seems to signal an ending better than 'wiggling wadling' would have done.

I am quite sure, too, that she did all this while keeping up routine social chat with her friends on either side – these sessions were more than usually chatty and informal – and equally sure that her talk fell short of asking them about the poem she was doing or showing them; she did say herself that she didn't talk about it. It seems difficult to resist the impression that she was working in much the same way as a 'mature' poet would, polishing and redrafting until her piece just felt right. It is not the quality of the final poem, but the process of its development that is the crucial feature in all this, of course. What is striking is what the girl is attempting to do, and the ways in which she goes about it: the way in which, having discovered a motif – the alliterative adjective phrase – she hammers away at it without for a moment letting it escape represents the clear-sighted working out of a poetic idea. And needless to say, there is little sign of concern at this stage for spelling, neatness, or the price of paper.

Perhaps it is worth suggesting that one effective way of preventing such fertile experimentation would be for the teacher to raise these considerations prematurely. At the stage when Lucy is 'playing around' with her idea it would be fatal and frivolous to attempt to divert a focus that is already intensely energized. The 'play' is a serious trying out of possibilities, a play of the mind and the verbal imagination, the creative consciousness at full stretch.

A personal style

It was part of Lucy's style of working that sometimes she did not write very much, often crossed out false starts, and did a great deal of doodling when she was stuck. Of six pieces of writing done over about sixteen continuous pages of her exercise book, there are crossed out false starts in four; sometimes these are changes of subject on the same idea, such as from dragonfly to dragon. In writing based on a television film called *Mordicus the Buzzard* she crossed out one and a half pages of attempts at poems, and then wrote two-thirds of a page of prose. On the poems page she wrote 'I gave up'. Yet there is clearly a good deal of effort being put into even the one or two abandoned pieces; reading these over, and a later piece of prose abandoned after two sides, against which she wrote 'I gave up too difficult', it strikes me only that her decisions to give up were right. The awareness that informed them was of a piece with that which shaped the revisions of the pigs poem.

It strikes me now, but unfortunately it didn't do so then, or not so clearly. My comments on her writing at this time (late in the year, when I knew her work well) included a good deal of approval: 'excellent for ideas', 'very ingenious', 'This sounds like a true-to-life diary', and so on. But they also reflect a preoccupation with 'shaky punctuation', 'can't-be-bothered' symptoms, spelling errors, and so on. This is understandable up to a point, and it would have been unfair to her to evade or soft-pedal any skills issue because she was so evidently able to immerse herself in writing. The trouble is not just that such judgements are much easier to make than those that recognize the autonomous writer in her, nor even that making negative judgements on one level seems sometimes of itself to blur perception of other attributes in the writing. It is more that the routine way of expressing such judgements threatens to become irrelevant when a child is engaged in a genuinely autonomous endeavour to write, and it is irrelevant because, as I have already suggested when talking about Lucy's pigs piece, the child is engaged on a different task. The comments are properly appropriate for the formed finishing-off stage; the writing is at an urgent searching-for-expression stage. In her 'Mordicus', where she crossed out one and a half sides of poem drafts and went on, on the next page, to write prose, I simply missed the significance of what she had been doing, by not seeing the drafts. My written comments, in short, did not often enough rise to the level of what she was doing.

In retrospect, all the abandonments, stops and starts, hesitations, doodlings, visual messiness, first draft errors, and so on, seem to be closely related to, even an expression of, a markedly autonomous creative impetus. It seems clear, for instance, that one reason she was willing to cross out and try again was that new ideas were always – or almost always – available. A piece called 'Underworld', at the beginning of the sixteen pages I referred to above, was crossed out after these two lines had been written:

The small fish swarmed in flocks across the sandy fields
When the leader stopped by a large piece of coral

She then embarked on a piece called 'h'Octupus h'our':

The octupus petroled the, . . .
dark, musty, sunken vessel
he wóófts his nose in the, . . .
dark places were fishes nessle.

The octupus changed from petrolling –
to rolling,
down down down stop . . .
dance dance dance plop!!

To give up on a not unpromising thing – the first line is lovely – for something else that comes to mind suggests both boldness and fertility. I liked the shape of the octupus piece, the ingenious rhymes, the use of very explicit punctuation to point movement, the coinage 'wóófts' (with two acute accents over the 'óó'), and so on. In particular, I found the evidently calculated pauses at the ends of lines 1 and 3, resembling an intake of breath at the most awkward point in the sentence, after 'the', uncannily right for signalling an entry into the dark. A single example such as that itself argues strongly, it seems to me, against any view of children's writing that implies that mainly a natural spontaneity is involved, and to a far less extent the conscious work of the shaping imagination. At any rate, the teacher's particular encounters with such examples of artistic activity are likely to form his conception of 'the child as artist', and my own conception is strongly shaped by examples such as these.

It becomes an uncomfortable paradox that on several occasions over the two years I taught her I felt the work she had done was 'disappointing'. It is hard to resist a tendency to expect the best, in solid quantities, all the time, and yet the slightest acquaintance with artistic endeavour and its attendant inclination to scruple – if that is not too grand a way of styling it – ought to make one wary of this all too professional expectation. It seems to me odd that evidence like that just offered should not of itself generate a perspective that is a good deal more open, less professionally mundane, than the one I employed from time to time. I can account for it only by suggesting that a certain bi-valence characterizes the socialized professional psyche, endorsing both the creative and many things that are antagonistic to it. This bi-valence might ideally take the healthy form of an open acknowledgement that pragmatic and creative perpectives are in routine conflict; more often the issue is disguised by a strategic belief in the capacity of institutions to deliver both at once. And perhaps a teacher can go from one to the other, from energetically recognizing conflict to not doing so, and in the latter phase betray something of his own beliefs in the creative.

To return to what was autonomous in Lucy's way of working: one other feature of her work seems worth noting, and that is its small-scale nature. She did not write much, and her most characteristic pieces were short poems, 'Dipper', for example:

Dipper Dipper
Dipping all the time
Splash splash splash
Sort of like a rhyme.

The concern for punctuation in the octopus poem, and for just the right word in the pigs poem, the interest in repeated sounds and sound values generally in all three, are suggestive of a close focus on the materiality of language; it is as if she sometimes doesn't write very much precisely because of this. It seems perfectly expressive of this trait that a year later than the pigs poem, she should spend a good deal of time revising one detail of a poem, working in the same artistically painstaking way. She had written the following lines about a painting:

> Just after winter
> just after dawn
>
> with a newly washed sky
> and a polished sun
> the grass had been hovered
> the river been swept
> the reeds had been combed
> the trees been scrubbed
>
> that's what happens
> just after winter
> just after dawn

The original began 'Just after dawn,/just after winter'; she changed the two lines around. She was then happy with the poem, except for the word 'scrubbed'. What was interesting was not so much the perceptive judgement that this was the case, but the refusal first to let the poem go with the one solecism sticking out awkwardly, and second the determination, pursued over twenty minutes or so, to find the word that would do. She eventually started to use a thesaurus. (It may be, though I cannot remember, that I suggested the thesaurus at this point.) At any rate, she finally discovered that 'trimmed' satisfied her, and the amended version included the line 'the trees been trimmed'. That was the only change, and its isolation seems to convey something clear about the essentially artistic motivation that impelled her to keep looking, rather than be satisfied with a poem that many might have been satisfied with, but which from her point of view was flawed, or unfinished. It is rather less restless as a search than were the varying attempts looked at above, but beneath that surface there seems to me to be a strong resemblance; the same artistic working style and autonomous resolve seem equally evident.

And yet, as I suggested, this commitment and care for detail were displayed by someone whose work seemed at times 'slapdash', even lazy. Looking back at these few achievements – as I should wish to describe them – I am struck first by the paradox of believing someone to be rather lazy (I didn't actually use that harsh term) who demonstrates such purposeful energy, and second by the absurdity of expecting a steady flow of such work. What was worrying, as in retrospect I re-evaluated what she had done, was that the negative judgements I was making – often without articulating them at all, or doing so obliquely or tentatively, and once forcibly – might have been responsible for the intermittent flow of her most vigorous commitment.

Equally they might not. A hard-headed approach might suggest that the kind of pussy-footing tentativeness implicit in the last paragraph is only too likely to result in children's 'getting away with it' and doing things 'when they feel like it' and so on. It would be helpful to be reassured in that way. In fact, the answer to the problem is another question; is it possible, through conveying, however tactfully, judgements that seem valid at the time, to undermine the development of just those valuable traits that one's judgement is meant to encourage? And in this case, is not the drive to get something right so private and unmistakable that the most the teacher can hope to do – in a way that was not even available here – is to encourage by addressing the particulars of the poem in a constructive way. Any broader judgement about the amount done this week or the tidiness of the final version is bound to seem somewhat frivolous, simply because such comments derive from a different frame of reference from the one that the child is operating with at the time.

It seems that there are two general points in this. First, this kind of 'autonomy', which is a particularly wayward and elusive, coming-and-going phenomenon, is very easily discouraged by the premature introduction of perspectives which may seem urgent matters for the teacher but which are not urgent for the child. Second, there is perhaps a logic in the idea that autonomy, if it is authentic, must exclude for the time being considerations which might weigh more heavily in a less non-directive context; if one values autonomy, that is, one takes the consequences, and one of them might well be that autonomy includes the idea that the child decides what autonomy consists in, and another that the child decides when autonomy comes to an end, when to draw the teacher back in. Certainly Lucy, in the first example above, was evidently in no need of 'help' for the period in which she was trying out her different versions, and only brought one for inspection after several trials.

Routine autonomy

This girl's efforts seem peculiarly divorced from the pace of what was happening to the rest of the class at that time. One facet of autonomous work may well be the severance of certain links – of time, and of topic, for instance – that normally bind the child socially to the work of the group, and no doubt one of the problems for teachers is to find out how to help the class to proceed as a group at the same time as creating the freedom for children to go in different ways, and at different speeds. But it would be unwise to imply that the autonomous is always wayward in this manner. What is equally striking is that within the routine framework of set tasks there are signs of a similar independence; they may make reflective emendations even in the haste of routine work, so that it becomes possible to see autonomy not as a somewhat digressive or even aberrant – though especially interesting – style of working, but as something woven into the fabric of the most commonplace-seeming lesson. Two examples will have to suffice, and although they are perhaps exceptional in respect of the fertility of the emendations, they are offered as examples of what occurs daily in routine contexts, as characteristic of the reflective behaviour of children as they work on their poems.

Karen, a girl of 9 in the class whose work was described in Chapter 3, was working on an imitation of a speech in Ted Hughes's play *The Coming of the Kings*. She was trying another few lines like those in which the host's wife berates him with laziness – 'have you' done this and that; these are Hughes's lines:

> Have you mended my wobbly mop?
> Have you nailed the carpet down?
> or flattened the nail that catches in my gown?
> or oiled the door and the kitchen pump?
> what are you standing there for, you lump?

Karen's attempt to imitate this speech, through three drafts all done on the same day, is an interesting and rather mysterious

Children's 'autonomy' 99

example of someone apparently learning more or less on her own, and very quickly, certain things about how to write a poem – about poetic craft, one might even say. Her first version is very awkward and uninspired:

> Have you mended my shoe,
> The one I flushed down the loo.
>
> Have you mended the door,
> That one that scratches the floor,
>
> Have you mended the mop,
> The one that goes flop.
>
> Have you mended my pen,
> The one that I used to write on the hen.
>
> Have you mended the spoon,
> The one I called a goon.
>
> Come and get a move on!

I wrote in the margin, in consultation during the lesson, 'The rhymes are a bit strange', and put '?' by the penultimate line. She said she thought the rhymes 'babyish', and decided to have a 'second go', in which she makes alterations that centre on the rhyming words:

> Have you mended the clock
> And the rusty lock.
>
> Have you mended the guest-room basin,
> I'll get you racin'!

Along with her first trite or meaningless rhymes she had discarded all five of the objects she chose; she started afresh with two only. I wrote 'better' opposite this. She had a third go the same evening, making a splendid alteration to one rhyming couplet, and providing the new objects with attributes that seem to make them more real:

> Have you mended the grandfather clock
> And the backdoor rusty lock.
>
> Have you mended the guest-room sink
> It's black and it's meant to be pink.

The improvements might seem less remarkable than Lucy's adaptations, but despite the brief discussion with me, the work Karen put in to develop this piece seems no less autonomous. It was while working on her own at her desk that she saw the value of specifying the objects more solidly by adding 'grandfather' to 'clock' and 'backdoor' to 'rusty lock'; that is, her struggle to write unbabyish rhymes enabled her to grasp, however temporarily, something fundamental about how to make a fiction credible. And neither that change, nor her substitution of 'sink' for 'basin', nor the invention of the lively colloquial line to go with it, came from remarks addressed specifically to those bits of the poem. I made no suggestion about rhythms or adding adjectives. I even wrote on this version, 'Interesting how much they improve. How did you get your ideas for improving and doing the 3rd go?'

There was no answer to this ('How did you get your ideas?'), and it remains mysterious to me that a girl who started the day content with 'Have you mended the spoon/The one I called a goon?' should end it solidly specifying 'rusty lock' by adding 'backdoor', and by changing 'basin' to 'sink' to accommodate the neat line 'It's black and it's meant to be pink'. I could say that of course she found the original rhymes 'babyish', and that this prompted the improvement: she saw she had done something beneath her capacities and remedied the situation. But this doesn't explain either the original lines or her perception of their 'babyishness'. The lines she finished with might have been available at first draft if she 'had concentrated', but equally it may be a shaky assumption to see the initial banality as a kind of not bothering. Rather, the development from initial banality to the conviction of the final version seems to parallel closely enough the dramatic process of 'simple' improvement as it is visible in the reworking of even major poets' poems.

Examples like this lead one to suspect that, particularly during the confusion of the working day, the teacher may find it hard to note or be aware of the extent to which children may display a capacity for original and independent invention of the kind I'm calling autonomous. The following example, drawn from the work examined in the previous chapter, shows how quickly an initial sketch – consisting in this case of 'notes' on slides – may within an hour or so be totally transformed, in ways which are not traceable to any explicit guidance from the teacher.

Nicholas's two pieces, notes and poem, were written in pencil on opposite pages; I had asked the class to make notes from the slides, writing down either what they saw or what the slide reminded them of, and then at greater leisure, during a double lesson, to 'try to turn the notes into a poem', as they had done on previous occasions.

> Arches, Venice when it wasn't under water. Teeth.
> bright lights. Most shapes are round. A building on its side. Six sided shapes. [He draws two.] A pentagon in the middle. Sea porcupine. A conker in a conker. With wings. Lily pads in families. Reflections on the water. Cogs rusting to a standstill. Nuts and bolts. Islands in the paradise. Complicated series of wires. Car lights. A snake coiled round a screw of many patterns.

The poem is the result of considerable selection and reorganization of ideas, and though it is perhaps not quite enough to circumvent the difficulty of the task itself (in that, as I noted, the slides were perhaps too miscellaneous to be pulled into one statement), the distance travelled between notes and this attempt is remarkable.

> Maths is bubblology
> combined to make lilies
> shapes joined together to make
> lopsided buildings.
>
> Maths is complex wires
> to make complex radars.
> Cogs make anything turn
> including themselves.
>
> Maths is nature going
> to extremes to make things
> nice. Hexagons which won't
> fit make friends with
> pentagons. Islands in the
> paradise quake and erupt.
> Then they bleed.

Two interesting metaphoric ideas are generated; nature going to extremes, and shapes making friends. He uses the words 'combine' and 'make' as means of linking disparate notions. He moves ideas about: lilies and pentagons. He introduces parallelisms (the first verse) and adds extensions to brief phrases in ways which have rhythmic conviction. And of course he omits a number of his initial ideas so that the final result is much less anarchic than the nature of the task itself might lead one to expect it would have been. There is, finally, a sense of developing wholeness behind the imaginative leaps of this particular fantasy, a sense that the mild surrealisms are to some extent deliberate and relished, not just an effect of the oddness of the task as it was set.

It might be thought that the sketches I have offered, and more particularly perhaps the last illustration, of a pupil developing notes quickly into poem, is a description of nothing very remarkable or unusual; that this is what happens all the time with certain creative children, and one should indeed expect it. What then is the value of characterizing such work as 'autonomous' in the way I have used the term? What is the usefulness of the category if one is aware anyway, as a matter of coure, of the rapidity with which some children do deploy their imaginative powers on tasks of this kind? Surely the familiar word 'creative' will do?

First, I am sceptical of the extent to which such activity is in fact recognized – in any detail, that is. The intimacy of the process, the minute-by-minute shaping lying behind the dramatic outcomes, seems insufficiently noted and seldom recorded, either in theory, or by teachers in any formal way. There are also two particular problems about the word 'creative'. One is that other aspects of the classroom can be described as creative – not least the teacher's own work; the word does not specifically point to what the pupil does. A greater difficulty is that in the absence of detailed empirical evidence of actual moment-by-moment 'creativity' the word tends to be used broadly, as an attribute of personality; it is used, that is, to categorize particular children as creative, not to pick out those transient pieces of behaviour in all children that are creative.

It seems useful, therefore, to deploy the term 'autonomous', and find contexts in which it is appropriate to do so, as a means of clarifying (if only a little) such episodes as that which I have just described. An adequate language for describing them seems not to exist. An account of such behaviour may be articulated by means of two traditional categories which are in various ways unsatisfactory, and indeed implicitly contradictory. On the one hand there is the rather complacent ideology of original creativity; on the other there is the characteristically exploitative or behaviouristic language that teachers have been socialized and educated into as a way of describing their dealings with children's minds. In Peter Abbs's *English Within the Arts*,[2] for example, the rhetoric of creativity, contemporary enough to value such things as 'process before product' and 'the phases of art-making', schematizes the artistic activity of the child without drawing on observed activity. His current version endorses 'the creative impulse', 'the expressive act', 'the cultural process of mimesis', 'the quest for personal meaning', and so on, without examining either the emergent manifestations of these desirable things moment by moment in the classroom, or their various contextual and personal sources and dependencies there. It is a book about 'teaching' but there is no classroom in it. At the other complementary extreme – each distortion seems to make necessary the other – the actor-centred language of the teacher who 'provides a stimulus', 'gets writing out of' children, and so on, characteristically fails to note in detail the extent to which the 'stimulus' works, or is taken up, or is irrelevant or to some degree defeated. This rhetoric predisposes its user to seeing children's activity as primarily a result of what the teacher does, and hence to a crucial degree to overlook the activity that actually occurs. In neither conception does the child function as a partner in an intellectual relationship.

In short, whether the language as we find it speaks in terms of a literary-expressive process, or a stimulus-response process, it tends to neglect the notion of learning as expressive of the routine creative interrelatedness of child and teacher, both socially and intellectually. Lacking this sense of reciprocal dependency it does not seek to separate out, from within the one context that relates them, on the one hand those passages or moments that are expressive of the child's autonomous endeavours, and on the other those interventions that the teacher makes which help elicit (causal terms offer themselves only too readily) or in some way contribute to this autonomy. The absence of an appropriate theoretical perspective to account for the relation between 'spontaneity' and 'stimulus' makes necessary some strenuous attempt either to reconcile them or to speak differently or both. This then would be my reply to the suggestion, made hypothetically above, that there is little point in seeking to rename activity that we all recognize by calling it 'autonomous'. Unless it is described in some such alternative way it is in danger of being not recognized; an inheritance of inadequate ways of describing the classroom prevents it. Looking at the work of Lucy or Nicholas through the filter of the 'spontaneity'/'stimulus' dichotomy, we have to classify them as 'typically artistic'; as essentially doing their own spontaneous thing, being different, unpredictable, self-absorbed, in a sense out of touch with what the teacher offers, and remote from what the other children are doing.

To inflict a kind of 'artistic' stereotype on a few children also makes it possible to imply that the artistic efforts of the less creative are dependent on 'stimulus'. The one perspective helps to legitimate the other. Discarding the dualism of this way of thinking leaves one free, on the other hand, to assume the normality of the kind of autonomous creativity I have described. My own response to encountering examples like those above is to suspect that the spontaneity and creativity of children litters the surface of may lessons in ways which our normal habits of categorizing classroom behaviour make it hard for us to see and even harder to explain.

Autonomy and dependency

The free creative energy that Nicholas exercised emerged from a set task. I wished to make the point that autonomy is part of routine situations and is in that sense unexceptional. It may also be seen in this routine context as emerging from a dependency, and it is in this light that I should like to consider the next group of writings, as an example of a close 'dependency' generating – or going hand in hand with – autonomy. The dependency in this case is on a text, Rex Warner's *Men and Gods*, in that part of the story of Ceyx and Halcyone[3] where Iris goes to the 'drowsy court of Sleep' to tell him to send Ceyx a dream to say that her husband has died. I had asked a class of 11-year-olds – not so far referred to – to find the most dramatic sentence in the story, and to write it out. We talked about why they were chosen, and I asked them to write a poem or two about these dramatic moments. Matthew, aged 10, wrote two pieces, each lined out like prose, and more or less without punctuation:

Sleep

Deep in the heavens is a cave a cave of sleep, nothing moving nothing talking just silence only the noise of the stream. Nothing but silence only the images of dreams and the sleepy Nes mist.

Rainbow

darting through the air like a bright light the meany colours of the rainbow shining to earth as the colours form men begain to wander is it the god Iris with her thousand colourd viel or the heavens signaling

These were transferred, in our weekly session in the computer room, to the word-processor. I lined out the second for him, added punctuation, and corrected his spelling. The first he worked on himself, later, producing this:

Sleep

Deep in the heavens is a cave,
a cave,
nothing moving
nothing talking.
just silence only the noise of the stream of forgetfulness.
nothing but silence only the images of dreams,
and the coldness of the mist of sleep.

It is worth noting how independent of the text Matthew has become at this first draft stage. Something autonomous is immediately generated in a situation which might have served to bind him to the original words. His first version is dependent on the original only for the inspiration of the subject and the atmosphere of the cave. Phrases like 'deep in the heavens' and 'the images of dreams' do not occur in the text. And when he puts his piece on the word-processor, he adds 'of forgetfulness' after 'stream'. Warner has 'It is the home of utter silence, though from the end of the cave there flows the stream of Lethe, river of forgetfulness, whose sliding waves, gently stirring the pebbles over which they run, invite to sleep.' What Matthew has done, in two stages, is transform that poetic prose statement into a line – and a bit – of his own poetry. He also alters his own ending, turning a meaningless phrase into 'the coldness of the mist of sleep'. Again, Warner's language is different; it deploys different collocations. There is only a literal mist (mentioned once); the mist of sleep metaphor is Matthew's. Nor is cold alluded to, or anything described as cold until the very last paragraph of the story more than three pages later. The idea of cold is more likely transposed, with total appropriateness, it seems to me, from the 'cold lips' of Ceyx (at the end of the story), in the same synthesizing movement of the mind that perhaps is perceptible in each of these rapidly sketched visions of the drama of the tale.

These pieces were done quickly at one session. Given this, and given Matthew's characteristic 'haste', shaky spelling, and punctuation, it seems unsurprising to me, though a matter for regret and reflection, that my first reading of them again, as with Lucy at times, missed the greater part of what I am now trying to draw attention to; I failed to note the extent of the transformation that had taken place, seeing yet another 'dashed off effort'. What was not observed then was the amount of poetic work, under the surface almost, that had taken place as he wrote them out. And it is interesting that, once I had intervened to line out one piece and 'correct' it, he made no other emendations himself. It was equally true of his first version of 'Rainbow' that the phraseology – apart from 'thousand coloured veil' – was his own; the lovely image of the heavens 'signalling' at the end may have arisen from the context of the shipwreck, but there seems to be no verbal connection.

In at the window

If there is a flavour of paradox about stressing the role of the autonomous in routine situations that appear to be directed, it seems to me helpful in that it tends to make complex what has often been left simple. There is, though, a sense in which it also intimates an interesting truth about 'the creative'. It has been observed often enough that artistic and other kinds of creation frequently seem to take place after a period of incubation

Children's 'autonomy' 107

succeeds a period of hard work; what may also be seen sometimes in children's writing is the abrupt emergence of successful writing out of the shadow of honest but not very fruitful labour on a different subject. This is very speculative, but perhaps it is a speculation worth making, if children do write poems which seem to 'fly in at the window', as Wallace Stevens put it,[4] in that particular way.

The following poem was written during a period of concentrated effort on a quite different topic from the subject of the poem. Catherine's class had been writing poems about shapes – the work described in the previous chapter. She simply asked to write something else; there was no suggestion of a topic, no discussion about any aspect of what she wrote:

Depression

This is something hidden
   within you.
Your own thoughts,
Your own feelings,
Things you've said
Meaning different things
   to different people.
People turning against you
   for false and unknown reasons
The looks people give you,
   meaning hatred and spite.
Being turned out of things
Doing everything wrong.
All this is depression,
Something you have to live with.

The quality of the poem, its courage even, is less the issue here, of course, than the manner of its production. It could hardly be less dependent, directly, on the particular context in which it was written: asking to be allowed to write something different, to set to one side the topic I set up as an encouraging influence. And yet it is clear that she is not 'on her own' in any absolute sense. She has asked to write: 'can I say something that's important to me personally?' The relation she wishes to take up to her own writing is the one which the teacher would like often to be able to set up, a relation in which children 'simply write'. But it is difficult to set up directly. It is only temporarily that children become 'real writers', as Catherine did here, and they sometimes appear to do this when the focus of their routine work is elsewhere, but when something liberates in them a desire to do something that is particularly personal.

There is a kind of irony in this. The teacher 'sets up' work not just in the hope that good poems will be written along lines he suggests, but also with the idea that sooner or later children will wish to write independently of any such suggestions. One can provide for this as a contingency but not directly provoke it or request it – or at least if one requests it more than occasionally it is apt to seem both a vacuous request and a burdensome freedom. In Catherine's case, the personal urgency of what she wrote might well have depended on the absence of any direct appeal to personal feeling; it may have been possible only as a by-product of something else.

Such situations may have relevance for the vexed question of the relation between spontaneity and hard work. Writers have often enough stressed the need for both, but sometimes seem less inclined to clarify the relation between them. Wallace Stevens remarks that he 'almost always dislikes anything that doesn't fly in at the window'. At the same time he says, 'Writing poetry is a conscious activity. While poems may very well occur, they had very much better be caused.'[5] It may well be that in classrooms the poems or near-poems that are caused are obliquely responsible for those that fly in at the window. The ease with which a fine spontaneous poem can suddenly steal out from behind a laborious attempt at something else ought to temper any unilateral commitment to either the spontaneous or the caused. Embraced as infallible method, neither 'works'; seen rather as complementary rhythms of teaching which appeal to and mirror complementary rhythms of the child's mind as it imagines and thinks, both work.

Producing autonomy-subjects

In this sense, spontaneity itself might seem occasionally to be caused; that paradoxical suggestion would seem to have substance if spontaneity arose in particular kinds of situation that the teacher could construct. I shall give what seems to me to be an example of this happening. From time to time, like many teachers, I have suggested to children towards the end of a term or a year, that they might like to gather together a small file of their best work to take home – including three or four poems. This often seems to generate new poems, particularly if children haven't yet done the three or four asked for, or if they are dissatisfied with the ones they have done. Guy wrote two extra poems that I read only on the last day of term, when they were 'in best'. One was about Christmas and the other about garlic cheese; the second begins brightly: 'The tingle and the tang,/It's nicer than mirange' and ends 'You will love it,/Garlic cheese'. The unusual subject, independently chosen, for all that there are perhaps only two worthwhile lines in it, hints at an area of personal predilection and interest that Guy may be willing in the future to draw into his writing. Again, the significance is not in the quality of the finished piece, but in what the writing of it implies, or appears to, about his developing relation to writing.

There is a less dramatic but more significant side to this. Discernible from time to time in children's writing, alongside or emerging within the collective endeavours of the class working as a whole on one topic or theme, are signs of what seem to be individually authentic subjects, the particular ground of the child's imagination. The teacher is frequently in a better position than the child to recognize what this ground is. Donald Graves notes[6] how reluctant children can be to recognize the worth of their own knowledge as a source of material for writing: 'A child who regularly cared for cows, helped with milking, and assisted his father with the birth of a new calf, had no idea he possessed knowledge of any significance.' He adds: 'Those schools who help children to know what they know provide one of the most important services any learner can receive.' Such an endeavour is central to the attempt to encourage children to write, and it is hardly surprising that children overlook what is imaginatively vital in their own knowledge if they are socialized into the belief that knowledge is the possession of teachers and adults generally.

One of the advantages of children attempting a small group of poems, as they did above, rather than just one, is also that in the variety the teacher can sometimes see real subjects surfacing; it is one of the ways to find out what children can write about.

110 Behind the Poem

The invitation to complement set subjects with subjects of their own, if they have any, or to have a group of pieces ready for an end-of-year file, when the file will include pieces that have been worked on together and other things of their own, seems to be one way of avoiding the danger of trying to thrust autonomy onto them. Children in this situation are still free not to be free, so to speak; they can confine what they do to what has been prepared for. I asked a group of 12 and 13-year-olds to have four poems ready by the end of term, from amongst the things that had been attempted or from their own ideas. One collective attempt had involved going out in the grounds, at Neil's suggestion, to look at objects we had tried to write about.

Neil wanted to write poems about dew and leaves, and tried several; one draft reads:

> Dew sparkles like nothing of this earth
> of untold beauty in the rays
> that leak through the mist.
>
> Dew appears over night but where
> from its beauty is untold yet no one knos
> where its from then morning comes first
> and rays of the glisten on dew.

But he also included three first versions of pieces of his own about the sea, which seem to reach into felt experience:

> The sea lets it waves calm for a while
> but somewhere else they are 10 feet high
> the sea is a place of it own
> shellfish and half of its contens
> are know to manking but the rest
> is a secret kept from mankind.

And:

> A boat sways among the waves
> you never know where you might go
> then hoist sails and you will flow
> with the wind among the waves
> set a cource to the North
> bearing 38 and through the waves
> you will go.

Here there seems to be a marked sense of impetus; there are felt moments of something like wonder: the sea is calm here but there are 10-foot waves somewhere else; it is secret, a place of its own. I knew he spent time sailing, but it is one thing to know where the sources of imaginative vitality might be, and another to expect as a matter of course, or ask directly, that they be drawn on. A direct approach would normally seem like an attempt to encroach on a private domain. For a child to have come to sense the possibilities inherent in writing in this way seems a crucial step.

Robert wrote three longish pieces, 'The Mine', 'Execution', and 'Hedgehog'. His tastes in reading inclined to the lurid and sensational, and 'Execution', flatly explicit and derivatively generalized, seems to reflect this. It ends:

Ready
Aim
fire
Blood rolled down my eyes
I felt sick, a heavy fever took over me.
A man came over and shot me in the head.

A second piece came from the walk Neil suggested. An apparently different facet of Robert's sensibility is called into play in his account of their finding a hedgehog curled up in some leaves at the foot of a tree:

In the dead of night,
a hedgehog fumbles through
Thick wet dewy grass,
his back roles like the sea,
as each leg goes up and down.
He curls up by an oak tree
To hope to survive the jaws of winter.
And when morning comes,
a child gently touches, the frozen carcass
With tender hands.

This, I felt, was a genuine expression of his sensibility. His writing two years earlier already had an observant relish to it, and, as in what he wrote on one particular project, was full of an empathizing awareness of natural life. 'I think Highland cattle are lovely but rather rough but look funy with their shaby hair drapped down to their eyes and the horns which curve round so the ends face each other.' There is a marked imaginative feel for others' experience: 'It must have been exciting making eel traps and seting them. Because their are lots of streams in the forest going down each morning cheking the trap in peace of the morning.' But the same intensity can produce alarm: 'Iv always found gypsies scarry sort of people its the clothes that give me the creeps they have lovely cloths but maybe to lovely.' And: 'It was quiet dangerous sleeping in a tent in the midle of a wood, some gypseies wernt to plesent to other gypseies.'

Perhaps the sense of alarm, the undernote of violence that his imagination presented to him when he thought about the gypsies, is the antecedent of that strain in his sensibility which calls out an awareness of threat. His third piece is full of menace, but this time the imaginative projection that seems natural to him finds a different, even a compassionate, kind of expression. Here is the second half of the poem:

> The only noise is the clinking of chains,
> Or a chisle splitting into rock,
> And the scream of some poor victim to the whip.
> The smell of pee
> The never ending choking dust which,
> scratches at your lungs.
> When will it end,
> I cannot imagin anything worse,
> I can not.

So that perhaps it would be a mistake to see the hedgehog piece alone as 'the genuine Robert'. It does seems to me to be genuinely him, but the synthesis of violence and compassion in 'Mine' might well represent, in a sensibility that responds quickly to the idea of pain, some maturing of the imagination to the point where the pressure of situations like executions and imprisonment demands to be handled. His real subjects are changing as his sensibility begins to accommodate more of the world.

Looking at the work of these and other children over a period of time, I see continuities in what they write and how they write, and begin to recognize what they write as an expression of what they are; I develop a sense of what their autonomy as writers consists in. In eventually seeing all children as writers, I see their autonomy as routine and as at the centre of writing. And 'seeing them as writers' is not an ideological posture or a provisional intellectual optimism; the expression sums up recollections of seeing children write and recognizing that they do much more than respond to set tasks. They come to confront and 'rework' themselves in writing, extending themselves in a way that can be impressive and moving.

There is another side to this feeling. For all its routine character, and for all that the teacher may see what individual children are doing and try to point to relations between autonomous commitment or inspiration and other things, every line that children write remains mysterious. If we say we try to understand where poems come from, all that we mean by that is from roughly what direction and during what conditions, and so on. The timing and manner of the poem's arrival are unpredictable. Children's poems come from their being stimulated but sometimes from boredom; from their being left too much alone or too much prodded (freely or even as punishments).

It is often hard to see any relation between the conscious activity of the teacher (and the pupil) and what for the pupil 'comes in at the window'. One particularly interesting – or inexplicable – 'connection' between pupils' autonomy and the teacher's activity seems to manifest itself when lovely poems appear seemingly from nowhere, after or during a time of intense absorption not directly related to the poem itself. The first is by Sarah, aged 13, the second by Alice, aged 9.

Trust

Trust is balancing
On a rocky precipice
Undecided –
With a gently blowing breeze,
Which suggests betrayal.

Tortoise

Plod, plod, plod,
Here comes the slowest animal,
Crawling the slowest crawl,
'I'm going to do a little run,
To mystify them all.'

Behind the Poem

A final example of the same mysterious kind comes from the class whose work formed the subject of the first chapter. Zoe's writings during that first term were among the least 'visible', neither worryingly 'nondescript', nor marked by any evident positive character. Though she registered clearly as a determined and positive girl with a sense of fun, I saw her so indistinctly as a writer that in a sense she escaped notice. She was not in fact mentioned in the chapter, and I recall thinking of her as a 'tryer', with the patronizing connotations that word has. She then wrote the following poem three or so weeks into the second term, in one lesson and without any discussion with me or anyone. During the lesson the children were free to read or write, and if they wrote to opt for working on one of the set subjects we had worked on or something of their own. I remember the sense of quietly urgent enthusiasm about her as she wrote:

The Murder and Cat

Cat sat in the attic
By the boy
Who was not a boy
But a murdered boy.
Up came humans
From the outside world
Muttering, crying
Took the boy
And cat watched the boy
With green flashing eyes.
And he slank away
Following the boy
Until he could see the boy no more.
Cat walked into the darkness once again
And sat waiting,
Waiting
For someone
Perhaps the boy
To stroke him again.

5
Intervention

A suggestion

The examples from the work of Neil and Robert show how a growing acquaintance with the work of a class produces the sense that the teacher is learning something about individual imaginations, and about the experiences that are important biographically. But of course it goes beyond learning; the teacher is likely to want to use this knowledge, and to say, in effect, 'These are the things you write well about'. In this way the teacher is trying to show children something about themselves, and about writing, and trying to ensure that for some of the time at least they write on 'real' subjects. One might completely misread the child, mistaking where true feelings and interests are. For Ted Hughes, in *Poetry in the Making*, 'Your genuine interests are the clue to your genuine feelings, like floats over sunken lobster-pots';[1] but the attempt to recognize this feature of children's autonomy – through the endorsement of a particular selection of their feelings and interests as 'genuine' – is an especially precarious intervention.

At the same time, such interventions seem unavoidable. It would have seemed like a kind of neglect not to say to Neil and Robert that some of their writing seemed especially alive. In one sense all the teacher's activity is interventionist, and this points perhaps to a problem with the term itself. Even when one 'stands back', like a parent who has given enough advice for the time being, it is a very watchful posture, a variant form of one's presence, not an absence, or an experimental neglect. Within the dialogic intimacy of relationships that are as close as family or teaching relationships, not doing something is doing something in a different way; and just as there are ways of being parents that cannot 'leave children alone', so there are styles of teaching that in essence take up that position. The traditional model of the teacher as transmitter of information, beliefs, values, and so on, involves a diminished capacity for that kind of 'standing back' intervention.

Of course, all that I have said about beginning lessons and so on has been about various kinds about intervention in this wide sense. What I wish to look at now, though, is intervention in a narrower and more commonly used sense. In particular, I want to try to describe various kinds of direct involvement with individual pieces of work – the kinds of intervention that might be considered 'help'. And it seems especially important here to distinguish true creative interventions from various species of interference. Marie Peel remarks[2] that 'one needs the catalyst of the teacher's imagination'. The catalyst metaphor – like the Socratic midwife image – seems to focus appropriately on both the crucial and at the same time peripheral and temporary activity of the teacher. In general, the popularity amongst teachers of ways of describing their work which are mechanistically causal leads them sometimes to undervalue both the central force of the child's own contribution and the effect of their own more subtly encouraging gestures – the how rather than the self-evident whats.

The last chapter was an attempt to bring the activity of the child into the foreground; I wish now to try to illustrate some ways in which the imagination of the teacher has to work alongside that of the child as catalyst or midwife to the child's endeavours. It is evident that much of the material which in the last chapter illustrated the work of the child might well be used, if the process had been described beyond a certain point, or simply from the other viewpoint, to illustrate the teacher's contribution. In other words, the distinction between child's and teacher's contributions is made for the sake of examining them in an isolation they seldom have socially, as I hope is clear from earlier accounts of process. The final poem, as one might expect if some sort of dialogic relationship has been established, however transitorily, between pupil and teacher, could be described as the child's 'own' without one being able to say that it has been written 'without help'; the point being that children, like 'real' poets, need 'help' – stimulation, encouragement, helpful criticism – to write what is their own.

The most direct kind of intervention involves the teacher in direct consultation with the child about particular poems. Sam, aged 9, produced the following in response to an invitation to a class to 'imitate' a poem they liked. He chose A.A. Milne's poem 'When I Was One':[3]

When I was one I think of me beginning to grow
When I was two
   I learned to swim
When I was three
   I met my nan
When I was four
   I learned to talk
When I was five
   I climbed a tree
When I was six
   I got a bike
When I was seven
   I came here
When I was eight
   I fell out of a tree
When I was nine
   I went to see the Mary Rose
When I'm 100
   I hope to be in a coffin with moss over it.

This seems a rather lifeless imitation of the original; except for the last line, and perhaps the delayed fall out of the tree, its humour has escaped him. But the exception seemed to signal a willingness to try his own sense of humour out, to be amusing in his own voice. I said I thought the last line was funny. Why didn't he add a funny bit to the end of all the other lines as well?

Behind the Poem

His second version was written in three colours. Purple was used for the last line, which now became: 'I hope to be in a coffin with a British flag on the top and moss on the outside.' Blue ink was used for the rest of the first version, and then in red, on separate lines, he added the following phrases:

    ... grow/ a mm or two
    ... swim/ an inch or two
    ... nan/ who gave me a banana
    ... talk/ with a dummy in my mouth
    ... tree/ and fell out
    ... bike/ which fell to pieces
    ... here/ looking worried
    ... tree/ with a broken spleen
    ... Mary Rose/ or what was left of it

Each phrase he adds counters the flatness of his first attempt. With a nice self-deprecating humour he uses banality and catastrophe to draw an amusing self-portrait. And this comes from a second look at a model, itself amusing, which had not at first drawn out this humour. In this case, one intervention seemed enough to help transform something almost lifeless into a poem. Almost lifeless, but not entirely; I have already mentioned the adage that says that the strength of a poem, unlike that of a chain, is the strength of its strongest link. The touch of humour in the first version was a strong 'link'.

Intervention and interference

One way of construing Marie Peel's remark quoted on p.116 would be to suggest that not only does the teacher need 'ideas' but that the ideas, at their most productive, need to be poetic or writerly ideas; the teacher needs, as it were, to go alongside the child-as-writer in his role of teacher-as-writer in order to be responsive to the nuance of the child's attempts. The teacher's moments of direct intervention as 'critic' are part of the process of the making of the poem. Every so often, a dramatic transformation like the one above takes place. At other times, nothing at all would come of such a suggestion. One might take Pound's revisions of Eliot's original version of *The Waste Land*[4] as the type of this teacherly and essentially poetic intervention.

The teacher's interventions can thus be creative without amounting to trespass; it is a creative gesture to help unfold what is implicit in the child's original version. And yet this might appear to beg the question; if the teacher's contribution is creative, in what sense can it be said that what he 'creates' is implicit in another mind? An idea – such as, 'Why not write more funny lines like this? – is either the teacher's, as in this case, or the child's; and the poem is either that much more or less the child's 'own' depending on how one answers the question.

This may well be true. If one were in fact trying to establish which part of the river of the child's mind comes from this or that source, there would be more of a problem than there is. I need to do this for the child's poem no more than the reader needs to come to that kind of decision as to whose poem *The Waste Land* really is. It is conventionally possible to say *The Waste Land* is by T. S. Eliot without adding that of course he had help with it. In other words, the problem is a philosophical problem about the practice of all literature. Poems are accepted as poems without testimonials being required as to their authenticity, and without such help as the writer has received – through critical reading and suggestions from friends and professionally – needing to be publicly acknowledged and 'allowed for'. It is inconsistent to point to how children have been 'helped' without drawing attention to ways in which all artists are helped; it simply undermines the artistic status of what children do. The teacher-pupil relation, which is the soil from which children's 'own' poems spring, is in a sense just one variant of the general situation in which artistic endeavour draws on supportive contexts.

The crucial issue, then, is not whether the poem is the child's 'own, unaided' work or not; I have already suggested that the most independent poems do not proceed out of nowhere. The question is the manner in which context impinges on the writer, and the distinction to be made is between intervention and interference. A passage in I. Hansen's well-known book *The Year's Turning*[5] exemplifies what seems to me to be a common willingness to confuse the two. In discussing a communal poem – one written by the class together – she says that images about chimneys 'fingering the sky' and so on were 'near cliché':

120 Behind the Poem

> I reminded the class of a photograph ... showing a group of angry workers ... outside a factory ... What are the unionists called who prevent strike-breakers entering their place of work? After a moment the lines read: 'Grim/ The factory chimneys picketed the sky'.

Clearly, 'picketed' is her image, not any child's, and what she asks them to find is the idea and the word for it in her head. One might wonder how far, in teaching generally, 'encouragement to write' takes the form of eliciting topics, sentiments, modes of expression, language itself even, which articulate, directly or more insidiously, such a dependency.

Interventions which do not interfere are more difficult; they involve the teacher not in direct self-expression but in subduing self-expression in the effort of imagining one's way into another imagination. The teacher's suggestions then derive from a sense of what the child is attempting and are not superimposed on it. I should argue that the suggestion made to Sam to write some more funny lines was not made *ab initio*, but was a response to what he had already said. Nor could it be said that his response to the idea was other than very fertile in itself; the added phrases are varied syntactically, beautifully appropriate, and more truthfully 'like life' than silly or farcical. This was, in my view, his poem; and yet the example also makes clear the futility of thinking in either/or terms, of a poem as being either entirely the product of a milieu or entirely the work of a creative individual.

Working at it

There is no impropriety involved, then, no necessary undercutting of the pupil's autonomy, in accepting one's teacherly role as midwife, or catalyst, or elicitor of writing. On the contrary, the act of writing always takes place in a social context, in which the publisher's reader, the friend, the colleague, the precursors in the same field, all have their say in what gets written. The teacher combines in himself a number of roles that are normally distinct; he can operate as publisher's reader and friend and publisher and so on, as well as having commissioned the work in the first place, and being the usual weekly audience. And just as they can

Intervention 121

mishandle any of those roles, or be felt to trespass, so can the teacher. Possessing such roles, he can commission them to write what they actively prefer not to, publish what they would like to destroy, drily proofread when praise would help, be the same weekly dead audience, or just forget to deal with the correspondence. There is a permanent precariousness in the enterprise, and the possibilities of mishandling the relationship are numerous.

One implication of this is that intervention includes very different kinds of relationship with different children. Some are greedy for suggestions; others fastidiously ghost away to their seats at any sign of advice. In the same way, what sufficed for Sam would not be enough in a different situation, or for another child. A casual remark, a nudge, was enough to set him to work, but with many children the perception that they have something to say may be slower in coming. I shall describe a more extended or laborious intervention and offer it as an example of working with a less 'naturally' imaginative sensibility in a way which still, I think, avoids trespass.

Keith, also aged 9, had a strong literal streak that was sometimes resistant to imaginative suggestion; on one occasion, having read to the class the poem with the lines 'I saw a white swan make/Another white swan on the lake' he said the lines 'didn't really make sense ... swans have cygnets and they're grey'. But he was keen to write, and to 'improve', and brought back to me a comment I had written in the margin of a poem about Hercules going into the underworld (one of those discussed above, p.55): my comment in the margin had been 'Could it be more dramatic?' How could he do that, he wanted to know? This is what he had written:

Hercules gets to a river full of blood.
A boat lying ashore,
It was made of dead wood.
A man was on it,
He asked the man for a ride

I first asked him did he see what I meant saying his lines weren't very dramatic? Yes. Then this short interchange took place.

122 Behind the Poem

    Self: Could you find a line that wasn't very...
    (intending 'dramatic')
    K: (interrupting) 'A man was on it.'
    Self: How important was the man?
    K: Not sure.
    Self: OK, what kind of man?
    K: Old?
    (I inserted 'old' before 'man' to read 'an old man'.)
    Self: Anything else? what he looked...
    K: Showing through... bones... bony (I wrote this in)
    Self: OK, an old bony man. Which is better?
    K: The second.
    Self: 'is on' – like on a bus, Is that like it?
    K: No?
    Self: Is he doing anything? What did he do... his job?
    K: Take people across.
    Self: So what's he doing?
    K: Riding.
    Self: Riding sounds like a...
    K: Holding a pole.
    Self: Anything else?
    K: Shouting.

And very quickly, much more than with the adjective 'old' and 'bony', Keith found the phrase 'in an old ratty voice', which I also then wrote on his first version. I asked if there were other lines he could choose to treat in the same way as we had done, while he wrote his second version. He said yes, and went away to try it, but this second attempt in the event contained only the additions put in during our talk, so that it would be possible to see him as producing ideas only under guidance. Many teachers would be inclined to say that not only are such conversations time-consuming and impossible to organize for everybody, but what is at issue here is whether such a degree of 'help' amounts to something beyond authentic intervention.

Several things might be said in defence of such consultations, as Donald Graves calls them. First, all the added words and phrases were produced by the child, and with greater fluency at the end of the short conversation, it seems to me, than at the beginning; this seems to imply that the initial restraint or failure to dramatize may be as much due to an unfamiliarity with the purpose of poetic/dramatic language as with any essential 'lack' of imagination; it is partly, perhaps, a meta-communicative difficulty – what do poems try to do? Second, even if no more was added to this poem than those few phrases, there is some real sense of possibility implied in the expansion of an initially laconic statement, so that the experience of expanding a line or two in the direction of greater 'drama' is there to be drawn on subsequently.

Interestingly, in Keith's case, there were signs of his 'loosening up' generally as a writer. Two months later he wrote the following piece, which seems as expansive as the first piece was cramped.

The Plains of Tanzania

In the quiet plains of Tanzania.
Masses of herds of wildebeest.
Wander in the sun.
A few zebras joining them.
Sometimes a cheetah might come.
But it does not succeed here.
The wildebeests just roam round,
they are not afraid.
In the quiet plains of Tanzania the wildbeest wander.

This seems to me the work of someone more at ease perhaps with the subject, but also more at ease with the language he uses; the last line is a confident expansive gesture. Whether or not there might have been a connection between the experience of making the Heracles piece of writing 'more dramatic' and the more realized presence of this subject, I can't presume; what might be said is that my intention in seeking to expand the initially cramped poem was to present to him the possibilities of his own language, and that he has arrived at something like that kind of possession here. It seems to be an expression of that self-belief I tried to create for him.

It is also worth noting that there is no logical difference between a belief that children like Keith are 'loosened up' and urged towards confidence by some such means as I have described, and any other belief that teachers have which links a programme with an outcome. Such assertions are continually made: care with measurement teaches children to observe, learning a language helps them to understand a country, work with grammar helps written syntax, and so on. What is dubious is not so much, for all the frequent implausibility of the assertions themselves, the actual postulating of connections; this has to be implicit in the work of teaching for the teacher to be persuaded of its worth. The problem is their formulation in confidently causal form. A consequence is that, in the absence of evidence demonstrating the validity of particular connections, what legitimates them is the different social value placed on different activities. It seems somewhat more self-evident that children should be able to handle computers, or learn a language, than they should be able to put into words their feelings about, say, the pet that died. The higher-status activity – teaching computing – produces worthwhile 'results' because it is a higher-status activity, not because the results of teaching computing are any more demonstrable or real than the results of teaching children to write.

My suggestion that Keith 'loosened up' comes low down on the list of persuasive types of professional assertion; the professional audience for it – at a staff meeting, say – hears something quite subjective, about the speaker, whereas an analogously subjective judgement in a field higher up is heard as descriptively useful. A consequence of the low subject status of the writing of poems is that intervention of the kind I am describing has a comparable status. Structures reinforce this difference, not surprisingly, since they exist partly to give expression to it. For example, when teachers suggest that 'there isn't time' for the kind of conversations I am suggesting are valuable, they are not only presupposing a particular time-frame, and endorsing styles of intervention which fit better into it; they are also devaluing the more gradual interventions that form a crucial part of many teachers' work.

It is arguable that all connections the teacher entertains between his work and what children do are nebulous. They are certainly never available for inspection, but teachers' day-to-day language is soaked in unverifiable assumptions as to causality. Neither of the two examples of intervention that I have offered are given as explanations of the completing of a poem, only as accounts of process in which the teacher becomes implicated in a way that remains, finally, obscure. It is possible that Keith would have improved this poem in his own way, and that the remark I made was gratuitous; or that he wrote that version out of deference to this suggestion, and without real personal conviction –

though clearly I did not think that was the case. And, more clearly, there may be no connection at all between his Tanzania poem and what happened earlier.

Communal writing

The teacher's availability for individual 'consultation'[6] represents the possibility of more pointed discussion about a particular child's writing than is available in the class lesson. In being addressed to everyone's problems this all too often addresses no one's. Interventionist consultation of that kind may be looked on not just as editorial assistance, but as a directly personal kind of teaching; and of course the efficacy of the teaching arises partly from the fact that a child comes to consider a particular poem or line or phrase in the context of some general notion about poetry. The teacher is likely to introduce these generalities without being aware of doing so. But if he says that he likes the sound of those two lines, or the way those two words nearly rhyme, or the fact that that adjective is unusual but fresh and right, he has provided, alongside or rather within the encouragement, some notions of what poetry aims to be.

It would be unilluminating, though, to reserve the term 'intervention' for describing aspects of the teacher's encounters with individuals, and not use it of his encounters with a whole class. The same kinds of question may be asked of a class working on a communal poem, for instance, as those asked of individuals about their pieces. I mentioned earlier that with one class I employed, more or less by accident, a story/poem distinction to enable them to judge the suitability of phrases and sentences thrown up as suggestion for inclusion. That seems thoroughly interventionist.

I made the same communal kind of beginning with another class, in discussing how to start a poem together about Ariadne being left on Naxos by Odysseus. Two alternative first lines were offered: 'She woke up to find', and 'Waking'. Falling into the same distinction as before, I asked whether one sounded more like the beginning of a poem than the beginning of a story. 'Waking' sounded more like a poem starting, several said, so we kept that. The first suggestion for the next phrase was 'On a silent island'. So should 'Waking' be on its own, or joined up? On its own. Why? 'It sounds finished', someone said; and someone else: ' "Waking on a silent island" would be too long'. I asked for the next lines; immediately, 'no camp fire,/no voices'. 'Is that like a poem?' 'Yes', Oliver said, 'in a story you'd say "There was no camp fire" '.

What seemed to be happening was that the questions, simple as they were, prodded the children towards clarifying for themselves what it was the 'poem', as distinct from the 'story', was trying to do. The perceptions, or suggestions, that 'waking' sounded more like a poem starting, that it should be on its own, and that next there should be two phrases and not two sentences, emerged from their being confronted with alternatives; the children appeared to be coming towards some sense of what a poem is by seeing its practice as in crucial ways differing from the habits of prose narrative. Since what is being interposed, then, by the teacher, is a meta-communicative question, it seems that their sense of the manner and possibilities of the poem in general filled out in the same movement that developed that particular communal beginning. The interventionist attitude, and the interventionist questions, created choices that need not necessarily have existed, or occurred to the children, if they had been 'simply writing'.

The intervention was not didactic in the sense that it explicitly taught a story/poem distinction; but it taught it by assuming or presupposing it, and it seems important that at some point such a presupposition should be confronted, not left to become a taken-for-granted dichotomy. The poem could be written as story, obviously; the story could be written 'poetically'; the problem would remain of what we mean by these expressions, but it would be a live problem not a dead one. At the same time, the decisions as to whether to use 'Waking' rather than a complete sentence for the opening, and to break the first line after 'Waking', were the children's. That is, although there was strong intervention at the level of deciding the rules for the game (poem or story) and where and when it should be played, there was relatively little interference with its progress and outcome.

Instead of 'intervention', why not just say 'teaching'? 'Intervention' might sound like jargon, with a fatal hint of sociology about it. But the trouble with the word 'teaching' is that everyone knows what it means: it thus means what any user means by it. On the other hand, intervention, which is not synonymous with teaching, seems a useful term for separating out and summing up certain crucial aspects of it; and it implicitly calls attention to an alternative non-interventionist procedure or phase. It is also a relatively unspoilt term, needing desirable clarification when it is used; needless to say, that is not true of 'teaching'.

For my purposes, 'intervention' usefully suggests the intermittent nature of the teacher's role in its more active-looking aspects. Initially, in the work under consideration, intervention amounted to trying to set up a particular ambiance, which was here a discussion, a social means of confronting a particular question. I was a protagonist in that social situation; the possibility of intervention was sustained by means of it, in the sense that such a discussion allowed me to intervene with questions relevant to the purpose I had set up, and at the same time to leave the talk and the decision-making to the other protagonists, the children. 'Teaching' would too often imply a didactic intrusiveness in such situations; and in a stimulus–response model there is an uncomfortable sense that at the response stage, when the stimulus is 'taking effect', the provider of the stimulus is quiescent, or has withdrawn. In a dialogue such as the one I have described, intervention is continuously present as a possibility, but the aim is that it should be so in a way which avoids intrusion or trespass.

One or two brief interviews with children after the discussion make clear the value of intervention as a posture sustained beyond the initial impetus. The class wrote private endings to the Ariadne poem that was begun communally. I read a number of these out loud the next day, asking them what lines and words they liked. One poem by Neil ended strikingly: 'silence drumming through her heart', and having read the whole piece I asked 'Which word in the poem . . . ?' A chorus of 'drumming' interrupted the question. I said they were good judges of their own writing, then they worked on at their myth poems, and one or two came to me and asked what I thought. These brief interviews show them quite seriously wrestling with artistic problems. Some of these may have occurred to them as a result of hearing the others' poems read out, but one cannot be sure – though there seems no doubt that reading aloud not only sets some spirit of emulation afoot, but breeds a kind of confidence as well.

Marion had done her own ending to the communal start, but it was rather uncertain.

Waking
On a silent island.

Alone she wanders full of pity.
No cheerful voice
No campfire smoke.

She sees the ship
it sails on through the misty cloud.
The birds they twitter as silent as silent could be.
The tigers they roam.
With a quiet step.
The beasts are approaching
But she doesn't care.
The god of wine
Approaches near
And his drunken friend.
She cheers up well
And she is his wife forever.

I wrote beneath this first draft, a shade too firmly perhaps, 'You're not sure where you're going here – what you want to say'. My first individual intervention then, through marking, was negative. We had already decided in discussion that one of the difficulties about writing a sad poem set on a seashore was that it was normally a cheery sort of place, and perhaps I felt that Marion (whose own cheeriness and bounce were unflagging) had lost the sense of Ariadne's grief. She came back the next day with a second version, called 'Ariadne' again, but with 'Waking on a silent island' as a sub-title outside the poem. This was more serious, as if she had listened to the tone of what others had written; she prefaced it by saying 'It's really bad':

The sand is dry and cool.
She stumbles in a rocky pool.
And the tigers roam
And roar,
A sail or is it two?
Has passed the misty shore,

Could it be Theseus
Going away.

I remember saying 'The last line could rhyme', hearing the lovely 'roar/shore' rhyme and wanting the poem closed that way. Her friend, leaning over, said 'home'. I said it was really good, and wrote 'A very good poem. The roar–shore rhyme is lovely – and the words sound natural, like someone talking. What was Mary's suggestion?' By the following day the end had been altered, but to: 'Going away/with a black sail/and no goodbye'. Both she and her friend, it turned out, had forgotten the 'home' rhyme her friend had suggested. When I reminded her, she decided to alter the end again, so that it read 'Going away,/Going home'.

Intervention was in this case a diverse kind of influence: marking, reading aloud of others' work, a friend's comment, re-marking, and a reminder. It is so varied that one might speak of a context of interventions. The image I find useful and keep returning to is that of the eco-system. The rudiments of such a system are perhaps present in the way that the various activities in their different phases and pursued by different protagonists seemed to exhibit some degree of close and integral interrelationship. Children's poems emerge and flourish, perhaps, in a teaching habitat that is more complex than is often assumed.

More communal writing

The example above, in which one pupil suggested a rhyme to another, points to another aspect of intervention, the way in which the teacher may ensure that other pupils' influence is brought to bear on what is being written, by devising opportunities for them to comment on each others' work. This may happen to a degree without conscious planning, as in the example above; when children read their pieces to each other informally or when they read them to the class, the responses sometimes reach to particulars in ways that encourage the child to alter a poem, or leave it unaltered; either way, they influence and intervene. Marion, the girl who wrote the Ariadne poem, was reading aloud a first version of a riddle. This short interchange took place, with teacher and two other children each contributing a small influence:

> Self: Which line perhaps doesn't fit?
> Mary: 'The sky is high'
> Emily: It's a nice line though.

Mary, the girl who had earlier suggested the rhyme to her, felt confident to criticize; and there was also a spontaneous expression of support for it. It is not, I think, too much to see in such moments the first steps towards establishing a freedom for children to learn how to criticize and be criticized: by which I do not mean that they are learning Spartan virtues of confidence and resilience, but that reciprocal involvement in each other's work can extend and enrich the social context in which they write.

The possible fertility of reciprocal criticism might be suggested by one or two examples of children in small groups discussing their first versions of poems about the Ceyx and Halcyone story – the work I referred to in the previous chapter. They had put their poems on the word-processor, and each group of three or four had processed copies of all the poems written by the group. They talked about each poem, and wrote down their comments on the printout; they were then taken away by the writer, who could make use of them or not.

Lisa's poem 'The Kingfisher' ends:

> As she leaped into the air she flew,
> She flew high,
> She flew low,
> Now she was a kingfisher,
> With her long beak she picked up her husband,
> And flew off together.

Three out of four girls wrote on their copies, after they had talked for a while. Naomi picked out four lines at the beginning and wrote 'good'. She wrote 'good' opposite the first line quoted here, and underlined 'she picked up her husband', writing opposite that: 'make clearer please'. She inserted a 'they' before 'flew' in the last line. Elaine wrote, 'I think she should say that

Ceyx turned into a kingfisher too'. And Jane put a ring round 'picked up her husband' and wrote 'change this'.

David's first hand-written version of 'The Speechless Cave' ran:

The spechless cave
Is all dark and misty,

And not a single sawned,
All sad and secker,
Faces white and whear,

With the king of sleep apon his cache,
In blak and white he lies asleep,
With his sleeping son by his side.
And the sleeping people all around,
Arfter beath has come there way,

His first word-processed version, for discussion, omitted 'he lies asleep'; otherwise it was the same, apart from three spelling changes: 'sawned' to 'souned', 'beath' to 'death', and 'there' to 'ther'. Two boys wrote comments. Guy wrote 'good' opposite the first two lines; changed the spelling of 'secker' to 'scary', 'souned' to 'sound', and 'whear' to 'wheary'; crossed out the line about the king asleep, adding the phrase 'the king asleep' to the next line; added 'the cave' to the penultimate line; and wrote 'needs some looking at otherwise its good'. Matthew wrote a general comment: 'very good apart from he has mist out commers'; and crossed out 'on his couch'.

David himself, as if following Guy, crossed out the line 'with the king asleep on his couch', adding 'the king asleep' to the next line. But his final version, interestingly, keeps the line that the others wanted him to modify or discard, and alters the next:

With the king asleep on his couch
In black and white he lies asleep.

So that, despite his extreme uncertainty, in certain ways, in handling language, he exhibits at least the suggestion of a willingness here to construct something afresh, and not be prodded by others into their definitive version of a line. It seems a very small increment, but such movements sometimes are best appreciated against the background of a habitual lack of confidence.

Guy wrote a poem about Isis. His first word-processed version reads:

> As Isis dances over the rainbow
> She glances into the cave
> She is amazed by the quietness
> Her cloak shines round her in the cave.
> The dreams cluster round her.
> She can't keep her eyes open
> As she sighs in pity for Ceyx and Halcyone.

He had already done three handwritten versions in one double period earlier in the week, with minor but interesting changes. He had first written the sentence from the story that appealed to him: 'When Iris had entered this caven and brushed away the dreams that clustered round her, the sacred place was lit up with the shining of her garments.' His third line at first read: 'She is amazed and dazed of the quietness of the cave'; he brackets out 'dazed' and 'of the cave', but his next version keeps the second phrase and has: 'She is amazed by the quietness of the cave'. Finally, 'She is amazed by the quietness'. The next line was at first 'Her cloak lights the cave', and he had written 'Keep' alongside this and the next three lines, but that line becomes in the third version 'Her cloak shines round her in the cave'.

He had thus spent some time thinking about the poem and working on it before talking over it with his friends. Their ideas seemed helpful. Matthew's comments were: 'The king can't keep his eyes open. I like she sighs in pity for Cayx and Halcyone'. David wrote 'good', and added 'she must go in /and the darkness in the cave' though it was not clear where it should go. Guy himself added 'as she walks out' after 'round her', and again extended the third line to 'she is amazed by the quietness and darkness of the cave', as if picking up David's suggestion.

The final version, which is now in two sections, reads:

> As Isis dances over the rainbow
> She glances into the cave,
> She must go in,
> She is amazed by the quietness,
> Her cloak shines around her.

The dreams cluster round her,
As she walks out.
She can't keep her eyes open,
As she sighs in pity for Ceyx and Halcyone.

Guy has taken up David's suggestion of the extra line 'she must go in'; it adds a narrative – and psychological – link that was missing, then is balanced by his own addition of a similar link 'As she walks out', as if Matthew's suggestion had prompted his own alteration. He makes two more changes, taking out 'of the cave' after 'quietness', and writing it all out in two sections, which again suggests a greater awareness than at the beginning of the narrative of the poem, the going in and the coming out.

Apart from the sheer amount of work that goes into developing this short poem to the point where it is 'finished', what seems particularly interesting is the way in which both his own autonomous shaping of the lines and the suggestions of his friends contribute to the final poem. And perhaps this was not simply a cumulative effect. Their ideas seemed helpful, not just on their account, but as a means of prodding him into even sharper awareness of the rhythm and feel of what he had written. One can only guess at the encouragement the others' praise might give, but it can do no harm for a friend to say he likes certain things, particularly when their choice of things to like seems so appropriate.

Renewal

Comments and criticisms from friends can work in a more profound way, stimulating the writer not just to attend to those genuine difficulties that they point to, but to rewrite so substantially that the piece changes its character. In the following example, friends' interventions seem to have had an effect going beyond what they refer to, provoking more than critical awareness. His emendations are not confined to tidying the piece up, but become the stimulus for re-creating at a different level. Here is the first version of the poem which William, aged 11, wrote about a photograph:

Desolate,
A broken chair,
ready to welcome Anything that comes in
The window pains knocked out.
The seethrough livingroom,
inviting people to sit down,
bits of rotting wood,
hanging from the cealing.
A once grand piano,
lying smashed to bits
Looking like a ship,
wrecked beneath the sea.
It's richness gone from it,
Sleeping on the floor,
A feeling of lonliness
as I first enter the house.
I brush away the cobweb's
and sit down on the chair,
which seems to share a sadness,
with the rest of the house.
The shadows follow me,
as I walk down the passageway,
I walk out as another tile falls,
And smashes on the floor.
The noise echo's through the hollow house.
As I walk down the street,
A funny thing occurs,
In a row of bombedout houses,
There is one standing perfectly alright,
Tomorrows victem prehaps?

Three friends worked in a group reading each others' poems, talking about them, and writing comments; I had asked them to say – in writing – what they thought were the 'good lines' and the good phrases and words, and also to say whether anything could be left out or altered to improve the poem, and finally to add any general comments they wanted to make. The good lines chosen from William's first version were 'Desolate', 'A once grand piano', 'which seems to share a sadness', 'The shadows follow me', 'I brush away the cobweb's', 'The noise echo's through the hollow house'. They liked these words and phrases: 'shadows',

Intervention 135

'victem', 'desolate', 'seethrough livingroom', 'cobwebs'. There is an interesting list of lines that 'could be left out': 'As I walk down the street', 'and sit down on the chair', 'hanging from the cealing', 'I walk out as another tile falls', 'Looking like a ship'. Their general comment is: 'Make the lines more scarry. Its a bit too long!'

This criticism seems to me, first, very helpful. The two friends have chosen for approval some of the more vital and dramatic lines in the piece, so giving William some sense of where the strength of his poem lies; they have underscored this endorsement by implying that the properties of cobwebs and shadow are important. Their suggestions as to what to leave out point to real redundancies; two of these, the ship simile and the falling tile line, involve dropping other lines. The general comment about the piece being too long seems fair and helpful too. In his second version, below, he keeps in no line they find dispensable, and, except for the word 'victem', drops nothing that they like.

Desolate,
a broken chair in the doorway.
readyto welcome things in.
The see-through living room
inviting people to sit down.
a once grand piano
smashed to bits.
I enter the house,
which is lonely with neglect.
I brush away the cobwebs
as a little creature
runs across the floor.
The shadows follow me,
a noise from behind
echoes through the hollow house.
Darkness,
something brushes past me
and scuttles away.
The chair stares at me.
It seems to share a sadness
with the rest of the house.
The silence looms ahead of me
in this eery place.

It seems as if, as in Guy's case above but more markedly, their ideas have not just been incorporated but have served as a foundation for general rewriting, in which William's own new ideas seem both to derive directly from theirs, and to be generated in the process of trying to accommodate what they say. He seems to agree that it could be made more frightening, adding two moments of that kind, and that it could be shorter, cutting the first version by seven lines. He appears, though, not just to take up their criticism but to take them up and go beyond them. For example, he removes not just 'hanging from the cealing', but the rotting wood as well, not just 'As I walk down the street', but the rest of the section beginning with that line. It is as if, having had it suggested to him that there is too much mention of walking, sitting down, and going out, he sees that the real point is not the abundance of objects but the atmosphere of fear surrounding what is there. He 'makes it more scarry' by making fewer objects do more work, by having the chair 'stare' and the silence 'loom ahead'. The 'I enter' that is retained – in a better place than in the first version – is made somewhat more definite by not being in a subordinate clause. In fact there are five fewer subordinate clauses, which itself helps prevent tension being dissipated. The same heightened feeling for evenness of tone may account for his introducing, each in an important place, the words 'darkness' and 'silence', which help to give meaning to details and make for a clearer narrative structure.

Intervention by way of advice and criticism from classmates and in particular friends seems to be helpful in several ways, not just as a way of improving poems. It may be seen in particular as a way of enriching the social context in which poems come to be written. Relations between children are changed by collaboration, and their own relation to writing seems likely to be altered, becoming more critical in response to friends' comments but also more serious in response to their evident willingness to take each other's work seriously. This later point is worth stressing, since it is clearly possible to argue that the firmest foundation for writing is for the child to feel a capacity for writing, to enjoy it, to feel that writing is important not just as a way of pleasing others but as a way of pleasing oneself, or rather of being oneself. To push the idea a little further, what the teacher also has in mind for the long term is not only that such attitudes should become a foundation for writing *per se*, but that writing, through being important personally, should become one of the foundations of the self of the writer.

The previous example brings the account of intervention in a circle round to the writer's autonomy again. I have tried to show how the teacher can hand over to pupils some of the interventionist roles that he attempts himself, and how this enriches the context for writing, giving it a broader social dimension. In this case the result seems to have been that the writer's own autonomous relation to his writing has been refreshed and renewed. His starting again seems to have emerged from talking about his writing to friends. What might have been set up here, however briefly, is the kind of social writing environment which is conducive to helpful reading and criticism, rewriting, and broadly based commitment generally.

It is not just the improvements that are accomplished in the writing that argue for this, it is also the way in which the writing itself begins to draw sustenance – as a social act, not in terms of its quality as writing – from the relationships in which it comes to be embedded. Where writing and the discussion of it are, however transitorily, a part of children's social interaction with each other, and do not stand out nakedly against a different background, then writing has become a 'natural' activity.

The following are examples of written comment on each others' work made in the same class at the same time as William's work was being discussed. I discern in them some evidence of the validity of assuming that children readily accommodate their relationships with friends to include talking about each others' writing.

> You've got some lines about people playing and some about the countryside and they don't go together
>
> Try and make it Rhime (if you can) and think of more Idea's for the first and third verses. Leave out 'the street which mums makes sure their kids don't play on after school' and 'inside a chair' MORE!!!!!!!!!!!!
>
> 'The clawing fingers
> Grabbing at the water'. . . I like the clawing fingers.
>
> 'Swarm of foam', swarm is interesting

'A moon giving
a waterfall to the earth', kind of wierd (I like it)

'They sit on cloud
and have a picnic', you can't sit on a cloud, it's a nice idea (funny)

'rushing road of water.' I like the idea of a road

'a well behaved waterfall.' I don't like this

Many fine poems are written without the benefit of such supportive talk. At the same time, writing in the classroom, as in some sense a collective activity, is enriched by such a sharing around of awareness. Insights are shaped, likes and dislikes endorsed and argued over, ideas adopted and renewed; doubts are allayed, confidence strengthened. The fertile and independent activity of the mind that is evident in the comments quoted above is brought into being and carefully nurtured over time by a pedagogic style in which intervention is crucial.

Part 4

Context

6
Literary models

Imitation and the creative

The descriptions of process in the early chapters include accounts of children writing in response to literature: after reading the Hercules legend, for instance. Some of the work that teachers do implies that the 'imitation' of literary models has a peculiar value; if children can plausibly invent another Hercules story one feels they have gained access to something in the culture and through that to something in themselves. When they write riddles, or haiku, or ballads, or attempt free verse Lawrentian animal poems, it seems that more is involved than earnest parody or creative plagiarism. The piece below was written by a boy of 11 after reading Ted Hughes's play, *The Coming of the Kings*.[1] The starting point for writing was the line, 'Listen, the snow is falling', which begins the minstrel's last speech. First come the minstrel's words in the play itself:

> Listen. The snow is falling.
> Snow is falling on all the roads.
> Falling on to the hills, on to the eyelashes of sheep.
> Falling into the chimneys and on to the doorsteps,
> Into the frozen well, into the dark forest.
> Slowly the heavens are falling.

Every snowflake is an angel.
The angels are settling on the world.
The world will be white with angels.
The world will be deep in angels.

Thomas's 'imitation' makes use of the same opening line and is structurally similar:

Listen, the snow is falling.
Snow is falling on icy rivers,
Falling on snow-capped mountains and white mice;
Falling on bare trees and small fishes,
Into clothes being worn and onto fast streams.
Falling onto cows' tails and donkeys,
Over houses and around lonely caravans and faraway rocks.
Into mouths and under feet,
Falling over roaring lions and bleating goats.
The falling snow is like babies;
The babies will conquer the world,
The babies will cover this earth.

At first glance, perhaps, this seems not to go beyond pleasing parody and, clearly, certain basic features derive from the original speech: context, syntactic structure, spatial range, and so on. It is an achievement, though, even to reconstruct some of these. But the strengths of Thomas's piece are not simply parodic. He re-creates from the original. His piece is more adjectival, for instance, using eleven or so adjectives to Hughes's two; the adjectives are also made to work, towards suggestions of fragility in 'bare trees and small fishes', and isolation in 'lonely caravans and faraway rocks'. His ear seems to sense that within the line the adjectives should go in semantically related pairs ('snow-capped' and 'white'), echoing the parallelism and the balance of the lines. The dynamic sense of space in the Hughes passage has also been taken up and even recharged, with remarkably disparate particulars (caravans, rocks, clothes, cows' tails, mouths, and so on); the range seems as global as in Hughes's lines, but the effect is still small-scale and humanized, and a kind of compassionate awareness informs the whole. These successes – and the imaginative energy of it all – are his own.

Thomas's imitation came to mind twelve months later when

reading the play again with the class whose work on Heracles I described in Chapter 3. I read his piece aloud to the class, together with the passage it originated from. I asked them to look for other lines which they could use to begin their own pieces with. Their unerring choice of 'poetic' lines – about silence, and stars, and so on – was interesting. There had been, a day or two before, a discussion about the different styles of the play: the comic, the poetic, and that which seemed neither, and they had wrestled with the meaning of these. The minstrel's mystical utterances were puzzling: 'This doesn't make sense.' 'It's not meant to.' 'It's not funny either.'

A child saying that the minstrel's language 'is not meant to' make sense has grasped something difficult and important. Other insights followed. Anna pointed out that the minstrel 'was imaginative', and 'magical', and talked 'in poems', and was 'a bit batty'. Christine described the innkeeper as 'a fool with a lot of brains, frightened of his wife.' I had also asked why the wife, for instance, used rhyme, but the minstrel did not: 'Because it's funny.' So that they had noted the dramatic use of rhyme for the comic, and the freer styles for the more serious parts of the play. Their perceptiveness encouraged me to continue, and to broach the difficult business of imitating the comic, the serious, the magical. When I read back to them their choice of lines to start from, which as I suggested went for the most part for the most eloquently magical and poetic moments, and then read Thomas's piece again, Keith asked: 'Is it a poem?' 'Are they like poems, the speeches we've listed?' 'Yes.'

I suggested that they should try 'a few', rather as they had attempted a number of short poems on Heracles. 'When you've tried four or five different ones, you'll like one or two.'

The children's imitations of Hughes's manner for the minstrel were thus set in the context of Thomas's earlier attempt, though I ruled out more imitations of that particular speech. There is a general issue of some interest here, in the context of the notion of imitation. Thomas's poem to an extent functioned as an incentive, by virtue of being a successful model of imitation. Such poems become influences, not through encouraging a spontaneous wish to emulate so much as by showing that it can be done interestingly and well. Any poem written in school which children enjoy reading and having read to them, particularly if it is preserved in some publication like a magazine, for instance, as this was, helps others to write similar kinds of poem. The influence of peers sometimes seems more potent in this regard than that of established poets. In that sense children's writing is often imitative, not of literary models but of other children's writing.

I have introduced this issue here to make the question of derivativeness and originality less straightforwardly obvious. There is arguably a greater resemblance between the two kinds of relation to previous poems – the successful example as stimulus, and the fine passage as model for imitation – than might at first be apparent. In this broad sense, all writing is imitative of what has gone before. For the Russian poet Akhmatova the relation between originality and imitation was not at all straightforward:

> Do not repeat – your soul is rich –
> The thing that someone said before;
> But who knows perhaps poetry itself
> Is just one splendid quotation.[2]

The child writes a completely fresh and original animal poem, let us say. But there is a tradition of writing about animals which makes the actual project of such a poem plausible; and if other children's poems exist in published form in the school the tradition is locally vitalized and more immediately accessible. The child's new poem quotes, metaphorically, both sources.

If the writer cannot avoid 'quotation', the imitation of a model may have the freely creative character of all writing. An imitation that lacks originality does so because it is unsuccessful as writing, not in consequence of its being an example of an unoriginal kind of writing. Imitation is not disguised or attenuated plagiarism, or a strategy by means of which children may be guided into the literary culture. It is an inescapable part of writing, in that the context of writing is other writing, whether it lies in the background as something they have just read recently, or is foregrounded, as here, to the explicitness of an attempt at emulation.

In other words, it is more a matter of the pointedness of the attempt at imitating which differentiates 'working from models' from other sorts of writing. In a sense imitation is always there. The routine fact of writing always having a relation with other writing not only implies that one may claim for explicit 'imitation' the creative possibilities of writing in general. It also suggests that even within explicitly imitative writing there may be influences passing into the work by a kind of cultural osmosis that one may not immediately recognize. With Chinese poems in translation, for example, with which most of this chapter will be concerned, some of what one wishes pupils to 'absorb' might be described in terms of 'spiritual outlook', 'emotional tone', and so on. These are hardly 'outcomes' for the pragmatist to evaluate; there are no criteria in terms of which to measure success. The teacher is thrown back on her resources as a reader in order to respond to whatever her pupils may have drawn into their writing from the poems they use as models.

Writing in a literary context

Pieces of writing, whether they are by children or 'writers', are related by inspiration, shared endeavour, emulation, and so on, to whatever writings surround them, or provide the context for them. The question of imitation, using models, is not a matter of whether one does, or should, and to what extent. Imitation is implicit in the act of writing. The question then turns from consideration of the intrinsic 'value' of models and returns to the way in which models function to draw out pupils' creative energies.

Much of what children write, when they attempt poems and seem to fail, may be seen as issuing more from their displacement from such a context, a lack of awareness of the literary ways of the culture – including their own peers' poems – than from a lack of 'the poetic' in them. At the same time, these denuded possibilities represent what at any time emerges from their contact, or lack of contact, with the literary culture. Clumsy rhymes are not a disease to be cured by quarantining children off in a compound of free verse; they are a satisfying way of exercising words, and children who experiment and play around with them for long enough will start to learn 'how to use' them. An example was given in an earlier chapter of a girl learning very quickly about rhyme, when faced by the need to write better ones. What she learnt 'freed' the particular poem she was working on.

What seems to be happening when children in such a fashion somehow take over for themselves an aspect of the literary tradition? A child inventing amusing rhymes, for instance, is being funny, but is also finding a new way of being funny, and so adding to the self. 'Absorbing' literary models in general, whether at the level of discrete device or at the level of genre, means creating for the self new possibilities of speaking poetically. The process of imitating forms such as the ballad or the riddle need not then be thought of as some kind of prelude to the 'real thing', to authentically creative writing.

One might even suggest that a reason for working with models in children's writing is that far from such work being less creative than other more original work, it is creative not just for the individual child but much more broadly. The conventional way of regarding the relation between the 'professional' poet's poem and the child's poem may be that while the one reaches out to 'literature' in general, the other is narrowly an expression of the child's own growth, of the development of self. This omits on the one hand the value to the self of the adult poet's work (as 'psychology', it belongs to aesthetics not art), and on the other the relation to literary culture in general that is represented by the child's poem. The reason for not talking about the value to the poet of his work is that it conflicts with the view current until recently that the poem is an 'object in words', with no biographical strings attached. It would in fact be good for the teacher's view of the poem if this position were modified or abandoned, because he is in a position to see that the theoretical severance of the 'therapeutic' or 'expressive' values of the activity of making a poem from the 'aesthetic' values of the 'poem itself' is no help to him when he wishes to argue for the value not just of poems, but of the value of trying to write them. In order to teach he has to assume that the two values are really one, and not separable.

The reason for not talking about the value of the child's poem to the culture is that no such claim as to its significance is customarily made. However, if there is in this sense only the poem, not the child's poem and the real poem, then the claim that children's poems belong to, and so add to, the literary culture just as they are seen to add to the self, that in fact they do what the adult poet's do, may not seem particularly large and naive. The categories, moreover, are not literary, or to do with value. Many children's poems would 'pass' as 'real' poems, and the reverse is equally conceivable. Supposing the reader did not know that the riddle already quoted had been written by a girl of 11?

> I have two waists
> and one noise in my life time.
> I have a hat that I can't put on;
> And when I scatter
> I bring laughter.

What else is there to say about this except that, like all successful poems, it is not replaceable? It is difficult to speak of its 'value' without making the claim for it that one makes for any good poem. The implication then seems to be, if it has 'passed' as a poem, that the significance of children's using models is no different from when the 'real' poet deploys the sonnet, or returns to the four-line stanza form, or like Pound writes 'Chinese' poems that are English poetry. This riddle derives sustenance from a tradition, and restores for a moment something of the possibilities of that tradition.

That claim adds some legitimation to one's work with children's poems, but it is children writing, not 'literature', that is the teacher's concern. The crucial pedagogic question is how to interpret a tradition to the children. To attempt a view of how this may take place in practice, I shall describe some recent work with a group of 12 and 13-year-old boys and girls, in which our model was a group of Chinese poems in translation.

In the week before this began, I made a note to the effect that I was very uncertain whether the time was ripe to introduce Chinese poems. I had already thought that if we did work on them it would be through the idea of the journey, and this allowed me to say merely that we would look at some journeys, with the idea of perhaps writing one ourselves – no more than that, nor a commitment to prose or poem. The tentative start was perhaps due to having not for a year or two worked in this way; I was not sure if the poems I chose to read with them initially would be well received, and hence the rather tight-lipped introduction, which would allow me to retreat to the kind of 'essay' story that they had to practise for exam purposes.

In Hughes and Heaney's *The Rattle Bag*[3] there are several of Pound's Chinese translations, and I decided to try three that related to journeys and departures, and so on, and with them Pound's translation of 'The Seafarer'. It was the insights displayed during the lesson that suggested I could go further; one example will have to suffice. At the end of 'Taking Leave of a Friend' the emotion of severance is somehow, in a moment of chracteristic reticence, displaced onto and carried by the two men's horses: 'Our horses neigh to each other/as we are departing'. Someone observed of the horses, 'It wouldn't be a departure without them.' This insight seemed almost startlingly to signify how well children of 12 and 13 might be able to respond to the poems. What had been picked up immediately was the distinctive way in which in Chinese poems the emotional power frequently flows, in a kind of metonymy, through natural surroundings and objects and creatures close to the protagonists. The young pupil saw that the poem's portrayal of the grief of that leave-taking was bound up with the presence of the horses; she saw, without of course thinking of it in quite this way, that the core of the poem was that their neighing to each other was a way of evoking both the literal silence of the men at parting, and things that might have been said but which the poet leaves expressively unsaid.

This critical sensitivity is worth stressing, because my main impression of their own poems later was that they could only have been written by children who understood something of the way the models they drew on worked. We might put the insight recounted above alongside something James Liu says[4] about images in Chinese poems, that they frequently 'put two objects side by side without making any overt or covert comparison between them', resulting in various effects: juxtaposition, comparison, substitution, transference; the girl had sensed the operation of such a transference mechanism.

The insights of the first lesson encouraged me to type out a small collection of poems from the three anthologies I had: the old Penguin collection of Chinese verse,[5] Arthur Waley's *Chinese Poems*,[6] and *The White Pony*, a collection by Robert Payne.[7] I included several four- and five-line pieces, since a small-scale poem often seems to make for closer scrutiny. We read 'Old Soldier',[8] 'Soldier's Song',[9] and 'Dreaming of My Dead Wife'.[10] I wished to hold to our initial emphasis on journeys, departures, separations, and work in that confined but characteristic terrain. After I read aloud 'Old Soldier' there was an audible spontaneous 'that's good'.

Old Soldier

Riding on a skinny horse

the old soldier

comes dimly from the wood
and out of the morning mist
and returns dimly into the mist.

Day after day
he is carried steadily
he knows not where:
on his sword there is
a little dust,
a little rust,
a little frost,
a little brightness,
a little blood shining in the morning sun.

Despite the approval, or perhaps because of it, there was a discussion (which I invited) about whether it was a poem or not. 'Well, is that a poem?' 'The way you read it it was.'

I was about to read aloud a bit from *Roget's Thesaurus* to try to make it sound poem-like, when Marlene said that 'Old Soldier' 'could be prose'. I tried to read it as if it were, and then one or two of the children did, but we agreed there was a residual 'strangeness' that resisted our handling the poem in that way.

This discussion may have helped to open up possibilities for writing. It could well have suggested to the children that certain kinds of writing might turn out to be poems once they were looked into, despite having a surface that closely resembled prose and having no affinities even with the free verse feel of the other poems we had just read. Whether or not this happened here I can only guess, but the discussion did lead us back to examining the

Literary models 149

'simplicity' of 'Old Soldier', built as it is out of an apparently endless journey, early morning mist, and – especially – a sword which summarizes in symbolic terms the history (and presumably the future, since he returns to the mist) of the soldier's aimless odyssey. We asked what the 'little rust' meant: he's been wandering for a long time; what the 'little frost' meant: perhaps that he had been sleeping on his horse. And so on. The exploration of the poems proceeded by way of their breaking into the enigmas of the concrete details. It became evident that they were there for a reason. Their 'appreciation' of the poem had, again, seemed perceptive.

In the poem that we next read, 'Dreaming of my Dead Wife', there is a similar gathering together or focusing of emotion in an object, which is here a feature of the protagonist's natural surroundings:

> It seems to me that the place
> where my heart breaks each year
> is the pine ridge on a moonlit night.

I had referred to some of the poems we read as 'stories', and now stressed that there was 'more to the story' than is often apparent on first reading. The point was taken up. There was a comment that the phrase 'each year' makes the poem sadder by making the reader think of a longer period of time. Shona pointed out how 'factual' the poems were. Someone else drew attention to the fact that certain objects – the pines, the dust, the frost – recurred in different poems. This, together with the evident appreciation of their 'factuality', made me feel that I could press even further. The remark that the poems were very 'factual' seemed particularly important, but their responses in general indicated a growing alertness to the kind of emotions being portrayed, and to the way they were handled.

What seems interesting in retrospect is the way in which we focused on the emotional resonance of physical presences in the poems, mountains, streams, and so on. I say 'we' not 'I' because their comments, like that about 'factuality', led that way too. Having become convinced of the children's capacity to work from an awareness of this central feature of the poems, and wanting to keep some record of the session, I suggested we drew up a list of items that recurred in the poems, the objects and natural features that writers made use of: pines, frost, mist, and so on. Interestingly, someone asked, 'Can I write down "separation", and "grief"?' I suggested a separate column for abstract words like that. In view of the successful 'factuality' of their own poems later, it was perhaps important – this is again a thought that occurs in retrospect – to make this distinction continuously; they themselves seemed to feel that it was possible to construct poems out of what was 'factual', and keep to a minimum the large abstract words like 'grief' and 'separation'. Another reason for recording words in this way – apart from focusing on them in the act of searching for them and writing them out – was that I felt that if the whole idea was going to work, it would have to be something that was put to one side and resumed; it needed time to mature.

The class also needed time, I felt, to absorb more of the flavour of the poems, so far as I felt able to interpret it to them, and within the confines of the idea of absence, the journey, and so on. In the next lesson, therefore, I gave out five brief poems from *The White Pony*. I read them aloud, and after each heard comments spontaneously delivered – 'don't like that' and 'like that' – suggesting firm preferences. I asked them to choose any one of the five, write it out, and underline any object they felt drawn to in any way. It was, I noted, a 'rather directive morning'. Even so, the limitation of focus to journeys, absence, and so on, and the epigrammatic brevity of the poems, made it possible to dwell on the different ways in which a similar emotion – grief at parting, particularly – was expressed, and how natural surroundings and other objects were deployed to carry it, or echo it, or in some way be implicated in it. We looked particularly at the endings of three poems (the second of which, I realized too late to make use of the fact, is a more literal version of the Pound piece which has the horses neighing at parting):

For a while I gazed upon the lake
And there was only a white cloud rolling among green hills.

The setting sun, the affection of an old friend.
So you go, waving your hands –
Only the bark of the deer.

Literary models 151

My thoughts of you are like the creeping grass
That grows and spreads without end.

The focus, again, was on the concrete: the grass, the cloud, the deer barking (which Pound rejected in favour of the two horses; the deer now seems less neatly parallel, and more remote). Linda asked if we should write down the various items – grass, mountains, lake – as we had done before, and we did so, since this way of building up a vocabulary of ideas seemed useful. In the list also went the colours that the writers used for mountains, lakes, and so on.

In all this there were the dangers, perhaps not avoided, of swamping the children with too much reading (about ten medium-length poems and five short ones) and attempts at joint criticism. At the same time, the critical judgements that they made tempted me to suggest they made a provisional attempt at writing their own 'Chinese' poems. I decided to take the project this one stage further before putting it to one side; I had already asked a friend to come in and observe these lessons, in the hope of using an observer's detachment as a means of seeing more clearly what we were doing.

I had also had in mind for a while the idea of using a video camera to take close-ups of still photographs, so as to scrutinize them with a class in detail on the television screen. I intended to concentrate on three or four favourite Chinese landscape paintings. Inevitably, the camera gave in after I had filmed two pictures, though I had five or six minutes of film of these two. I made photocopies of the ones I missed, and some others, and to stimulate awareness – or the memory – further, I wrote out a long list of titles of both poems and pictures. I reasoned that inspiration might be triggered by the titles themselves, which are often not only evocative, but 'set a scene': 'Spring River', 'Secret Parting', 'Ice in a Stream'. The plethora of resources – typed sheets of poems, photocopies, a list of titles, a ten-minute video of two paintings – was a problem, just at the point where one wanted a sharp focus so that the children could write. It remained a problem on the day the children saw the interrupted video and began to write. I had earlier given out envelope files to everyone so that the papers would be manageable, but papers that go into files often stay there.

An observer's notes from the lesson might be brought in at this point. The record begins:

> RH writing about a journey, a departure, a leave-taking... 'this is a bit of an experiment'. Shows video and comments on content, people, time of year and what he likes... 'I love the shape of the leaves', 'I love the little bridges' (this helps introduce the idea of appreciation and aesthetic considerations).
>
> Pupils asked to select four or five pictures from those going round the class, that might interest them.
>
> Possible that the distribution task caused some problems and I wondered if this could have been overcome, especially with a small group, if you had arranged the resources on tables round the room and got the pupils to travel around, as if at an exhibition, rather than getting the resources to travel round the room. As it was the pupils coped well and there was no problem.
>
> Titles list much in demand.
>
> Longish period for writing. RH moves round room helping, in a way that was not possible for me. Pupils invited to read aloud their work, very reluctant to do so, tendency to play down own efforts. RH upgrades efforts, and asks if writing captures the atmosphere of the paintings. Emphasis on working quickly, moving from one poem to another and not getting bogged down with something that is not working. Pupils less willing than those in the morning to comment on other pupils' work. For these older pupils the emotional content they were dealing with may have inhibited reading aloud. I wonder if this sharing might be better done in smallish groups, although I appreciate your stress on reading poems aloud.

Some concluding comments from the observer, based on seeing five lessons during the day, are interesting.

> The resources were high quality items presented to the pupils on video, in pictures, in photocopy. The pupils seemed fully able to cope with the amount of material which, at first, I thought might be overwhelming. To a large extent I felt the pupils were able to cope because of the way you handled the material – the pace was leisurely, reflecting, interesting, the atmosphere of the Chinese journeys, in which arrival was far less important than the experience of the journey.
>
> The relationship you set up with the pupils was one based on mutual exploration, an enterprise in which all parties were discovering, and this was marked by your comments such as 'I love the shape of the leaves', and in the way you received the pupils' suggestions. Your ability to enhance the pupils' suggestions through genuine enthusiasm struck me as significant in the process of extending pupils' willingness to make... aesthetic awareness an enjoyable occupation.

He noted in general 'the willingness of pupils to share their perceptions with one another in the public arena', but remarked that this was less evident with the older pupils: 'Perhaps the older pupils feel more comfortable working in a private rather than a public arena.'

I shared most of these reservations, particularly those about the difficulty of handling so many resources. I felt it had not gone very well. There had been, for all the interest in the video and the photocopied pictures, and the sense that they were able to draw something from them, a feeling of stiffness and overcomplicatedness about it all, which made me feel that the writing would probably be less interesting than I had hoped.

At the same time, this kind of stiffness is something many teachers will recognize in work that is more than usually planned, or newly resourced. It would also have been possible to interpret these awkward aspects of the lesson, like the children's reluctance to read their poems aloud, as indicating the basic 'difficulty' of drawing children of that age into Chinese poems to the point where they could confidently try their own. It would demonstrate that the idea of using such a model as a base for peι_ nal writing with pupils of that age is fraught with implausibilities. Backing off at this point would be tempting. Or if not that, it might at least be wise to draw breath, and do something else for a few lessons. Perhaps the sombre tone of most of the original poems argued for this too; a simple change of mood would be refreshing.

But the writing itself, when read at leisure away from the classroom, was much more encouraging than the lesson had led me to expect, and this suggested that it might be wise to spend another session on the quick first drafts. The observer noted, of the stiffish lesson he observed, that my efforts 'were necessarily concentrated on the starting processes of getting out ideas for writing, and these were very successful in unlocking a range of ideas in the pupils' minds. What I would take to be the next stage – that of focusing some of the ideas for writing – I was less able to observe, as a stranger.' But he also said that 'this focusing process was taking place' already in the lesson he saw. All I had felt at the time, though, was that despite an abundance of lively ideas their writing seemed not to rearticulate the perceptiveness with which they had responded to the poems themselves.

Particularly during routine marking, it is possible to overlook the gains that children have made in pieces of writing.

Half-consciously, and despite a commitment to a search for what is good rather than what is less successful, a filter of expectations relating to the finished piece can descend and obscure the truth of the child's attempt to shift into new terrain. What had looked plagiaristic, in some cases perfunctory, in the classroom, took on a different significance with a more appreciative reading.

I copied extracts from their quick first drafts. The emphasis on working quickly on three or four topics – after a slow, contemplative build-up over two weeks – did not seem to have produced superficiality. Indeed, one or two things appeared that seemed satisfyingly complete, and in no need of redrafting. Linda wrote a short piece called 'Spring Notes', one of four she attempted:

> As the bamboo flute breathes,
> Soft notes come dancing out.
> They are swept away,
> Their music mingling
> With the whistling wind.

I looked for signs of the pupils' having absorbed something of the spirit of what they had been reading. I felt that several influences were discernible as deriving from the models. The poetic materials of flute and wind, and the shortness (and completeness) of the piece, are at the most straightforward level of influence. One might also see in the wistfulness of the piece, and particularly in the overlaying of one perception by another, an influence at a deeper level, going beyond parody or perhaps even beyond conscious imitation. The 'contradiction' between the sweeping away of the notes and their mingling with the wind – they do not and do still exist at the same time – reads more like appropriate ambiguity than confusion.

Anna attempted six poems. Here are two first drafts, already satisfyingly complete:

The Lotus

> You came to me
> like the blossoming of a lotus,
> and flourished on my pond,
> and withered and dropped away,
> and died like the passing of a butterfly.

A Lock of Her Hair

My gaze rests on your chair
where you used to sit,
combing your hair,
and as I gaze
I see your face,
white as a lily.
For your face was pale,
and your eyes,
green as the ferns by the wayside.
I was the envy of the spirits,
and they took you for their own.

The emotional tone of these is comparable to that of two poignant love poems which we read, 'Since You, Sir, Went Away'[11] and 'Dreaming of My Dead Wife'. From the latter poem Anna took the image of a man dreaming that he sees his wife dress her hair, but she modified it beautifully, removing the suggestion of hallucination or dream to say something more direct and powerful, making the chair – which is not in the model – the focus of longing. The ferns image used in another poem to suggest neglect – 'sweet ferns flourish by the wayside' – is transposed into an image of beauty: a radical change effected with remarkable artistic economy. Such moments seem particularly creative – more Pound than Waley.

These pieces are already interesting in other ways. Just as the Elizabethan sonneteer inherited a vocabulary of objects – rose, nectar, honey, stars, skies, and so on – in terms of which to realize and convey passion, so the existence of a ready-made world here, consisting of a structure of objects imbued with poetic resonance, gives to the writer a store of meanings on which she can draw. It is not of course that resonances are intrinsic to objects, but that a conventional association of object and significance creates a meaning that can be taken up with the word. These pupils are already handling some of this vocabulary as if they are aware that the object has meaning of itself; they may be unaware of shades of significance, but they are making use of a creative freedom implicit in a tradition, even in translation. Their own poems are becoming uncluttered, quiet, even poignant.

But it is not a matter of absorbing something of a tradition for its own sake. What is interesting is that thereby such young writers are enabled to articulate their emotional experience (assuming for the moment that it is theirs) in a way they are not likely to have done before, using 'correlatives', including objects (like the lotus) which they have not actually met in experience. What is more, the object is handled with a flexibility of significance – ferns are neglect or beauty, for instance – that suggests they are still creatively free to rework what is given. What seems worth stressing is that even objects that children are acquainted with in daily life – ferns, say – may at this point be given to the child as a resource by the tradition. Ferns do not characteristically appear in children's poems, and yet they are available to perception: similarly, although mountains, mist, rivers, boats, and so on may be written about without the intercession of a tradition, they are revalued by it, charged with significance – departures, journeys, distance, absence – which are not 'really there'; so that one great advantage of going to this tradition is that such meanings are thereby made possible for the child, whose imagination by the age of 12 and 13 clearly encompasses them.

Why not appeal direct to the children's experience of separation, departure, travel, and so on? First, there is a good artistic reason why emotions like separation may be better handled when the situation is transposed, or disguised. There is also the question of the child's right to privacy. Much of the subject-matter of the poems is painful, and writing could not be asked for on similar subjects if there were any implication that the child either should search for actual experiences to handle in this way, or should reveal whether or not the poem alluded to a real-life situation. Beyond this, the value of distancing the milieu – from contemporary western experience – may well be that it helps the child to see something permanent about such situations, and hence to see them seriously. Anna's poem 'A Lock of Her Hair' seems to me both totally and movingly serious, and I can hardly conceive of her having written it from within her own inheritance – traditional love poetry, mild porn idyll, magazine romance, pop lyric, and so on.

There were signs in most of the work of an attempt to draw on the classroom experience so far described. I felt that the qualities we had talked about had infiltrated what they had written; to

Literary models 157

some extent it even seemed as if this reflected a conscious and deliberate shaping of materials encountered in the models. Emma tried a piece about returning home after long absence, similar in theme to 'Soldier's Song'; in the Chinese poem, these lines occur:

> On the way home I met some villagers.
> I asked them who was living in my home.
> 'Far, far away is your house
> Tombs are built among the pine trees...
>
> In the courtyard grow the wild rice shoots;
> The sweet ferns flourish by the roadside.'
> I cook rice in the grain,
> And prepare a soup of ferns.
> As soon as dinner is ready,
> I do not know who to call.
> When I stagger out to look to the east,
> Tears fall and wet my clothes.

Emma combined this theme with that of the dead wife:

> Your wife is dead and gone,
> the villagers told me,
> She is buried under those trees.
> A sad death,
> people mourned for her.
>
> I went to the broken house,
> which had not survived the years.
> The garden was covered in moss,
> and inside, the long ferns ruled the floor.
> I looked over the years gone by
> and wept.

The final three lines seem in particular to create something quite new, not only out of the tears and the ferns, but in looking 'over the years gone by'. She also made three starts at a piece about a stream:

> As the day broke,
> a crisp coldness
> gripped the stream,

158   Behind the Poem

Then:

> As the water made the long journey down the mountains,

Then:

> I rush down the mountain valleys.

I said I preferred the second beginning. She had two versions of another complete piece, which seemed inspired by one of the pictures I had videoed of two fishermen, one with a flute.

> Every morning,
> he sat in his boat,
> listening to the drumming of the water.
> The still notes of a flute wavered
> in the air
> and he relaxed once more.

Emma ticked this, having crossed out the one she wrote next:

> As he lies on the boat
> listening to the drumming of the water,
> the still notes of a flute
> waver in the air.

The shorter and in some ways more satisfying version seems an interesting criticism of the first, and yet a preference for a more explicit statement is then made. (Her final, third version, done later in the term, left out 'and he relaxed once more'.)

John, a boy I thought of as having what is called 'difficulty with sentence construction', constructed these sentences for a piece called 'Snow in a Mountain Pass':

> The snow fell, whispering down all night,
> The fire gleamed red,
> red as a mad dog's eyes.
>
> My sleep was as deep as the lake,
> As quiet as the butterfly's flight.

And Martin, a boy with little confidence in writing who

Literary models 159

nevertheless displayed flashes of sensitivity, wrote about 'the ringing mountain paths' and the 'mountains humming in the spring air'. Marlene began her poem called 'Goodbye For Now' in this way:

> I watched you sail away,
> This was when my face was unwrinkled with youth.
> I was new to the earth and unblemished
> but now the red leaves pile high outside my door.

The way in which the piled leaves become a kind of metonymy (of 'comparison', perhaps, in James Liu's terms) for the woman's ageing seems true to the spirit of the poems she had read. The nearest image to that amongst what we had read was the line 'Stray leaves turn red in the cold autumn'. Though leaves and doorways occurred in the poems we read, the use to which she puts them here is her own.

It seemed evident, then, that the class as a whole had begun in some ways to write in the manner, and even the spirit, of the models we had studied. My interpretation was that they were beginning to write original poems in the manner of Chinese poems in translation. They had done so by means of a concentrated bout of writing that began on Monday (for three-quarters of an hour or so), continued on Wednesday morning (half an hour) after a discussion of Monday's efforts, and was completed – or curtailed – after another hour's work on the same day. The stress had all the time been on an initial attempt, possibly brief, maybe even abandoned, to 'get going' on a number of ideas. It was 'a bit of an experiment', as I had said, and perhaps some of their success in it was related to the willingness they appeared to display to try things out and take risks. I had said things originally about the unfamiliarity of the milieu we were entering, and the need, therefore, not to be concerned unduly if it seemed that we weren't getting anywhere, or if we kept needing to 'try again.'

It was at this point that we put the work to one side, though I did say that I had begun to find the pieces they were doing so interesting that I wondered whether it might be worthwhile collecting them in a small booklet to take home at the end of term. In the interim, while we were engaged in other work, I mulled over how best to develop the writing beyond the point where we had left it. Eventually I decided to try to draw them into the criticism and evaluation of their work, intending to use their written comments as a way of generating discussion and provoking redrafting. Accordingly I typed out at least one poem from each pupil as they had been written or begun in the sessions between 17 and 19 February and, on 13 March, presented these sheets of poems to the class; I suggested that they should pencil comments on what they liked and what they didn't like, and hand them back to the writer, and repeated that I thought we should try to produce a small collection for the end of term.

I also suggested that it might be good to have some drawings relating to the subjects of the poems. This suggestion was taken up during the following lesson, and two or three attempts were made at sketches in the manner of Chinese landscapes – sometimes with my book of reproductions in front of them, sometimes not. Over the next few days, with regular visits to the art room in English lessons and at other times, a collection of drawings and paintings was gradually put together. This was done more or less without further comment from me; several children tried drawings at different times, but a few were so striking that the others retired. Four or five drawings seemed beautifully to express the mood of the poems, and this seemed to lift the enterprise, making it look generally more interesting and worthwhile.

The suggestions and comments added to the first versions, and some of the autonomous revisions done at some stage before the lesson on 13 March, were interesting, and I shall look at these in a moment. There were initial signs of a difficulty with the idea of handling work in this way, as if the invitation had been to find things that were wrong, stupid, and so on. 'Criticism' would normally, of course, imply a judgemental posture rather than an exploratory one. Thus Anna wrote 'weird' of this line of Shona's: 'The crisp, even pace of the donkey, like the crisp, even snow by the river', and 'Crazy' against these lines, also by Shona:

> Alone,
> on the edge of the cliff,
> waiting to see you return.
> The tree grows wrinkled
> and old.

Literary models 161

Shona herself wrote 'Don't use it – ghastly' against a short piece she had called 'Departure at Dawn':

> The spray at the prow of the boat,
> as you go.
>
> The sun behind the clouds,
> as you go.

I wrote on her book that I liked it, but Shona sustained her distaste for a while, until comments from others, and my comment repeated, induced her to include it. Despite such uncertainties, mainly due to individual reluctance to approve of their own pieces, their comments and suggestions as a whole revealed a capacity to function critically within this new milieu; their interventions seemed to me to be in the spirit of the models. I had expected reflexive attention to what had been written to seem less creative than the original impetus, but there was evidence of a capacity to sustain it both in commenting for others and in making use of others' comments in redrafting.

I collated the various comments, which had been jotted down on separate sheets, added them onto the first typed sheet, and handed them back. The writer was therefore presented with his or her first draft and various suggestions. Thus:

> *Sleeping on Horseback*
>
> I strode along the singing morning,
> singing in the light breeze of air.
> I wondered where my lonely horse
> would want to take me to next.
>
> Suggestions: change 'sleeping' to 'wandering' in title. Add 'in' after 'along' in line 1. Change 'singing' to 'whistling' in line 2. Omit 'to' in last line.

John's revised and final version incorporated all of these suggestions (none of them mine), and he added 'in' after 'along' in line 1, which normalized the idiom. The last verse of Edward's first draft of 'The Early Boat Journey' read:

> Then the giant city drew steadily nearer,
> with its magnificent splendours and grace
> and its great rising skyscrapers
> which pierce through the clouds of the sky.

162 *Behind the Poem*

The suggestions read: 'All in the last verse – pierce is perhaps too sharp... giant city and giant skyscrapers make it sound unlike Ancient China.' I had written, 'Why not have objects in line 9?' ('Away and away we sailed.') He made alterations on the typed sheet on the basis of these suggestions. His version of the last verse now read:

> Then the small village steadily drew nearer,
> holding out its humbleness and poverty,
> focused on its small wooden huts
> sprawled around the bare countryside.

He then bracketed the whole verse, and wrote 'leave out completely?' Seeing that then his poem finished with the lines: 'the vision of the temple fading away,/as did the tall sycamore trees,' he left out the limp last line.

Though the decisions were made by Edward alone, I am not sure how far these changes might be described as 'his own'. Following the pupil's comment, I said that 'skyscrapers' brought the poem out from the ancient world which was the context of our writing, and then regretted intimating that we ought to remain there, and said in effect that it was no matter, that indeed there was an advantage in bringing the poem into this century. But by then, perhaps, the prejudice had been picked up. Nor can I remember whether the idea that the last verse be left out was originally his or mine. It was discussed, and I have argued earlier for the legitimacy and necessity of such dialogue, if the writer sees the potentialities of his poem.

Several other kinds of change took place. The more informal the situation, the more these different ways of looking back over what has been written flow into and modify or endorse or cancel out each other. And the further on we were, with the need to finalize versions for publication in booklet form, the more fluid, natural, and in a sense urgent the process became. From early on in the work, pupils made their own changes apart from our lesson spent improving things, and there were resistances to suggestions about change; and towards the end there were editorial interventions of the kind that occur when such a product is being brought to completion. Very often there was a good deal of talk, mostly between two or three friends, or at random across the room,

Literary models   163

though not much at all in set groups. The examples that follow are from various stages, but they convey a similar sense that the changes are made in the general direction – there were only one or two exceptions, it seemed to me – of making the writing more genuinely expressive of the spirit of the models.

I had written in Anna's book, hearing the single rhyme chair/hair in her poem 'A Lock of Hair', 'Does the single rhyme fit in?' She changed the first four lines to read:

My gaze rests on your [chair deleted] stool,
Where you used to sit
combing your hair,
And as I [gaze deleted] look

The title was changed too, to 'Combing Your Hair'. The only change that did not originate with her was the idea of dropping the one rhyming sound; I now felt it was fine as it was, so that it becomes a cautionary example of the coercion possible even through such questions as the one I asked.

Experimenting with the first drafts of other poems produced other changes in harmony with the sensibility of the poems she had been reading. Her original beginning of 'The Lotus' was 'When I married you,/A bud appeared.' She removed both lines, substituting the lovelier, more oblique but less ambiguous, 'You came to me/Like the blossoming of a lotus.' An intermediate, prosaic 'and went' at the end of the first line was deleted too. She did this without being prompted by any comment, written or oral.

Marlene's poem, first called 'Goodbye For Now', then 'Leaving', shows in draft forms a struggle going on about how to end. After the line 'my tears wet my face', she had tried and crossed out several variants: 'For your body is in the grave, with earth', 'For now you are buried', 'For now your body is covered with dust', and at one point two of these together, finally settling on 'For your memory is covered with dust'. This was despite discussing transposing the last two lines, ending with the image of the leaves: 'now the red leaves pile high before my door', and my bracketing 'memory' (at the final editorial stage) and writing 'object?' She kept to her own version, therefore, which finally was:

Leaving

I watched you sail away.
This was when my face was unwrinkled with youth.
I was new to the earth and unblemished,
but now the red leaves pile high before my door.
My tears wet my face,
for your memory is covered with dust.

A retreat from the over-explicit also appears through Paul's first drafts of 'Sad Memories of a Brother'. His first draft had the lines 'I prayed for your safety/But I prayed in vain/for as steel hit steel/an arrow flew through the clear sky'. After 'steel hit steel' he then added (writing between the lines) 'And the noise echoed in the valley'. The reference to steel was then deleted, displaced by the image of the echo, and the unnecessary line 'I prayed in vain' went out too, so that the lines now read: 'I prayed for your safety/But the noise echoed in the valley', which is more ominously reticent. At the foot of the first draft of another poem, 'The Grey Mountain', I wrote 'I like the feeling of this – are there not too many lines, though?' Paul crossed through about twelve lines of explicit narrative – 'And when the snow comes and the rain falls/I'll think of you and your warmth and care.../I remember the tears and remember the joy.../ The first chance you have/you must come and see us', and so on – leaving the poem as it now stands:

Sad Memories of a Brother

I remember the day,
I remember the weather,
The grey cloud gathering over the distant mountain
As you climbed your shiny grey horse.
As you rode away slowly,
I prayed for your safety,
But the noise echoed in the valley
   flooded by rainfall and morning dew;
An arrow flew through the clear sky,
Past your fierce warrior enemy
And into your heart.
I remember that day.

To her originally complete short poem, 'Alone,/on the edge of

Literary models 165

the cliff,/waiting to see you return', Shona added, a day or two later, 'The tree grows wrinkled and old'. When I asked why, she said, 'I wanted to get the feeling of growing old.' It is interesting that she has done so by recourse to metonymic association of the kind that James Liu drew attention to; in the fashion of the Chinese poem, the figurative vibration occurs in a speciously 'literal' statement:

> Alone,
> on the edge of the cliff,
> waiting to see you return.
> The tree grows wrinkled
> and old.

It seems interesting that a girl of 12 senses the possibility of this way of speaking, and realizes that the object she has requisitioned to function as a symbol of ageing seems to be physically and spiritually close enough at hand to be implicated in her feeling without strain or overt comment on her part. Perhaps the Chinese poems that we read encouraged the children to construct their own poems by means of quiet operations of a similar kind.

Two final examples:

> In solitude he slips away
> with no-one to guide him
> but the moon's glow,
> watching him,
> far below.

And:

> The sun behind the clouds
> as you go.
>
> The spray at the prow of the boat,
> as you go.

The moon in the first poem seems to offer the distant figure a watchful concern that is otherwise denied to it; and in the second, because there is nothing else described or referred to, the vital images of the sun and, particularly, the spray seem, in articulating the poignancy of the departure, to energize the watcher's regret. The writers thus seem to have sensed how imaginative and even strictly figurative power can work through materials lying close to hand, drawing them into the poetic moment and yet at the same time leaving them as they are. And just as the understated directness of the models, with a syntax shorn both of unnecessary connectives and adjectival or adverbial luxuriance, helped to make the original meanings available to these young readers, so it seems to have enabled the young writer to rise to real emotional strength without needing to attempt elaborate syntax, unusual metaphor, difficult vocabulary, and so on. Certainly the final collection of poems, in which every member of the class was represented, had a simplicity, seriousness, and restraint which I have to see as an expression of their immersion in Chinese poems embodying such values.

7
The world out there

'Taking the mind a walk'

In turning now from cultural forms to the world of external reality, and suggesting that the poetry which children have in them is to be discovered also in their direct encounters with the world, I am not arguing for attention to be paid to 'the world' as a source of inspiration parallel to but separate from literature; I am suggesting, rather, that the teacher's work is to avoid splitting apart children's experience of cultural forms from their experience of the world, and to do this as much by returning to external reality in a studious fashion in order to see what is there, as by focusing on literary reality. One might say that children need to work through given cultural forms in order to express their relations with the world they inhabit, and to contemplate the world they inhabit in order to have anything to say at all by means of the forms they employ.

A primary level of apprehension of the world, through the senses' perceptions of it, seems to be more accessible for the teacher than experience in more complex forms. It is basic, common to everyone, and neutral enough to make any focus on the contemplative, on just looking, hearing, noticing, seem possible. With pets, say, as a 'topic,' children are immediately plunged into compassionate issues, strong emotional reactions,

168 *Behind the Poem*

private memories, and so on; these are of course exactly the things the teacher hopes children will, to some extent, wish to handle in their writing. But if one's intentions are essentially to convey something about the writer's primary duty of fidelity to the truth of what his senses tell him, in order to write strongly or sensitively about anything – not least living creatures – then continually to go back to this primary level of experiencing seems a necessary part of writing.

At any rate, those were the motives for an attempt with a 'mixed ability' class of third-year secondary pupils to look at the world of physical reality, through a stress on a conscious attending to matters that in routine perception – when one is engaged in just living, walking about, working, noticing the weather, and so on – are to some extent passed over. The value of arresting one's brisk transit amongst objects and locations seems to be that they can thus be looked at freshly again, retrieved from the neglect of casual attention, and fully acknowledged, by both senses and mind. What has begun to be forgotten – if it was ever known in this sense – is subjected to rediscovery. These blades of grass are no longer the ones routine perception looked away from; they assume particularity, they possess unsuspected colour or shadow, their very bladedness prods one towards metaphor; insect behaviour, or a memory, may expand such a moment towards narrative even. Some of the poetry which is susceptible of being released through increased awareness of the physical world may then find its way into the child's mind. Objects lifted in this fashion from the stream of forgetful attention in which they lie can give off a kind of rawness which, if not necessarily the motive for the poem, is a stuff which is present in it.

It might be said that it is adults not children who need the physical world to be renovated, and perhaps there is truth in this; and in school, it may be older children who benefit. Perhaps, but the experience of working with children in this way suggests in fact that it is susceptible of renewal or more intense apprehension, perhaps because after all there are different ways even for the child of 8 or 9 to encounter the world. Unselfconscious immersion in their own immediate surroundings seems one; another is the set of physical milieux that they are socialized into, which they experience as it is mediated to them by adults; and a further selection comes to them in representational images in

The world out there 169

different media. Children's closest world physically sometimes seems furthest away as a resource for writing, in the sense that they see no particular reason for recapitulating what is so familiar, and they can be puzzled by the teacher's odd interest in the details of the places where they play, their previous classrooms, and so on. But beyond this, it seems quite possible that children may well miss or skim over the same things that adults do, through the same exposure to an anaesthetizing flow of visual representation, through often having to experience the world at the same urgent pace as the adult, and so on.

The work I wish to describe endorsed for me the truth of this perspective. The class worked for a period of weeks, from early December well into the spring term, on the original Penguin English Project publication, *I Took My Mind a Walk*.[1] Many of the examples are short prose notes, and one of the interesting things about the work seems to me to be the emergence of poems from contexts in which prose seemed more immediately appropriate as a way to write about what we were doing. All the examples are from the four files which were the random survivals from the work of the whole class at the end of the year, the others having been taken home. The title *I Took My Mind A Walk* is from the first line of Norman MacCaig's poem, 'An Ordinary Day',[2] which is also the first piece in the Penguin anthology. Our early work developed out of thinking about the last two verses of the poem:

And my mind observed to me,
Or I to it, how ordinary
Extraordinary things are or

How extraordinary ordinary
Things are, like the nature of the mind
And the process of observing.

At the same time we read the second poem in the anthology, 'Observation' by W. Hart-Smith,[3] which similarly intimates that a particular way of looking can produce its own vision, 'looking into a different direction':

Now and then concentrating
on the very small,

focusing my attention
on a very small area

like this crack in sandstone
perpetually wet with seepage,

getting so close
to moss liverwort and fern

it becomes a forest ...
Someone seeing me

staring so fixedly
at nothing

might be excused
for thinking me vague, abstracted,

lost in introspection.
No, I am awake, absorbed,
just looking in a different direction.

Between the two poems are eight pages of observations and drawings from Leonardo da Vinci's notebooks, a beautiful illustration, of course, of observing the 'extraordinary' in ordinary things:

> Observe the motion of the surface of the water, how it resembles that of hair, which has two movements – one depends on the weight of the hair, the other on the direction of the curls; thus the water forms whirling eddies, one part following the impetus of the chief current, and the other following the incidental motion and return flow.

I suggested initially that everyone should compile a set of observations, over a period of days, on the lines of the Leonardo notebook entries. I intended that the first writing they did should be a kind of imitative taking on of the role of 'artist', a kind of writing in role. To suggest that 13- and 14-year-olds should imitate the gestures of a (presumably unfamiliar) stance towards reality seemed preferable to asking them baldly to 'observe'. The Leonardo extract might offer some kind of foothold for assuming a posture that would be difficult to take up 'naturally'. The fact that Leonardo thought it worthwhile, for example, to observe the flight of birds, and record what he saw in some detail, might legitimize the recording of any observations of birds that pupils made.

The world out there 171

One boy, John, produced three sides of observations about 'crows' – more likely they were rooks. They are sometimes sharply perceptive and firmly focused, in a way that suggests his taking up the stance that 'the artist' takes:

> A crow always lands with both feet on the ground at once and touches down then jumps up again to stop itself toppling forward.

And:

> Crows take off from the ground by jumping up and flapping their wings and at first flying low to the ground then suddenly gaining height.

And:

> If a crow is frightened by anything it will never use its walking motion across the ground, it will jump along with both feet at once.

The same Wordsworthian keeping of the eye 'steadily on the object' is apparent in one and a half sides on a patch of tulips, which a Leonardo entry about leaves might have helped to bring to the surface:

> I like the tulips that stay, sometimes even as much as 3–4 weeks, split bud with a pointed green tight leaves clamping in the bud.

And:

> If you pick up the dying remains of the previous flowers, there you will find many different insects; usually when you disturb the remains the insects will go under the ground then come back up in a few minutes' time.

Again, what seems as valuable as the quality of the observations themselves is the consistency, even the integrity, of the relation taken up by the boy to his subjects; he has taken on the artist's purposeful vision.

It was evident to the class that there was also a markedly speculative element in Leonardo. As well as the artist observing closely, there was a 'scientist' impatient to interpret his observations and to theorize. I suggested that the class should attempt, in a second round of observations, the imitation of this feature of his manner; they should record observations in the speculative way Leonardo the 'scientist' had done. John, now calling himself 'Professor J', enquires about a familiar scene:

> If snow falls evenly why, when it falls on stones, does it give a flat coat of snow if the stones are uneven?

His observation of some ants is also speculative:

> Ants always seem to get lost after collecting their food, they drag their catch this way and that until after much trying they reach the certain crack in the ground, more by luck than skill.
> Ants may be tremendously strong but are not very brilliant. They not only get lost they carry things far too large to get home and (which) they have to abandon on the way, or things totally indigestible.

Again, the observations and speculations appear to reflect the boy's willingness to take on a role, a conventionalized relation to reality. He does see the ants in a somewhat new light, does ask a question about the evenness of snowfall that presumably had not occurred to him in quite the way it has done here. Moreover, in contradistinction to routine writing in science, the personal mode preserves an emotional colouring that makes the record potentially useful as a source of the poetic. For instance, the phrase 'carry things far too large to get home' implies, particularly round the idea of 'home', a kind of empathizing identification with the ants' plight.

The observations of another boy, Mark, as 'Professor M', are in some ways more detailed and more purposefully in role.

> 7.35 am Front door to the house
> Icicles never seem to go to a fine point: explanation: the minimum size of the drip dictates the size of the point.
>
> 7.30 pm Back door
> As I swapped the dogs around so that one went out and the other came in, I noticed that they touched noses: explanation: some kind of scent communication, saying where the dog has been, what it has done... need further observations and research.

The world out there 173

The range of subjects touched on in the space of a page or two is itself interesting. Some of the notes made almost casually, *en passant*, are arresting and sharp. For instance:

> Quite unexpectedly I came across a large spider making a shelter with leaves and broken glass to get away from the snow.

And:

> There are no lichens on the wall near the pavement. Reason – too much water or some chemical in the tarmac.

The way in which this kind of attention might modulate into a metaphoric perception is suggested by several of his entries. One example will suffice:

> I saw something I had never noticed before: snowballs that had smashed against a wall had all taken up the same shape. They were like dead volcanoes with cold larva flows lining the slopes. Explanation: the same vibration sequences could have formed these shapes or was it just coinsedence.

A third journal manner was tried about two weeks after the first 'artist' attempt. I asked the class to write as 'themselves', taking 'their minds a walk', noting down features of their external surroundings at any time of the day, anything that seemed to them interesting to 'observe'. Paradoxically – although in retrospect not unexpectedly – this seemed to be more difficult than the 'in role' pieces, in that aspects of the roles they had been previously encouraged to take up seemed to persist, so that they were 'taking for a walk' those perspectives already assumed.

John wrote:

> Round the bottoms of the trees I noticed that in the flat untrodden snow was very small holes which were quite deep. Possibly from the snow melting on the trees and the water dropping on the snow.

Then wrote, still also speculating:

> It's bitterly, beautifully cold. Why does everything look so sharp?...
> I ask myself, why do all the shadows look so sharp on such a bright day? Is it because the light from the sun has a more penetrating power because of the lack of clouds and heat haze, yet it is steaming in place of the heat haze. Strange.

Others seemed to move easily into a journal manner that was observant but less 'artistic' or 'scientific' – more 'natural', one might say. A girl, Fiona:

> A frozen plastic bag lies screwed up on the ground like a prawn cracker. When touched it's solid and cold.
> On the grass-roller the frost only covers one side of it. The other side has melted in the sun. There is no frost on any of the bolts either.
> The mud is solid and slippery. The grass crunches beneath your feet.

The 'prawn cracker' metaphor, the detail of the bolts on the roller, the juxtaposition of 'solid and slippery', suggest an attentiveness that is both engaged and 'natural'. Her next piece, done at the beginning of the spring term, was a two-side set of impressions of light and reflections, particularly sunlight; they are more in the 'scientist' vein:

> As the light hits the sea it reflects and this gives the water a glossy, transparent look. As you look ahead you can see this, but as you get to the place you were looking at the glossy look disappears and if you look ahead again the next bit is glossy and as you reach that place the glossy look disappears again.
> As light strikes a spider's web the whole web seems to glisten like tiny pieces of broken glass. The light darts off in different directions when it hits the water and this is what gives it the glistening effect.

What appeared to be happening in the journal entries of the class as a whole was that they had become a means of looking at external realities. The isolation of observing from any more connected activity legitimized the short two- or three-line note, a 'genre' which was perhaps crucial in that it released the students from the need to assemble large structures, allowing them to concentrate on detail. An accepted brevity – the artist's succinct jottings – provided a frame within which images that might ordinarily have been passed over without comment or notice, were attended to, contemplated, and made significant. In this process the linguistic frame seemed to serve to direct the experience just as the experience of observing particulars conduced to establishing a frame. The small details like the bolts on the roller and the holes in the snow seem to acquire (given the excision of any connections with surrounding narrative or description) a modest autonomy and resonance of their own; to be curiously worth mentioning. Similarly, the raising of speculative questions at this level of particularity in natural phenomena is also made possible by isolating the observation; stopping to ask 'simple' questions would not be possible in more connected writing, or in more connected activities.

It also seems possible – and again this was not planned but only dimly anticipated – that the focusing observation in the journals functioned as a kind of poetic groundwork. This was evident in Mark's empathizing with the ants trying 'to get home' and the spider making a 'shelter', and in the metaphoric perspectives that he and Fiona took on when looking at the marks of snowballs, which he saw as dead volcanoes, and at the frozen crisp bag, which she saw as a prawn cracker. Another girl, Jane, generated metaphoric views of most of the things she looked at for any length of time: 'Veins standing out like rivers.' 'Hands are like tools.' And watching football:

> The ball is put down so gently you would think it was made of glass, but it is then kicked as if it was hated.
> The sun struck the sign like a single squirt of orange juice on a plate.

It may be that the degree of metaphoric statement in some of the notes derived from prior discussion of the Norman MacCaig poem, in which the ordinary becomes extraordinary in metaphor. I suggested at one point, talking about the poem, that objects looked at hard and long tend to make one think of something resembling them in some way, and that when MacCaig saw that 'Long weeds in the clear water did Eastern dances' he was giving an example of a kind of experience that is available to anyone who is prepared to see in that intent way. A suggestion that they should *try* to see metaphorically produced, in some notes, a perhaps over-metaphoric manner.

> The spray flies everywhere and the river swirls as if captured and unable to find a way out of its cell. The water in the stream runs its obstacle course over stones, wood and litter. It seems in a great hurry, as though late for a date. Further on it turns brown and goes much slower but with a certain threatening look, like the school bully just waiting for his chance to knock you down. The water reaches a whirlpool. Here it travels round and round with all the litter and garbage in a never-ending dance.

This willed manner perhaps suggests that the experience one wishes to encourage is somehow being subverted, presumably by being directively promoted. There is clearly a paradox latent in the idea of saying, in effect, '*try* to have a genuine experience', and this example seems to show how the 'offer' or request can infiltrate or distort the 'experience' and threaten or even annihilate it.

However, even though some of the writing seemed trite or false, much did not, and seemed almost to be waiting, as I suggested, for shaping into a more poetic mode of expression. At this point we returned to the poem 'Observation' by W. Hart-Smith.

For use with a different class the previous year, I had taken some close-up photographs of a number of things – cherry blossom, a rabbit's eye, an uncoiling fern, and so on. They looked very suitable to accompany the poem, but it also seemed important to take some pictures for or with this particular class. About 11 or 12 December there was a heavy frost, following snow, and on the spur of the moment we went round the school grounds, taking pictures, some in close-up, of fungi on a tree trunk, litter frozen in the snow, the roller on the cricket field, and so on. The snow obligingly began again before we got back into the class room, and we took pictures of snow on hair and glasses, snow melting in the hand, snow on cars, and so on.

At the beginning of the next term, I decided to use a close-up of hoar frost on the roller from the batch we had taken, and one or two of the original close-ups I had done. This was a unilateral decision; it was a pity, perhaps, that the class didn't have the opportunity of talking about the respective merits of the photographs and making their own choices; though they saw all those we had taken, the ones picked out for communal use were picked out by the teacher. Even so, there was perhaps some justification for that if one's intention was to focus with the whole class on a small number of pictures, and to produce some poems in a part-communal fashion, rather than to take a larger number of pictures and give the class the opportunity of constructing a tape–slide sequence from them, choosing their own slides.

Reproduced below are three poems that emerged, written by Derek, Fiona, and John. It is important to note that they are constructed partly from ideas that emerged as the class as a whole discussed the slide, and partly from the individual vision. The metaphors they have in common make clear the communal origin of the work, and to that extent render them less individually creative. At the same time, the form, manner, and tone of each poem are perhaps marked enough to allow one to hear individual voices.

'Hoar Frost on the Roller'

Derek: A wild land,
       Blue and sharp,
       So delicate,
       but so unfriendly.

       A choppy sea,
       or wild flames.
       Neglected and forgotten,
       and so still.

       An unwanted land,
       so rough,
       But so peaceful and still,
       It is harmless.

       The shape of swords,
       or a storm at sea.
       Perhaps a jungle,
       Or a fire.

       The sight is very chilling
       and lonely,
       But it could be nice,
       Like furs or bristles.

       A field on a hill,
       With many strange plants.
       But it is too rigid,
       And far too still

       The more you look,
       The more it changes.
       Firing missiles,
       Or a fire turned to stone.

Fiona: A blue fire swallowing everything in its path,
       Jagged, jumbled, tall and thin,
       A forest of tiny white trees,
       Spread about like plants on a hillside,

178   *Behind the Poem*

> Standing like bristles on a brush.
> Blue-white carpet covering everything.
> Silent and mysterious.

John: Reaching up in rigid spikes of white.
> The brilliance is dazzling in the early morning sun.
> Jagged crystal-like spires.
> The amazing angle at which they lean.
> The white-clearness of their tops.
> Their freezing look to chill all people.
> The edges of them melt in the still weak sun.
> They melt under the heat of the hand but not
>   without a fight, they freeze the hand first.
> Eventually they meet their match and die under the
>   sun, their remains trickle round the roller
>   and onto the ground.
> Finally nothing is left, all is dry.

The overlapping images and vocabulary that derive from their own comment in discussion are the images of fire, sea, hillside, jungle, and bristles, and words like jagged and still. The swords image, here used only by Derek, was also one, I think, that derived from talk.

But there is also evidence of original development beyond the shared start. Derek's striking opening seems to be his own: the land image, and the juxtaposition of sharpness with wildness, which pre-echoes the antithesis of delicacy and unfriendliness, came from himself. The emphasis on its neglected and forgotten and unwanted state, later underlined in 'very chilling' and 'lonely', and perhaps in 'far too still', spreads an even emotional tone over his poem which the discordant bits – 'it could be nice', for instance – hardly dispel; he perhaps felt that he *ought* to include the furs image because it had been mentioned. He was a shy boy, and the unfriendliness and loneliness of this land in the picture were perhaps only too real. In two poems written six days later he finds the fungi 'frightening', and the 'sharp thin stigmas' of the cherry blossoms are 'points' which look 'angry' and then 'look fierce'.

He also finds a shape for his poems which no one else used and which he kept to in all the nine poems he wrote in this section of his work. The four-line stanzas have a satisfying two-stress feel to them, they rhyme occasionally, and the sentences are completed pleasingly within the stanza, even if there is a good deal of filling in.

Fiona added little of her own to the ideas produced in discussion. Her poem does not perhaps read with the conviction that Derek's does. The approach I took may inhibit some children, who would prefer to be on their own from the start. On the other hand, John's version, like Derek's, avoids the rather derived manner that seems to weigh down Fiona's. His first line has a bold rhythm of its own, and the two phrase-lines – 'The amazing angle at which they lean/The white-clearness of their tops' – convey something like restrained wonder. After this beginning, his poem runs into a prosy dribble that lacks the observant stance of his earlier notes, though 'trickle round the roller' is exact.

The other close-up pictures (in slide form) were looked at a week or so later. The subjects were: a rabbit's eye, an uncoiling fern, fungi, lichen on bark, cherry blossoms, a drop of water. I asked the class to choose three of them, and suggested that later they could do a second version of one they liked, if they felt they could improve it. The offer was made in a rather directive way, perhaps, but having waited for three or four weeks before introducing the notion of having a second look at poems, so as to make the best of the original inspiration, I was reluctant to let it slip through diffidence. At the same time, such decisions often generate – perhaps ought always to generate – an anxiety lest what the pupils are doing is not what they themselves are doing at all, but what the teacher is doing through them. Martin Buber describes this perennial predicament: 'Through the teacher the selection of the effective world reaches the pupil. He fails the recipient when he presents this selection to him with a gesture of interference... Interference divides the soul into an obedient and a rebellious part. But a hidden influence proceeding from his integrity has an integrating force.'[4]

I mention Buber's dilemma here because of a strong doubt that arose at some point about the legitimacy of redirecting children's attention so firmly, or drastically, and towards things that might seem to them trivial; it was a sharp visitation of the perennial uncertainty about when legitimate intervention becomes intrusive, and it was prompted by hearing some false notes in the writing. Did the emphases that I was making 'proceed from integrity', or were the pupils taking it over with their 'obedient part'? It seems to me that there is frequently no answer, in the usual sense, to such questions; but that the teacher's doubt, however transitory, is valuable both in so far as it is productive – of a renewal of commitment, a recognition of having asked too much, and so on – and as a resource, as an alert scepticism which one can draw on to insulate against easy judgement. I have suggested that the small two- or three-line notes of observation modelled on the Leonardo entries were 'authentic'; they felt right. But a residual doubt lingered as to whether they could not be taken as very skilful adaptations to changes in the demands made on them, rather than as their own committed attempts to imitate a way of seeing and writing.

The pupils' own comments on the work, which are reproduced later, were not available at the time; there was only the work, and my responses to it, to suggest that there was a kind of genuine influence that cut quite deep. The poems that follow, written in response to the slides, seem to be genuinely and vitally metaphoric; trying to read them as poems in which metaphor – and close observation – had been skilfully but cerebrally 'worked in' seems impossible.

Derek wrote about the rabbit's face twice, once on 12 January and again in March. His first version is:

As you first glance,
The face is expressionless.
Not happy or sad,
Or good or bad.

But a closer look,
Shows the face with a thought,
He could be thinking,
About someone he knew.

The eye looks sorry,
It is a mirror.
Wet and shiny,
Looking at you.

Bristly hair surrounds the eye.
Bristly, but still soft.
With neat lines running down,
And two big eyes.

The second version was done after seeing the slides again, without intervening comment except for 'Again, very observant' written below the first attempt.

> The face is very serious.
> It must be thinking hard,
> Considering what to do,
> Or where to go.
>
> He stares at you,
> With a big wet eye.
> Does he know you're living,
> Or just a piece of stone?
>
> The eye knows not,
> Of the hair surrounding it.
> It knows not its colour,
> Yet it knows the mind.
>
> The light brown hairs,
> Lie soft on its face.
> The eyes blink,
> And the rabbit moves.

There seems to be a number of differences between the two attempts. In the second the mirror metaphor is dropped. He includes his own activity in the first – 'as you first glance', 'a closer look' – but not in the second; the rabbit moves in the second, as if Derek has in imagination gone beyond the still photograph. Similarly, in the second poem the rabbit's thoughts have more substance, suggesting that he has taken up a more questioning and genuinely empathizing stance. And yet there is a preoccupation in both versions with what lies behind the eye, with what is being thought; the preoccupation seems to develop, and in the second poem is more clearly stated, as if he had begun to find a subject: 'He stares at you/With a big wet eye./Does he know you're living,/Or just a piece of stone?' And comparing the two last verses, the static attempt just to record or describe in the first poem gives way to something which is both more fluently said, and more of an ending to the narrative of the piece, in that the last words 'the rabbit moves' put a conclusion to its 'considering ... where to go' in the first verse.

What seems interesting here is the way Derek has apparently

gone beyond the encouragement to observe and try out metaphor. He has looked hard at a slide and, in the first poem at least, used metaphor; but through this he has been led to try to grasp something in purely speculative terms. He has tried a subject that it is difficult or impossible to observe directly, or to express in metaphor.

He also attempted a quite autonomous piece. I noticed, after his second attempt at the rabbit's eye poem, that he had also written, two or three days after the first version, a third poem, called simply 'Eyes'. This was done without any suggestion from me:

When an eye looks at you
You wonder what it's thinking.
Thinking about you,
And what you are.

It slowly blinks
And you realise
That it is living
And thinking.

The eye looks tired,
Yet interested in you.
So it can't go to sleep
Until you have gone.

Looking at the original slide evidently led him quickly to this expression of a feeling of being watched. It suggests a personal source, in deep shyness. The image of the eye that 'can't go to sleep/Until you have gone' conveys a disturbing sense of being continuously under observation, not just by eyes, but by a functionary of some kind, at the moment neutrally 'interested' although it is the sinister note of the last two lines that stays in the mind.

This intervening poem seems to represent a wish to speak more personally than he did in the two versions of the other poem. Rather than the rabbit's eye as a suggestion of others looking, the subject simply and directly is others looking. But he would hardly have been led to the more directly personal poem without the initial subject acting as some sort of preparation. He seems to have been drawn to articulate and confront a personal

The world out there 183

difficulty by means of what began as neutral observation. In the three pieces together, he has found some expressive release, presumably, but not only that. He has found a way of writing in stanza form which he seems content to use and which conveys what he wishes to; he has also found some additional commitment to the idea of writing, if one can interpret that way his spontaneous attempt at a second poem.

Mark chose not to do a second version of any of these, but to write a new poem 'The Drip', which drew on his earlier notebook entry:

> A drip, peeps out of the hot tap,
> A steaming morsel of an ocean,
> A menial of it's kind,
> Glassy highlights line it's sides,
> The pale blue chamber has no colour,
> It falls, and disperses with a click.

This developed awareness seems to draw on his earlier studied observation of a drip forming at the end of an icicle. The paradoxical 'pale blue chamber' with 'no colour' is beautifully observed; 'Glassy highlights line it's sides' is both musical and the kind of close-up accurate perception that might testify to the 'hidden influence' – here not so hidden – of the earlier observations.

His other close-up poems contain sharply focused perceptions. Of the coiled fern shoot:

> It's head is hugging the stem.
> The bristles on it's side,
> Are still powdered with fine soil.

John chose to rewrite his hoar-frost poem. His second attempt is a rather draconian shortening of the first:

> The tall white spines reach to the skies.
> Their coldness digs deep into man.
> Their white cold look is dazzling.
> They are like snow-covered church spires with no building.
> They lean at amazing angles which make them even more
>   spine-chilling.

184   Behind the Poem

Some cumbersome lines at the end of the original have been left out, but so have some good things. The first line is changed from: 'Reaching up in rigid spikes of white' to: 'The tall white spines reach to the sky'. The enthusiasm of 'the amazing angles at which they lean' is ironed out to 'They lean at amazing angles which', and in general the second piece sounds like a retreat from the observation and experience which the first poem seemed to formulate. John's other close-up pieces also seemed to have less vitality, as if the enterprise had gone on too long.

The four pupils whose work has been scrutinized here also wrote brief comments at the end about what they felt they had learned or not learned from the project. I should like to put their remarks inside the frame of Buber's question, and ask whether they emerge from the ruminations of the 'obedient part' of the soul which responds in a divided way to the 'interference' of the teacher, or whether they reflect an influence proceeding from the 'integrity', or wholeness, of what they had been asked to do.

> John: I have learnt a lot about small objects of life everybody normally passes by without even a quick glance and I have observed them at a different angle to what they are normally observed. And this folder gave me great fun in compiling.
>
> Mark: This 'take your mind for a walk' project has been of great benefit to me, because it has taught me to be more alert to the world around me, and to look at things twice, whereas, before, I would only have glanced at. It has also taught me to exercise the power of my imagination more, a type of positive mind-bending to my advantage.
>
> In the project we have been taught to use 'metaphors' more, and better, so that we can see things from a new angle.

(Is the repeated 'it has taught me', 'we have been taught' the shadow of 'interference'? Are the speech marks round 'metaphors' an indication that the idea is taken on as, essentially, a piece of technical language?)

> Fiona: The whole idea is to look at what you usually pass by. On the whole it is a useful exercise. It encourages you to open your eyes and take an interest in the things that go on around you. You have to mix imagination with reality. The imagination needs something real there to work on and then the interest comes.

The world out there   185

Derek: In this project I found out a lot of things I didn't know, mainly through observing things. I now notice a lot more things [when] I walk around than I used to. The project helped us to see things differently.

Looking at Mark's work over the whole period – comprising about twenty-five sides of writing, stapled together – I wonder what forward movement there has been towards sharper observation, towards a feel or relish for metaphor, towards uncovering these features of his own poetic awareness. Even at the very beginning, he writes in his notes: 'That slushy mud that we played football in yesterday is now a time-trap, trapping the suspended particles in one position until the Key to let them out arrives. That Key is the sun'. He already observes in metaphor, unless the one reading of the MacCaig poem and the Leonardo notes itself evoked a metaphoric response. His later work, impressive as it is, may not owe its impressiveness to the project. He writes some notes on eyes about three weeks after the previous note: 'Eyelashes, superhuman vacuum brushes, infallible dust excluders. Invisible protection grills'; 'Eyelids, the human version of a car lubrication system'. He then does a page of observations of 'canal water' through a microscope.

Magnification 35X

I can identify only a very few of the animals, larva and insects in the water.
   You could see that the water flea's heart pumped blood all the way up its back in one big artery. I found out the sex of one of the water fleas because when I put a 'Georges Disc' over the flea to hold it still about 200 small fleas came out of the flea's mouth, thus proving it a female.

After this come two pages of carefully tabulated data on the birds using his garden over a four-day period, giving data, time of day, species, sex, and number; then one page on jackdaws: 'Unlike some birds it can walk by putting one foot in front of the other.'
This all seems to have as much to do with aptitudes and enthusiasms already developed in him as with the particular directed encouragements of the project, and yet the point

perhaps is that whatever may be the antecedents of this facility for close scrutiny and the reading of information, he is working in ways which not only suit him, but draw him into them, and through which he expresses his poetry and his science – a sceptical modest science that 'can identify only a few things in the canal water' – and that here these aptitudes have space to develop further. In that sense at least he is moving towards finding his own poetry, and doing so, interestingly, by associating the world of the poet and artist with the world of the scientist and careful observer. The drips on the icicle and the tap are seen metaphorically, but also observed intently and questioned hypothetically.

The jackdaws are looked at closely as individuals, but their appearances are also quantified and tabulated: '27th – early morning – 2; 28th – early morning – 2; 29th – early morning – 8.' There is an eager awareness at work that relishes the various forms of 'mind-bending' that have made him 'more alert to the world'; but to appreciate having the mind bent and the imagination's 'power' exercised might be the privilege of those whose minds can bend and whose imaginations have power.

In other words, there is never an answer, in such contexts, to the questions: 'How have they developed? What has been achieved?' Liam Hudson, writing about the contradiction between the apparent sterility of the training received by Turner and his own unfettered genius, suggests that the problem is particularly intractable: 'Anyone who assumes, as we are all prone to, that we create qualities by nurturing them, or even by opposing them, can make no sense of Turner at all.'[5] On the other hand, there is a remark of David Holbrook's which makes for a more hopeful resolution of one's dilemma, implying it would be better not to see the question simply in terms of influence and 'development' if we wish to see what is 'achieved': 'I develop merely by having a Shakespeare play ... if I truly have it, not because it has developed (stretched, improved, added to) me.'[6] The children's 'development' here is a matter of what they have actually done.

8
Other contexts

The previous two chapters attempted to describe something of the way in which the teacher sets out to use certain contexts, broadly so defined, as a means of eliciting poems from children. Writing poems in imitation of other poems, and making observations of the outside world, seem to open up distinct sets of possibilities that are worth discussion. There seems no reason why this should not be true of other areas that the teacher is drawn to, and to attempt to do greater justice to the idea of context in this sense I wish to look briefly at four more such milieux. The choice may seem somewhat arbitrary, as essentially reflecting a personal taste, but I would argue that each one is also 'important' in relation to children's writing, and even in some danger of being undervalued.

Film

The first of these contexts is film. 'Film' here is not video, but 16 mm and 35 mm film shown on a large screen. There seems to be a particular value, increasingly overlooked as video takes over from the large screen, in the child's experience of cinema proper; its size and relative formality, the darkness itself, help to restore some of the sense of occasion and significance that is dissipated by both the small-scale images and the casual social contexts of television. We also tend to forget that the cinema screen is not simply larger, but that its pictures have in consequence a richer grain than those of the television monitor, and that the larger images are also qualitatively different. It is thus the large screen more satisfyingly than the small that makes available the kind of awareness that Siegfried Kracauer thought it was the 'specific nature'[1] of film to provide, namely the experience of 'the redemption of physical reality'. What seems distinctive to film is that the audience is surrounded, in a way that is not as possible in other art forms or in experience lived through at a routine pace, by the immediate presences of a physical reality which even children can begin in routine perception to 'forget'. Kracauer suggests that the small, the large, the transient features of the physical world are, in particular, reclaimed by the camera for a different kind of attention.

This idea becomes interesting, and worth alluding to in a book about children's writing, because of its heuristic implications. If such a claim for film is valid, so that it is itself either a way of seeing things afresh or a strong encouragement towards it, then it is the poetry of film as much as its visual informativeness which ought to engage the teacher's attention. The difference between this emphasis and that of the previous chapter needs to be made clear. The claim there was for a close personal 'observation' akin to contemplation, a kind of slowed down or arrested attention; here the effect that produces the sense of seeing things differently still occurs at the routine pace of living – because the pictures are moving pictures – but alters the size of things and frames them so severely and selectively that something different again is uncovered.

I gave an example in the second chapter of such a use of film; film images of actual trees provided a way of escaping or enriching the banal statement 'the branches are bare'. It is as if the camera itself can, like a teacher, point out and stress that feature of a landscape, say, which the writer would wish to emphasize; the framing and selective underscoring of components of an experience accomplished by the camera is a first artistic step, so to speak, which can encourage the child to move further in that direction.

Alison, in her second year at secondary school, records the

beginning of the film *Terminus*, a documentary about Victoria Station, in this way:

> The begining of another day in London, a man is seen walking along a roof. His friend is looking at his bees.
>
> * * *
>
> The Station Master walks into his office and takes off his hat. He picks up the phone and calls the signal-box. He looks at his papers.
>
> * * *
>
> Feet and Faces.
>
> * * *
>
> Men and women say goodbye to relatives. The husband boards his train and waves goodbye to his family.
>
> * * *
>
> The cat (Betty) sits on the station-roof and watches station life.

The opening of the film complicates any picture we may have formed in advance of busy station reality by presenting the images of the cat, the man walking along a roof, the bee-hive, and so on. This immediate refusal of a stereotype involves breaking apart patterns of expectation. Some echoing sense of the disjunction of perceptions that are normally linked seems to be taken up by Alison here. She uses very short paragraphs and marks the breaks with asterisks. She describes what she sees neutrally, and without comment, apparently taking that stylistic cue from the camera. The result is curiously arresting. The 'objective' manner is kept up to the end of her piece; the last line is: 'Dirty water comes from the engine pistons.'

Aiming perhaps at the same dry or laconic manner, she also wrote a group of short interchanges between passenger and porter, ticket collector and traveller, and so on. These feel quite different, simply flat; there was perhaps nothing in the functional dialogue of the film to inspire or energize her attempt:

> I left my purse on the 3.15 to London.
> What colour was it?
> Blue with white spots.
> Was it big or small?
> Small.
> We'll let you know, what's your telephone number?
> 88693 and thank you.

190 Behind the Poem

She wrote later in the year about another film, *City of Gold*, a lyrically evocative documentary about the Yukon gold rush. She tried a poem and a story, and as in her *Terminus* writing, there seems to be a contrast between the writing which draws directly on the visual poetry she has encountered, and the 'invented' story, where the memorable imagery of the film recedes. The poem comes from a moment when the camera wanders through rooms left untouched since 1902. The ghostly owner of the house is the speaker, watching the children who visit it:

> The summer's here at last,
> The children come and plague my house,
> They are like flies to fly-paper.
> But that little girl is always by herself.
> She stares up at my picture,
> Her eyes like two big blue saucers,
> I wonder what she's thinking.
>
> My satin shoe lies decaying on the window-sill,
> It reminds me of a small boat lying in an ocean of dust.
> She is trying it on now, it's too big though,
> She is sitting in my rocking chair
> With a shawl round her shoulders,
> She looks like a baby bird in a soft nest.
> But though she can't see me,
> I see her.
> For I, the ghost of Sweet Sue,
> Shall haunt the house on Wisky Hill,
> For Ever.

Here, what is invented – the girl and her actions, none of which are in the film – emerges from what the camera sees, and sees with a particular poignancy: the shoe on the window-sill, the rocking chair, the portraits. One of the images she uses, the small boat, may have come from one of the stills seen earlier, and the idea itself may have been suggested by a passage in the commentary, which a colleague had painstakingly transcribed from the soundtrack in its entirety:

> You know, when we were playing house in Dawson, it never occurred to us that any of this meant anything, that one of these chairs, for instance, might be the very one in which Silent Sam Bonafield was

sitting the night he lost the M and N hotel in a poker game. It never occurred to us that each Victorian picture told its own story, that these two paintings had once been worth more than gold itself to a man who traded half his claim for them. No ghosts of the past returned to haunt us, here in those silent rooms.

The writing of the poem seems itself to be an expression of the poetic vision of the camera and its underscoring and narrative expansion in the commentary. In other words, the film has made the poem possible, and this time on both levels. It can happen, it seems, that once the poetry of such a film has surrounded children for twenty minutes or so, an unusually strong incentive exists to give verbal expression to whatever it is which somehow asks to be further articulated as language. Writing poems after reading other poems or stories involves starting afresh on a new creation; other writing can even numb the impulse to write. But encounters with other art forms can bring the poem nearer. Some of the 'inspiration' has been provided for the writer, and the charged experience of one work of art becomes the source of another.

In Alison's writing, making connections between the experience of film and the writing of the poem has involved stressing what the camera does to shape experience artistically, and I have suggested that the effects of this shaping were apparent in the prose piece she wrote on *Terminus*, in a deliberate disconnectedness which paralleled, or rearticulated, the camera's unusual emphases. This kind of prose has often seemed to me to be closer to the poem (or to that idea of the poem that I tend in practice to handle, which with children has excluded the longer narrative poem) than more extended and coherent narratives.

In the account that follows of some work on the film *Application*, with the same third-year secondary pupils whose work was the subject of the last chapter, I have included several prose extracts which seem either poetic in themselves, or imaginatively penetrating in ways that might anticipate and even 'prepare for' the poem itself. In that one or two pieces rework the poetry of the film into satisfying prose, they might serve as a reminder that a request for 'a poem' may not always be the most appropriate way of encouraging writing that is genuinely poetic, nor of course of responding to the poetry of such a film. This raises rather prematurely, also, the question I have so far avoided and which I shall touch on briefly in the last chapter, as to the status of 'poetic' prose. The work on the film was done just after the work on observation described in the previous chapter, and some of the children's emphases reflect that.

Application is a film about a woman in her late 50s who goes to make enquiries about moving into a 'home'. She is chilled by the encounter, particularly by the brisk impersonal interview, during which she is haunted – as the film suggests in sometimes hallucinatory moments of flashback – by images from her past. I suggested that the class write, as a poem or in any way they chose, either their own impressions of the film, or the woman's own impressions of her experience.

Derek wrote three sides of conversation between two boys who saw the film very differently. It begins:

> Ken: That film, 'Application', was boring, wasn't it? All it was, was buses and things.
>
> Sid: I don't know. It wasn't exactly like real life. So it was interesting. Kind of eerie.

He created one character whose questioning awareness goes to the heart of the film, and another who doesn't see why one should want to know about old people's homes. Derek thus used dramatic dialogue to articulate his own feel for the film, and his awareness of another's unawareness:

> Ken: We don't need to know about it, do we?
>
> Sid: No, but we only think about what being a child is like. Old people's lives must be very different.
>
> Ken: I still think it's a waste of time. Besides, some people find it depressing.
>
> Sid: Why?
>
> Ken: Well, I don't know. I mean it's all so quiet and miserable and they seem so unsociable.

A few lines later:

> Sid: You said even this way was boring. Can you imagine what it would be like if they just showed you what the routine was like every day?

It was saddening though when the camera showed you a closeup of the expression on their faces.

Ken: I thought it was boring. I mean it didn't tell you much, did it?

Sid: Of course it did. It gave you an idea of the atmosphere of the old people's home. Although it was obviously exaggerated.

Ken: That's all it seemed to show, anything showing gloom. And there could have been more speech in it.

Sid: I think it was better without speech. It let you get the idea of it yourself.

Later, near the end:

Ken: The interviewer was really snappy.

Sid: Well, it can't really be like that. But everything like that helped to make it more cold and therefore interesting.

In the introduction to his file, gathering together the term's work, Derek wrote of this conversation: 'Included in this file is an imaginery conversation between two boys about a film shown to them. Their first thought is that it is extremely dismal and not a nice thought at all, but later in the conversation they compare their life with an old person's. This is really observing another person's life from our own eyes.'

To respond to works of art it seems necessary to suspend judgement about what is before one, and 'simply look' without prejudice or preconception – however impossible that is, practically speaking. Both this capacity and a helpfully modest temperament – 'often just by looking at something you can understand more about it and its purposes' – are perhaps what give Derek's aware character the capacity to note that 'we only think what being a child is like; old people's lives must be very different', and to imagine what it would be like 'if they just showed you what the routine was like every day'. He is able to observe that the interviewer 'made it more cold and therefore interesting' and that 'it was better without speech. It let you get the idea of it yourself.'

It is interesting to compare Derek's perceptions at this point with his effort to read what lay behind the eyes in his poems in the last chapter. Both may be related to what he wrote in the introduction to his file, referred to above, that what matters is 'not so much what you know' about various things as 'how you interpret them'. The dialogue form here makes it possible for him to articulate a similar attempt to 'see things through other people's eyes', as he put it.

John's piece responds to the bleak poetry of the film. The beginning, where the woman looks up at the windows of the home, is vitally metaphoric:

> I see the building of my future home, towering high, the windows alight with morbid faces, shining on me. Their dull faces are not enticing, they garp [gawp] at me as though they are imprisoned and I am soon to join them, they ward me away.

'The windows alight with morbid faces' catches an early shot in the film where faces are discernible in each of a group of windows reflecting the light. John has taken the images of reflected light and 'morbid' faces and elided them to one disquieting metaphor. He goes on:

> Inside I am asked questions, I do not hear them, windmills, the sea, children, everything flashes in my mind until interrupted by the question again. I answer, not always completely truthfully, but I answer.

Mark wrote a poem in short broken statements in the woman's own voice. Each section tries out a metaphor, suggesting perhaps that at this disturbing moment she would see intensely in metaphor. He draws on an observation made a week or two earlier: 'I looked under a brick and counted over twelve woodlice and two or three centipedes and other such insects that I could not recognise. They were all in a group huddled together.' The juxtaposition of the brick and the insects returns in the poem; perhaps the huddling together of the old people in the home is also implied in the comparison.

Application

'I'
'I see a brick, a building brick.'
'I see faces, without expression, in this brick.'
'It's a cold brick.'

'I'
'I am an ant.'
'In an anthill of brick.'
'Lost in a labyrinth of interconnecting passages.'
'I'
'I am a prisoner of age.'
'At a geriatric Stalag 17.'
'What will they do with me?'
'I'
'I see pointless faces.'
'All are negative.'
'Soon, I too will vegetate.'
'And become another blank.'
'I . . .'

In the first verse the brick is the building itself. ('Building brick' is awkward, but the metaphor seems serviceable.) Then, without too much awkwardness, 'brick' becomes literal, and the space which he saw under the brick where insects were 'huddled together' changes to an 'anthill of brick' which is a metaphor for the home. 'Age' is personified as the enemy that incarcerates prisoners there, and Mark finally has the 'I' reduced to a 'blank', an event which takes place literally, or typographically, in the last line. The other isolated 'I's, placed before verbs, sounded more confident; the last one suggests hesitant emptiness or desolation, especially after the earlier bleak metaphors and bald statements. The film presses into service an image held in suspension in the mind, an image without significance until the encounter with the film released it. A request to write a poem about insects at the time might have produced something, but not this oddly strong vision. And clearly the fruitful relation between the experience of the film and that of the earlier observation legitimates both activities, and hints again at the need, when thinking of how to 'encourage' writing, to take into account those remoter 'ecological' kinds of influence.

Fiona found an altogether different, but equally interesting way of suggesting the woman's distress; it harks back to the notebook entries referred to earlier. I suggested that the brief two- or three-line notes in Leonardo's observations functioned both as a genre to imitate and a frame to observe through, and

Fiona has apparently taken both these over again in her reconstruction in words of the woman's experience. It begins:

> The old lady sitting under the hair-dryer reading her newspaper
>
> * * * *
>
> The tram silently going on its way. Only one person in it, the old lady. Everywhere is empty and still.

In a bare prose style perfectly suited to what she is doing – a style I should also call poetic – she goes on to describe two old men playing billiards in the home.

> An old shrivelled man with large ears stares blankly into space. He leans on his stick. He gets up and silently hits one of the balls that strikes another on the billiard table with no pockets. No-one speaks.
>
> * * * *
>
> The tram carries on silently as if in a dream

I find the disconnectedness of this moving and sympathetic. To separate 'He leans on his stick' from the previous sentence, and to see the old man as simply 'shrivelled ... with large ears' seems an expressive gesture, and no more distortive than the film itself is at that point. Then, in not ending the third sentence at 'one of the balls' or even at 'another' but only when she has drawn out this particular moment through the words 'strikes another on the billiard table with no pockets', she seems to be trying – successfully, I think – to re-create the tedium that the camera establishes as it watches the stroke and its effects; almost as if she were watching the ball go round the table, unemotionally, waiting for it to stop as one waits for the sentence to stop. Then 'No-one speaks'.

The description of the home itself is developed through several brief statements, disconnected from each other like the notebook entries: 'The women knit like machines. They stare at the needles but don't see them.' She then deals with the interview and the woman's memories, particularly the photographer who, we presume, is her dead lover or husband.

The screwed up face of the photographer, like a dead melon. A young face in a white bonnet smiles, the camera clicks.

* * * *

A woman walks over cobbles at dusk. A camera whirls, the white bonnet turns and the face is old and empty.

* * * *

A horse gallops along the shores of a sandy beach. The wind billows out the young girl's shirt. The wind blows her hair.

Again, there is a conscious discreteness, repeating 'the wind' as subject of two sentences, rather than, say, 'and blows her hair'. These even shorter statements continue to the end: 'Alone in her room the woman sits, lonely, sad, remembering.'

This transposition of film imagery into language seems to me genuinely creative. Possibly the isolation of each frame in the original observations of snow and so on encouraged a reductive emphasis to the essential particulars of the scenes in the home, an emphasis which fits the coldness of the places which the camera brings to the watcher's attention. And the camera observes in a style of its own; the way Fiona sees the old man – 'shrivelled ... with large ears' – is a re-creation of the camera's perception of that moment. But 're-creation' is also creation, for the kind of verbal distinction between 'stare at' and 'see', and the kind of verbal dislocation that I have mentioned, while they may be inspired by the dislocations of the film remain to be created as verbal statements with their own particular rhythms and sense of desolation. The dead melon image is not *in* the film, though the camera's eye, twisting the man's face through a distorting lens, allows Fiona's imagination to find it there. The poetry of the language is her own, even if the film's poetry made it possible.

Myth

Children's writing discussed in the last section seemed to show them entering imaginatively into experience that one might have thought was in some ways 'beyond them'. Perhaps the universalizing tendencies of art help to efface distances and bring remote experience within reach. Through myth particularly, it seems, it becomes possible for children to confront situations that would seem to them implausible, or meaningless, or just shocking, if they were presented realistically. This may be one reason why the teacher so often returns to myth. Already in this account I have drawn on the Heracles story, on several Greek tales – Ceyx and Halcyone, Theseus abandoning Ariadne, Pluto's abduction of Proserpine, and so on – on Hughes's version of Christ's nativity, and even on St George and the Dragon. And yet this stress, or imbalance as it would seem to some, is not accounted for in my case by rational consideration of the 'value' of such stories; it lies deeper, in the pleasure the teacher and the pupil derive from entering imaginative worlds constructed in poetic terms. Reading the Jason story recently to children, I was struck afresh not just by their relish for the tremendous pace and dramatic action of the tale, but by their responses on a different level, as when Orpheus calms the sea after a storm, or we discover that the white sand on the island of the Sirens is the bones of victims; and so on. Much of this pleasure may also come from the sense that a kind of truth is implicated: the sowing of the field with serpents' teeth, and the springing out of the ground of fully armed warriors, functions almost unconsciously as a metaphor for the relation between arming and war itself. Through a poetically conceived moment of drama children may extend their awareness of the origins of such violence; in this fashion myth confronts where explicitly naturalistic treatment may evade.

Myth never avoids the subject of death, in particular. But the accounts given in myth are not likely to sicken, or induce despair. Many of our own young children, in what is for most the comparatively well-fed comfort of life in western Europe, have confronted pictures of young children dying of hunger in Africa. They should know, one feels. And perhaps they should; but one can also believe that such scarifying images do little to help the child towards a balanced personal awareness of future extinction. And yet the images are seen, and presumably in some way they help to shape the child's developing conception of death. That seems to make it particularly necessary that children should imaginatively confront the largest issues in more thinkable, less annihilating forms; I should like to give some examples of a similar confrontation, this time with the idea of death as it appears in Australian aboriginal myth.

The following poem by Nicola, aged 11, was a reworking,

essentially similar to those in Chapter 2, of an Australian aboriginal myth:

Wuluwait, the Boatman of the Dead

Anagoi is dead, so I'm told.
Wuluwait has come, so I'm told.
No more mourning, rituals of old.
Arnhem land is one less, one less from the fold.
Anagoi is in his log coffin, beneath the ground.
Mokoi, his spirit, departs without a sound.
Wuluwait is at the shore, waiting there,
None will spy, none will dare.
Anagoi will sail along with an escort of dolphins.
When he gets to Purelko many times he will be speared
To cure him of his age and of his sins.
The plover has risen,
The spirits will be there,
Maybe he will suffer pain,
Maybe pain will be easy to bear.
I wonder what it is like to be slain?
Will he be scared of being speared again and again?
But I suppose the others have all taken their fill
If there is to be universal good will.

Another on the same subject by Edward, also 12, begins:

When my body finished lying in state
My makoi went to Wuluwait.
Wuluwait, the ghostly boatman of any waters,
Who took me, and will take my sons and daughters
To Purelko where he means to travel,
To Purelko where he means to travel.
The journey took long for Purelko is far
Beyond the rising sun and the setting star.

Perhaps even more than the poems on Heracles and Cyane, these seem to indicate not only how children can rise to the largest of subjects with a truth and seriousness which might seem surprising, but that they can do so by responding powerfully (as I should say they do here) to an unfamiliar mythic world. The poems' freshness may even in some measure derive from some kind of defamiliarization of the very idea of myth, accomplished here by going outside a traditional corpus of stories.

One might also argue for working from myth that it is a way to approach the largest subjects without confronting or being encumbered by the autobiographical material in which the child's urderstanding of myth is grounded. Whatever particular autobiographical experience of death might have been drawn on by the two pupils writing the poems above, all that they need to confront to write here is the colouration, the tone, the residual truth that such events may have left in their minds. They can write about death without going too close to their own lives. But though it is clear that no personal grief spills into what they write, it seems that personal reflections about death do find expression there: this 'long journey' will also 'take my sons and daughters'; they have to 'wonder what it is like to be slain'. And perhaps it is a youthful rather than a religious optimism which speaks in the lines about the plover rising, and universal goodwill. What seems interesting and important is that the simplicity and power of this myth, and perhaps its strangeness, has allowed children to speak elegaically, rather than confusedly, or out of despair or shock (or its opposite in hard-bitten acceptance of violent death); they have embraced a ritualized ceremonial form of speaking of the kind that confronts human experience as a totality.
experience as a totality.

Two more boys in the same class, both aged 12, seem to show that they can rise to an understanding of the 'adult' dilemma, or tragedy, of a quasi-mythic personage. Anthony, writing of Don Quixote:

> Astride a bony nag
> travelling in the dust and heat
> in his madness
> in his blindness
> for the peerless Dulcinea
> Dulcinea of La Mancha
> Duclinea watching over
> Dulcinea of his dreams
> Dulcinea never there
>
> From his books
> he got his madness,
> From his books
> he got his sorrow,
> Oh, foolish Don Quixote!

Other contexts 201

The boy's understanding of Quixote seems to emerge through the simple poignancy of it all, from the echoing 'madness', 'blindness', and 'peerless', through the repetitions of 'Dulcinea', the last of which strips the situation to its essentials.

The other boy, Stephen, sees a kind of death in the eyes, and relates it to thinking:

But look at his eyes –
they are the eyes of a dead man.
His face it is dark,
his eyes are sunken in . . .

He sits astride his horse,
thinking, thinking.

In general, it may be worth suggesting that any attempt to establish a context for writing needs to recognize that the preoccupations even of 8-year-olds in their writing are as likely to be deeply serious as they are comic, for all their enthusiasm for comic verse. The reason why myth seems to call out a responsively deep seriousness in children must lie somewhere in a need and a developing capacity to confront large issues; the genuinely threnodic feel of the aboriginal-myth poems represents a quite straightforward willingness to enter the idea of death, even the imagined future death of the young, the 'sons and daughters' of the dying. And with the Don Quixote poems, as in the sadness of 'Dulcinea never there' and the injunction to 'look at his eyes', there are gestures of true concern. Like the previous poems, they seem to represent the young mind's previsioning, through a mythic situation, of ordinary human insanity and its roots in the way the world is.

A poem in science

A context that can be more fruitful than it is often assumed to be is 'other subjects'. Poems may be written about 'nature', and, less often, about history and geography, but they seldom seem to be written from within maths, or science. The poem is even neglected for pragmatic purposes, such as putting into verse information that needs reassembling. Despite widening recognition of the alert freshness of much of children's writing, the notion dies hard that a statement in the form of a poem is less to do with the mind, less a focusing of the kind of awareness we call cognitive, than is a prose statement. There is still some difficulty involved in suggesting that there is 'scientific' value in poems that put into words the child's felt experience of science.

There are really two issues. One is the suitability of science as a subject for poetry: will children find something interesting to write about? Second, will the poems be science? It is easy to have doubts about saying yes to the first, and hard not to have them about doing so to the second. This second doubt is the real obstacle, perhaps – the belief that a poem somehow cannot be science. And yet there seems to be no particularly self-evident reason why a poem should not interrogate and interpret any field as satisfactorily as its conventional forms of expression, like the written-up experiment in science, the essay in English Literature, and so on. If we take the view that the poem is, amongst other things, a mode of intellectual apprehension, we might presume that it could have its place in any subject where understanding is needed. Science is no different in this respect from other disciplines; the example of a writer like Holub,[2] whose poems explore his own science, suggests precisely that.

I should like to describe two examples of attempts to encourage children to write poems from science, in this case an experiment-centred way of doing science. There were two things that we hoped for, first that the writings that emerged were poems, and second that they were science; because the second seemed the more problematic of the two aims, and unfamiliar terrain for both the children and myself, I thought of approaching the 'science' of an experiment by way of a focus first on its human context. This meant asking children to look not just at what substances and liquids were doing during an experiment, but also at what they themselves were doing. This seemed to be a 'way in' to looking at science itself.

The encouraging view of the science teacher I worked with was that there was every reason for children to try out such a way of looking at science and writing about it. I made a short video record of the class at work in small groups, doing an experiment on distillation. I played it back to them the following day during the English lesson, asking them to 'make notes' – short phrases or sentences written in pencil in their exercise books, with one 'note' or observation per line – of what interested them in the film, using the pause button to isolate images that seemed worth looking at. Some of these were in the experiment itself, like bubbles of ink frothing up, and steam, and water dripping. Others were children's gestures; for example, at one point Simon made conducting movements over a bunsen flame that had risen up. Arrested, this looked amusing. So did a moment when John peered under the beaker and pointed at the glowing red of the mesh that the beaker rested on. When the teacher had gathered them together to write down what had happened, Catherine twice performed an elaborate sweep of her whole arm to turn two pages of her exercise book. This was played over and over again, in response to demand. The 'human context' seemed more interesting than the 'experiment itself'.

I explained that I wanted them to use their 'notes' to write a first version of a piece of writing about the experiment: it could be poem, prose, or dialogue. If they chose to write a poem, they could do it in the same way we had already written poems, working from phrases, trying to make it sound different from a story. In a story one might say, 'Catherine made a sweeping gesture as she opened her book, and then two minutes later Tom pointed at the camera'; in a poem we would probably miss out 'two minutes later'. We were going to write an account not of the 'scientific' experiment itself, but of the class, of themselves, doing the experiment.

The day after they had written these notes, the science teacher and I made a second video of the experiment, from which the human context, so to speak, had been excised, leaving only the 'experiment itself'. The question of what actually an experiment is, whether it includes those who perform it, was a question I thought it might be possible to raise by juxtaposing the writing that emerged from the two different videos. (In the event that was not even attempted.) But this second video stayed close to the apparatus. The macro lens allowed us to go within an inch or so of objects, and the events that had seemed somewhat distant, hidden almost behind the boys and girls performing in the foreground of the first piece of film, became significant and at moments dramatic. This video was put by for later use, in line with my notion of working in two stages.

The first drafts showed the children writing poems from notes in the way they had done before. The unfamiliarity of what they had been asked to do was no obstacle to writing; they wrote as they usually did. Dominic's poem reflects the moments we had paused to look at, but is also very much his own view of things.

Distillation

Mr Coldwell comes round
The bunsen is lit,
'Goulding you stupid . . . ' Simon says.

John takes a peep
Under the gauze
'Look up there!' he says to me,
'It's all yellow and blue.'

The beaker flashes in the light,
George the giant sneezes,
And Simon looks up in disgust.

The owl seems to watch
Over the whole class,
But then its wing catches fire
What a brave owl

One-eyed Jack
Sits quietly,
And a baked bean can
Drifts towards the sea.

Rory posing,
Jacqeline whistling,

John points at the camera
To tell me that it's on
Then Mr Coldwell's voice gets higher,
'Look over here!' he says.

What an experiment!

'One-eyed Jack' and the bean can were part of the drawing the teacher put on the board to illustrate the idea of distillation, and there was a stuffed owl in a glass case that reflected the bunsen flame, producing an eery image of wings in flames. Dominic used these details with assurance; his notion of the owl watching over the whole class was not one that had been mentioned in commentary on the video, nor had we noted the can 'drifting out to sea'. I read it aloud to the class, and it was enthusiastically received with 'Brilliant', 'Really good', and so on.

The poems show clearly, I think, that as a subject for writing the science lesson in its social guise had been suitable, even fertile. Extracts from other poems show essentially the same attempt as Dominic made to embody the experience of the filmed lesson in poetic form. There is a good deal of ingenuity displayed in ordering and reordering the disparate particulars of their notes, and giving some coherence to them:

> Gesturing hands
> Brilliant blue flame.
> 'The bung should not be hot.'
> 'Achoo!'
> 'Bless you!'
> An owl in a case,
> A flame burning its side
> A different arrangement.

And:

> A pair of hands conducting
> The solute in the flask
> As the solute boiled away
> Someone sneezed in the background
> And still the solute boiled away.

Lists are written with a feel for rhythm:

> Stoppers, tongs, noses,
> Rulers, watches, tables,

Or for other sound values:

> A stream of steam
> fierce fluttering flames
> blue bubbling broth.

There is a hint at the humorous possibilities of technical language:

> Place the Side Arm Conical Flask
> On the tripod and gauze,

and even some wit:

> 'Has everybody got some water?'
> 'Yes!' everybody shouts.

These pieces answered the first question: they seemed to be quite as much poems as any other writing the class had done. But the second question, as to whether they were also 'science', is perhaps the more difficult and pertinent one. I had hoped that somehow the essential 'science' of what they were doing would be visible inside the description of the social event of the experiment, and that we could confront this science by looking at the second video, after this first familiarizing attempt. But several poems seemed to me to be essentially and only about the social situation of the experiment. One or two went even beyond that situation, to the intervention of the camera into the lesson:

> The camera was wobbeling
> faces were blured,
>
> The world outside was dull,
> Skin was turned light blue.
>
> The only voice I could hear clearly
> was the cameraman,
> Asking a siloute a question.
>
> Someone walks quickly past,
> He looks blured, see-through, like a ghost.

I felt that the poems from the science lesson were about something other than science; they did not themselves enact or articulate science; in humanizing what went on, seeing it socially, the science receded or disappeared. I hoped to confront that difficulty with the second video, where there were no human figures, and where the camera went much closer to the apparatus and, as it were, watched more attentively. Even so, for the moment, the first attempts were poems in the sense that their other poems were. Moreover the ways in which they had developed from the notes seemed to imply that the children felt they were engaged not on some ambiguous or implausibly different form of writing, the rules of which they were uncertain of, but on poems proper.

I shall return briefly to the first question, since one way to break the ice of the second question, so to speak, might well be by way of children's presuming that writing poems about a science lesson is like writing poems about anything else. This presumption is evident in the way many children worked on lines in their notes for use in their quick first drafts. This evidence of the shaping of raw material in the direction of the poem suggests that for them writing imaginatively from a science lesson flouted no important expectations about writing. This activity was evidently normal and straightforward, not suspicious or pointless, as is evident from examples of children working seriously on the rhythms and sound values of words:

Note: squirting steam
    fluttering flame
First draft:
    A stream of steam
    fierce fluttering flames

Here Dominic works to focus the humour more clearly and also to find a more satisfying rhythm:

Note: baked bean can floating about the island
First draft:
    And some wood
    drifts out to sea
Second draft:
    And a baked bean can
    Drifts towards the sea.

And in other ways the alterations suggest conscious reworking in the direction of the poem:

Note: explanations, steam, gas, hands
Draft: explanations, steam and gas

Note: Someone got so relaxed that he started whistling.
Draft: People whistling
      People getting relaxed.
Note: lots of steam, beaker shines in light, Humph sneezes.
Draft: As the solute boiled away
      Someone sneezed in the background
      And still the solute boiled away
Note: Noise in the background
Draft: The noise in the background
      Drained every other sound

Alongside these fertile inventions there were, of course, less creative moments – flat descriptive pieces that tended to recapitulate the notes without markedly shaping or developing them. Even so, it was intended only to be a preliminary sketch.

We returned to the subject after several lessons doing other things. The children still had not seen the second video. Their writing from that might well, one hoped, have more science and less social life in it. Through anxiety, perhaps, I introduced a perhaps fatal diversion back to their original notes. Without saying why I had chosen them, only that they were culled from the notes they had done while originally watching the first video, I gave them each a copy of the collection below. This was intended to reawaken some awareness of the original procedure of working from notes, but it all felt rather limp and the whole project unduly protracted, as if the very caution and deliberateness of the approach had undermined it. The novelty of the venture – it was the first time I had worked in the science classroom to draw on science for writing – presumably disposed me to over-insure against failure, or to imagine a difficulty where there was none. In unfamiliar areas, it is hard to see until afterwards when helpful preparation modulates into numbing over-preparation. Whatever uncertainty lay behind it, however, the interposition of this rather heavy flashback seemed to break the rhythm of what we were doing.

Distillation – lines from your notes

Will burning his fingers
Sneeze by Humph
'Distillerating', says Catherine

'You've got a problem – why've you got a problem, George?'
Simon, 'Cor, Lookat this!'
'The bung should not be hot.'
foaming ink
'Sir sir, look up there!'
hands conducting – condensation
big witches bubbles
Place the Side-arm Conical flask
murmurung, flames
explanations, steam, gas, hands
noses, tongs, rulers, hands
steam froth
'We did it, sir!'
staring at the bunsen
fluttering flames
people getting a 'real scientist' look
'Sir, it's on!'
conducting the experiment
swearing at the bunsen
Simon's group's steam is escaping
Lorna is losing a lot of steam
fogged up beaker
'Look up there!'
Catherine's hand waving the page over
People calling 'Sir!'
'Now your apparatus is very . . .'

I asked them to make similar notes on the second video and to try a first draft of a second poem. The results of this, I felt, and later said, were rather flat. There was much plain narration:

The bunsen roars,
The water crackles and spits,
The water condenses
And the gauze turns red.

And

Steam escapes from the flask, and forms ghostly effects,
Sharp water noises, like popping bubbles,
The water jumps up the delivery tube.

Passages with more life were rare:

> The bubbles bubble furiously,
> Blue bubbles in the flask,
> They look odd, BLUE bubbles,
> I'm glad I'm not in there!

When I asked the class why they seemed 'a bit flat', Edward said, 'Because there were people in the first', and Michael, 'Because it was the second time.' Which was the more important reason? Half and half, they said. Could they do poems about maths, I wondered? Yes, if there were people in them. And that is where we left it.

On basic mistake was presumably to have laboriously divided the idea in two. This may partly have derived, like the mistake referred to above, from the novelty and attendant uncertainty of the work. Trying to draw the children into writing a science poem by focusing on the social context of an experiment (which seems in one sense legitimately a part of science as practised) led to dwelling rather too exclusively on the appealing human features we noticed – the hands, the voices, and so on – and somehow not bringing forward the actual science they manipulated. Then later leaving the human context behind and trying to focus more closely on the process they were engaged in produced something oddly empty. It may be that the video itself was dull, though watching all the vigorous activity of the experiment in close-up seemed to me dramatic enough.

Whatever may have been the reason why certain kinds of meaning seemed to desert the second series of images, it seems worth noting that the sharp disjunction all this implied between science and a human context for it replicates the disjunction that is often assumed to exist between science and the human production of science. This may seem an unlikely note to introduce into such a discussion, but it may hint at a basic difficulty in many attempts to write across subject boundaries, and particularly to introduce imaginative writing amongst abstract concepts.

The difficulty seems to be that the attempt is circular. That is, the notion of writing poems in science implicitly seeks to redefine the activity of school science so as to include the poem.

Other contexts 211

In so doing, though, it may frequently assume that the epistemology it wishes to discard or in some way work against is adequate or necessary for current purposes, such as the subversion of that epistemology. Perhaps the reason why this particular venture seemed, in one sense, to fail, was that in order to get under way it worked rather too cautiously with the distinctions and categories it really meant to confront – particularly between an experiment and the people doing it. And it may be that my own judgement at the time that the children's poems were not really 'science' is compromised by the same outlook.

The science teacher's views, which I reproduce below, departed interestingly in two important respects from what I had expected. First, he saw the work in the laboratory as less to do with experimental science than I had assumed he would:

> The word experiment is a misnomer. In fact time rarely allows genuine experimentation. During practical sessions, science teachers invariably lead their pupils to make specific observations, whether consciously or unconsciously. This is not necessarily good 'science'.

To some extent he shared, therefore, without my being aware of it at the time, my notion that the tightly organized series of predictable 'observations' that children make in laboratories has little to do with observation proper. His endorsement of their poems as a genuine approach to observing in science is related to a scepticism about his own science as practised:

> When asked to write poems, based on the experiment, the children were liberated, and felt free to include any observation they had made. Being less constrained, they wrote on many aspects of the lesson, some of which would have been ignored in a formal write-up, yet were nonetheless important discoveries.

There is therefore an implication of unsuspected common ground between the teacher of science and the teacher of writing, not just at the social level of a willingness to work together, but at the deeper level of a shared epistemological outlook. Each of us feels that the knowledge arrived at through free observation and realized in the poem has value, and that the directed observations of the 'experiment' (incorrectly so named, in his view) have less. His reservations about junior-school science imply the necessity for its being open to accommodate the poem:

> As a breed science teachers often try to be too specific and stifle learning. At Primary School and Middle School level I feel there is a real place for poetry... At this level there is little justification for formal accounts of practical work. If we do wish children to write about an experiment there is no reason why it should not be in the form of a poem or a piece of imaginative prose.

The routine busy-ness of school life obscures the extent to which teachers' aims for children may resemble each other across different subject boundaries. The science teacher and I spent a certain amount of time discussing the practicalities of how to set up our venture, but none on exploring our notions of 'observation'. We did not discover until later that we had more common ground than we had presumed. His distrust of 'experimental' observation surprised me; my insistence on the importance of observing particulars closely in order to write at all surprised him. Given time to explore each others' intentions, many teachers may find such unsuspected areas of overlap. In particular, they may discover that children's poems articulate an awareness of subject contents which is as complete and complex as any other form of writing, and reflects the kind of 'discoveries' that the science teacher notes here. They may also come to endorse his conclusion:

> The only reservation I have in using poetry in my teaching is my personal lack of confidence with this form of writing. Having seen the potential of poetry, I would like to try again with other classes. However, I feel I would need some support.

Interdisciplinary projects

The work described in the previous section seemed to come up against the problem of boundaries at the same time as I tried to avoid it. One of the possibilities of routine interdisciplinary work may be that when poems are written alongside reports and maps and observations and calculations, as one kind of writing amongst several kinds that are all about the same object of knowledge, the poem may seem to be a way of knowing something, rather than simply a vehicle by means of which feelings are expressed. The more open style of working which is possible in projects that go out into the field also makes it likely that poems will be written in a less directed way, almost as a by-product of other activities. In consequence, the relation of children to writing may change; they feel that they are writing when they want to write, and about whatever aspect of the subject appeals to them, rather than being pointed in specific directions.

I shall describe briefly a project in which these possibilities did seem to some extent to be translated into actuality, and where the primary aim, which was envisaged as a combination of problem-solving and improvised drama, had at first no immediate relation to writing. A class of 9- and 10-year-olds was involved over a period of two and a half weeks, with two teachers, myself and John Freeman, the class's PE and Maths teacher. It was a one-off project at the end of the summer term, and ended in an Open Day. After a good deal of time spent discussing alternatives, we decided on a scheme that we thought would engage the children in as wide a variety of ways as seemed possible in the time.

There were to be two tasks for them. The first was for the children to find their way along a stream from the point where it entered a small river upstream to its source. They would have maps to help them, and could only use public footpaths and roads, along which we would accompany them. We were not to help them decide which way to go, and could only step in if they chose a dangerous track. They were going to take photographs as they went along. We were meanwhile going to video their efforts. The second task we would tell them when they had done the first.

The first task was successfully done, and the stream traced to its source in the hillside, in two visits of about two hours each. It was successful in the sense that there were no occasions when the exploration came to a dead halt, or when either teacher had to step outside the role of driver–supervisor–companion to become a guide or a resolver of problems; I recall one question about the direction a small tributary stream came from, and that was all.

We watched the video of the first task, up to the point where it was 'solved' when someone noticed a cluster of springs a few yards above the pond the stream had led us to. The second task, we then said, was to make another video of the stream, of whatever kind they felt they could make. They could decide what to do and they would be in it; we would be cameramen. Initially this decision was made because of the inordinate weight of the camera and battery pack; later it seemed a good thing anyway, as releasing them for other things.

There was a very long discussion about what kind of film to try – a story set along the stream, a documentary telling viewers about it, a rerun of the kind of 'accidental' film (as someone called it) that we had made already. There was much said about how an attempt to tell people about the stream, documentary fashion, would look artificial. There was little enthusiasm for a story, though one or two boys thought they would like to make one about 'the caves' – culverts between two ponds. Someone suggested a 'half-accidental' film, in which they would do the kind of things they had done before, but make it better; they would go over the same ground, recapitulating the details of tracing the stream, and invent scenes where they argued about which way to go. And so on. The phrase 'half-accidental' seemed very apt as a description of all this, and because it seemed realistic and practicable, and potentially amusing too, this was what in fact we attempted.

Up to this point the roles we had taken as teachers were similar; we consciously effaced our subject allegiances and talked as 'project' teachers; discussion was shared and each of us dealt with any topic that came up. Because of transport problems, we had then to divide the class, with one teacher working in the classroom and one out in the field with the camera. Partly because I was more familiar with the camera, partly because the first classroom work had been envisaged as working on a scaled-up version of the map, John worked in the classroom, while I had the outdoor work. Most of the five visits we then needed to make our film were with halves of the class, and the film was a relay of small groups handing on to each other. The half back at school concentrated on two things, the scaled-up version of the OS map, which eventually became a large hand-drawn map on the wall, and on careful written outlines of the scenes which their particular groups were intending to film. Then there were various other things that seemed to arise, some suggested by John or

Other contexts 215

myself, some not: reading about the trout they saw, identifying trees, trying to remember what had been said when people were guessing about the stream, writing down anything amusing that had been said or that happened. Any writing that was done was not only peripheral – initially – to the main tasks; it was also somehow prompted by what turned up.

This applied also to the poems that were eventually written towards the end of the two-and-a-half-week project, almost accidentally, and very rapidly as it turned out. On one level this seeming accidentality emerged, of course, from my year's work with them; the fluency of what they did was primed by their familiarity with me and each other, and their knowledge of how we had worked. And clearly, the relaxed and positive feel of John's own classroom worked to prepare the children in the same way; the differences in the content we worked with were less important than the similarities in the style with which we related to that content. The informality of the project, as far as writing was concerned, was thus a learned informality. But this stress on the children's preparedness does not undercut the point I am making about the intrinsic potential of such projects for writing; it means that to make the best of such opportunities the philosophy implicit in working out of doors, without strong subject boundaries, in a socially informal way, has to be continuous with the routine philosophy of the classroom. Moreover, in its epistemology that philosophy is clearly not a transmission philosophy; for either teacher to have strong transmission urges in such a context would feel immediately discordant. There is a clear connection, in other words, between the way the children's writing was produced and the beliefs and practices over a period of time of the two teachers working with them.

The writing itself began in a sense out of doors. The children had taken still photographs – of cornfield, paths, stream, bridge, old mill, pond, and so on – which turned out well. We mounted them – a visibly shared activity between two teachers – on A4 coloured paper and asked for writing 'about' the pictures, partly to identify them, partly because the photographs on their own didn't take up enough space. There was no specification that any particular kind of writing should be done, only 'writing to go with the pictures'; though we did say, I believe, that it 'could be' writing that tells people about the place, or tells them what we were doing, or it could be poems. We also provided a brief list of 'possible' subjects. This perfunctory 'preparation' may have been simple hurry; there had been the routine snags that extramural trips are heir to, one wasted visit due to camera failure, and one double-booked minibus. With Open Day approaching, and parents mustering over the horizon, a feeling-one's-way approach was becoming less feasible. It might be worth suggesting too, at this point, that while the thought of Open Day clearly motivated children to do well, it seemed mainly to function at the level of producing an exhibition that was pleasing to look at: while they took evident pains over writing out their poems on card, with the photographs, the fertility of their production seemed to derive from their original responses and experiences out of doors.

The kind of writing that was done at this point might even be taken to suggest 'a lack of guidance': 'This is a photo of Eleanor and Chloe by the big tree. They are both really hot, and are trying to get some shade. They are sitting on a stile . . . ', and so on.

There are fifteen of these prose accounts, and they are informative in a very plain kind of way, often 'repeating' what they saw in the photograph. This resembles the conventional way people write in photograph-albums, no doubt, but it is also a manner they might have been disposed towards by some of the poems done earlier that summer term, which were based on looking at prints and slides, translating pictures into words. 'This is a cut-down tree-trunk. It has got a criss-cross pattern on the wood.' 'On the left you have the pigs which were about three foot high.' 'As you can see the lily-pads are very close together, and that woods are all around the pond.' Yet, interestingly, children found various ways of escaping the convention and the frame. They edged the reader out of the picture to see things not there: 'just over to the left were men fishing'; 'At the bottom of this fountain was a round pool a cross looking face spat out the dirty water into a drain'; or to imagine differences between the picture and reality:'A seven-foot high water fountain. In real life it is much darker.' They told stories of what had happened on the trip, and repeated speculations made at the time: 'This meant that the trees stopped the sun from helping the corn grow there more than any where else.' One girl, Marion, dramatized a

Other contexts 217

picture of herself: 'Soon I will have to go and look at something else ... the owner of the trout farm has a very big house and he is a trout farmer.'

The suspension for a while of more formal teaching allowed one to take note of how some children may choose to write in the least coercive kind of situation. More than half the class tried poems to go with their photographs. Marion wrote three, all quickly. One, to accompany a picture of water spilling over a weir, was a little laborious:

> The lake is clear and smooth,
> With lots of greeny plants.
> It's as silent as could be,
> But, a rush of water tumbles off,
> An edge,
> Like an avalanche piercing the silence.

By contrast, 'The Mill' seems just right:

> Old and haunted,
> Standing alone,
> Expression is nothing,
> Its features are stone.
> Broken and used,
> Bright in its day,
> Now all it is,
> Is decay.

Clearly, one value of drawing on work done outdoors is that the experience they have there, whatever it is, can be recounted with an immediacy not always possible when writing from the classroom. A number of the poems suggest this, some particularly so:

> Walking through the wood,
> We are cooled by the shadow of the trees
> The sea of ferns lasts forever
> Capturing us in a prison.

Guy, writing about the cornfield, seems to describe a particular moment and no other. He feels the sky 'spread' as he runs down the path towards the middle of the field:

218 Behind the Poem

> Running through a field
> Fresh with wheat and corn,
> As the sky spreads itself,
> The sun comes streaming down.

The word 'fresh' seems to come from that particular experience; it is hard to imagine it being thought up in the classroom, where words like 'swaying' might be used.

Neil wrote about the fountain they had found:

> Looking up,
>   At the water spurting above him.
>   The water from the fountain,
>   Glistens in the morning air.
>   The old brickwork,
>   Dribbles out of its fishy face.

Again, it seems unlikely that this would have been written unless the fountain had for some reason lodged itself in their recollection of the visit. They had some fun with it, turning it up high and then down, splashing around in it, looking at their hands under water in it, touching the wet moss, and so on, and the two minutes or so of video at the fountain was one of the bits that they liked seeing over and over again. There was one moment when Peter, absorbed in a brief fantasy, sliced through the jet with his hand for a sword, with a quiet, private 'pow' clearly audible on the sound track.

A genuine interest, accidentally come upon, lies behind Neil's poem. They had found the fountain themselves, with its inscription and carved mouth. They had some small 'experience' there, and it seems important to note the difference between this, and the experience of being taken to or directed to look at it as part of the project. Neil's poem is a result, perhaps, of their not having been taken there, of their not being asked to write about it. Being there was in fact some sort of an experience because they weren't asked to have one.

If a project is extended enough, then, and sufficiently leisured and varied, at least some of the things that happen may have the kind of self-sufficiency and natural interest that warrant their being called 'experiences'. As unforeseen possibilities that may

Other contexts 219

take up time, divert and so on, these may be allowed for much more easily than they may be provided. The attempt to provide often negates; it negates what may not be foreseen within the provision, and lends a *trop voulu*, rushing-towards-it feel to certainly some of what emerges from focusing on things directly. If the teacher is to value genuine 'experience' – rather than planned happenings, or sensory involvement *per se*, which is less susceptible to deflation by direction – then perhaps he or she needs to stand even further back, once certain things have been arranged so that there is a chance that the valuable and unenvisagable may occur.

Certainly it seems to me here that not just the quality but the content and manner of the poems owe something to encounters with the environment that were only partly fabricated, and that the looseness of the framework allowed something one would like to call 'actual experience' to take place, often at the periphery of what we were doing. Implicit in this is the feeling that it was useful, as it happened, not to have mentioned poems until very late on, when the encounter with the fountain and other things had settled into their minds without having been shaped or interfered with by having to do something with them.

At the same time, the writing they did was subjected to the same process of revision and redrafting that they had grown accustomed to. The children were working on loose-leaf file paper at this point, and their trials and rewrites seemed no less numerous or careful than during the rest of the year, in situations where the process was under more reliable scrutiny. Emily, for example, tried out several versions of the poem quoted above, beginning 'Walking through the wood/we are cooled by the shadow of the trees.' She also tried one called 'Stream' that was eventually abandoned, but not after she had tried three versions, and at one point written a list of possible words for one line of it: tumbling, tripping, running, jumping, fumbling, dancing. (She had earlier in the term used the word 'fumbling' in a piece about shipwreck, where she described sea-water 'fumbling down ladders'.)

Guy had several poems in three or four drafts and, of those who chose to do poems, most were willing to rework what they were writing. The social informality and general looseness of the project framework seemed to have no negative effects on their willingness either to write poems, or to do the kind of quite intensive work on them that I have described. I am arguing rather that such a situation creates the kind of social context for writing that is particularly fertile, so that what one observed was in a sense not surprising. I should relate it also to the suspension, not of the idea of distinct disciplines, but of the idea that their distinctness needs to be expressed in unnecessary social separation of the work in those disciplines. In an earlier chapter I used the metaphor of an eco-system, suggesting that the teacher's concern is ultimately with an ecology of writing. The drawing of other subject disciplines into the network of activities surrounding the child makes the environment for writing both more complex and more rich in possibilities.

Part 5

Relations

9
Products and relations

Relation as product

The interdisciplinary work just described issued in a video film shaped and improvised by children, maps, photographs, and written products of a particular kind, all with a specific audience, namely visiting parents on open day. Some of the drive to do well stemmed from the children's wanting not just to do good work to show their parents, but from wanting the exhibition to be a success on the day. Whatever one says about children's writing has sooner or later to concern itself with the question of the material form the writing takes, and what is then done with it – which means who reads it or listens to it or ignores it. The issues of product and audience, to use the shorthand expressions, have been bedevilled by the glamorous expectations of the training institutions. They have stressed to students not just the possibilities of eventually finding satisfying products and audiences, but the need to find a stimulating variety of both as a routine matter, and somehow have conveyed the stressful assumption that children's writing should continuously transform itself by leaving the exercise book for the display board, the entrance hall, the magazine, the letters to zoos, and so on.

It is not merely stressful for students and young teachers. The quality of the relation the child takes up with his work is not well served by such an unremitting emphasis, any more than it is by the arcane notion that the exercise book should 'look good because it is a record'. The display neurosis which results in pressure on children continuously to exhibit negates that part of their freedom which is artistically indispensable, the freedom regularly to make a hash of things. That is crudely said, perhaps, but it still seems as if the messy trial-and-error side of creation is endorsed only in non-pragmatic prestigious areas such as Craft, Design, and Technology (and less often there than might be expected) and not in the verbal arts. Shaping and throwing pots and glazing them is highly precarious, and recognized to be so; and time and space, and the material and psychological ambiance of the workshop, are indispensable to it. End-of-term theatre is equally privileged in the sense that it has time to make mistakes and attempt its various drafts, though it may draw on children's performing gifts exclusively. And of course on the artistic periphery of computing, in computer graphics, it can be accepted that an enormous amount must be 'crossed out', abandoned for restarts, and so on. But writing has not yet claimed these privileges; writing a poem is not yet high-status fabrication.

This neglect of the creative is, of course, not confined to the place of poetry in schools. It is paralleled, endorsed, and culturally transmitted by the absence of non-discursive writing in traditional literary courses, where it is still possible to become BA Hons English without having written a word of fiction, or a single poem or paragraph of autobiography. And the place of children's independent composition in music and drama at any school level below that of formal examination courses still seems uncertain; the concert with pieces written by children, and the play developed from children's ideas and improvisations, are still less frequently heard than children's performances of the products of adult creativity. There would be nothing odd about this if the essential purpose of artistic life in schools were to transmit a heritage, but if it is the creative potential of the child that schools seek to develop, in every way possible, then this neglect of the most effective means of doing that suggests deep reservations about the value of the art of the child, and some confusion about the ideology of creativity.

Another way of saying this would be to suggest that the aim of artistic activity in school is that children should be continuously involved as creators or makers of art; their finished paintings, stories, and plays should be the end-'products', the outcomes, of a process of artistic involvement. That is, the teacher values the product not only or even primarily for its own sake but because of the relation it enables the child to take up, through it, to his writing and painting. What one therefore seeks, and continually returns to as the long-term project which transcends this or that product or this or that teacher or institution, is a particular relation between a human being and a human activity. That sounds portentous, no doubt, but it is hard to explain the pleasure the teacher takes in children's enthusiasm other than by thinking of it as indicating how they relate to the work at a particular point and what this might imply for the development of that relation in future. This sounds a less absurd idea when it is propounded in a more acceptable context, say sport. It would sound legitimate to say that teachers are pleased to see children enjoy football partly because they hope that they will grow up to enjoy playing football. In effect, this is equivalent to saying that a central pedagogic purpose that is sought through school football is the establishing of a certain relation between child and game. Similarly with writing.

One of the poems I have most valued in recent years is this:

> At the top of the Downs
> the water is running down the road.
> It is rushing from hills
> Into puddles.

It was written by a boy of 9 who at the time had enormous difficulties with language. To have asked whether it was really a poem, or whether it was any good as a poem, would have been beside the point. It was written, with great difficulty, in a few minutes in a minibus in the rain, and he read it, just, into a video camera on the hilltop just afterwards. It joined the class collection of videoed poems which was played back to several audiences at the time, and which is still played to others. But John's achievement, in inventing what he and others could think of as a poem, at the end of a year of what seemed like agonizingly little progress, meant that he had for the moment taken up a

Products and relations 225

relation with writing that was hopeful and positive, quite different from the failure which he often took for granted. Moreover, the film preserved this altered relation in tangible form.

Teachers 'read' children continuously in this way, for hints of a shift in the relation they have taken up with work. Another example shows the routine side of the process, rather than the dramatic breakthrough. A boy of 12 stopped me in the dining hall to ask what I thought of three or four first-draft poems. Such outside-the-classroom questions are frequently put to teachers, and tend to suggest something clear about a child's relation to work, simply because they are outside the classroom. In Ben's case, because of who he was – a boy who didn't think that he did any memorable writing – it suggested his taking up a more optimistic view of what he might do; evidently the poems had become important, and the perception that they had altered my expectations for him. In other words, in terms of the teacher's aims for the child, the altered relation evident in an extra increment of commitment is as much a valuable 'product' of teaching as the kind of material 'product' that seems so much more substantial, or even real. There is a connection between the two, clearly, and in this chapter I shall attempt to describe it. I wish to argue that the value of a material product, such as a magazine, while it is in part intrinsic, clearly, is more particularly that it can both express and help to set up a desirable relation between child and poem; in this sense the relation represents the future and not just the present, having an existence that outlives the product. A 'relation' sounds a nebulous thing, but it is the solid product that is ephemeral.

It is therefore difficult to speak about products without attempting to make clear what relations are embodied in them, or about relations without noting how they are embodied. It also seems an obvious point, but worth stressing because of its importance, that there is no necessary connection between types of product and qualities of relation. The scratchy poem in the drab exercise book may have been done in a spirit of casual eagerness; the pieces in the beautifully produced magazine may have been wrung out of compliant children by a merciless enthusiasm. Teachers' own zeal can distort the process of writing if, as sometimes happens, publication takes place without the children's spontaneous support or keen, freely offered endorsement; the basically laudable desire to publish their work can become an egocentric drive to exhibit the 'results' of teaching, in which the teacher can see those 'results' but no longer the children's relation to them.

Each mistake is a mirror-image of the other. One mistake is to stifle the future, the possible developing relation, by a too insistent regard for the present. The other is to be so daunted by the precariousness of the possible and emergent that one underestimates the need to draw out from what is happening an actual project which may be placed before children and towards which they may work. And this demands a crucial intervention. One knows in advance, from previous observation, something that children do not, that it is possible for them to become deeply involved in a project they cannot clearly prefigure. This kind of confidence, though, seems possible only with a class one knows well, well enough, in fact, to anticipate the gap between their own conception of what they do and one's own conception of what they might do. One even trusts in the robustness of the personal relationship one has established with them to draw them on further at times than might seem wise.

This was true of the work I shall describe in illustration of these issues. In this case it was with the class whose work on an interdisciplinary project was the subject of the last section of the previous chapter. Towards the end of the spring term I said to them that 'I wanted to' produce a booklet of their poems, with something from everybody in it, and on a particular 'theme'. I hadn't thought of a theme, but I was sure we would find one, or we could take one of the themes that people had done good things on already and try that. This project was unilaterally decided on, then. In the meantime there was another product that we had started putting together, a file of writing 'in best' taken from their exercise books and rewritten (and in the process often developed considerably) to be assembled inside coloured covers that they had already started to embellish. The idea of this was to have something to take home at the end of the year. So poems for the booklet might come from the personal file.

All this suggests a routine attempt to give children the feeling that their work is valued and worthwhile. What is worth trying to describe, however, is the way in which the teacher does more

Products and relations 227

with such a project as a booklet of poems than simply 'have an idea', which is announced and legislated on and put into execution. Indeed, if any point has been clearly made so far it is that such simplified accounts of teaching are pictures of something that does not take place. The product expresses a relation with writing which can be authentic or inauthentic, and descriptions of how products come about need also to be accounts of a relation which is implicit in them and which, one trusts, legitimates them. In this case, then, what signs were there that made a unilateral decision to produce a class booklet of poems anything other than an imposition? To answer this question, it seems necessary to look back at the period leading up to that decision.

A relation emerging

Any teacher concerned to draw out rather than impose is likely over several months to have noted, or less consciously come to be aware of, indicators of what is possible, precisely because she is on the look-out for them, not merely seeking to perform a curriculum. Legitimating moments lie around the mind, such as stray remarks made by children over a period of time that recede, but not without leaving traces of their significance. 'Getting to know' a class thus means a gradual accumulation of slight but distinct traces of knowledge about what they might come to achieve. Unless one's focus is myopically on the course, the unit, the module, it is indeed difficult not to gather such knowledge.

To say that the teacher looks for signs of a relation developing between children and the poems they write is not to say one discounts intellectual capacity, artistic awareness, and so on (though the solidity of those categories is I hope here seen to be very much at issue); it means that a perception of children's capacities is also a perception of the personal feelings that seem to accompany their deployment. Boredom and pleasure are kept in sight together with the range of gifts and giftedness. For example, I was rather worried early in the year by one 10-year-old girl in the class, Janet, who expressed some withering scepticism about writing of her own that interested me more than it did her; my concern proved legitimate, since her reservations about what she did, though they moderated somewhat, were never quite displaced.

On the other hand, various interchanges I recorded, also early in the year, implied some kind of general endorsement of the whole business of talking about poems and writing them. I described earlier (p. 127) how I was struck with the class's response when I read to them a ten-line poem written by Neil, about Ariadne, ending with the lines, 'Left alone on a silent island,/Sadness drumming through her heart'. I asked whether there was a particular line they noticed as I read it; the last, several immediately said; and was there any word in that line? A 'chorus' (as I wrote at the time) of 'drumming' answered the question. Such instances may seem trivial, and on one level they no doubt are; this answer did, though, seem to reveal not only one kind of question that could henceforward profitably be asked, but something about the kind of enthusiasm that might be drawn on again.

Even so, the teacher can be concerned about asking too much of a class too soon. In mid-November I read aloud some myth poems written by another class, and after much uncertainty asked them also to attempt some. It was Janet, thoughtful but cautious, who pointed out that one difficulty in writing about Ariadne is that the seashore is normally a happy place for children; her sceptical perspective was so positive that perhaps it helped me to decide to proceed positively. I made the following note, which refers back, after the poems they subsequently wrote, to the lesson when I asked the children to write them: "Several minutes' hesitation – push it now or come back later? Response here really encouraging. Confirmed rightness of decision to carry on.' I quote the remark because though such assurance is misplaced, in that it seems wrong to say that one is right where there is no way of seeing beyond an immediate outcome, it represents the kind of intuitive on-going response to what happens that is the basis of the decisions one makes.

This point was made in Chapter 2. I also suggested there that several perspectives implicit in that chapter would receive lengthier treatment, but I think it was also clear there that my concerns were as much with how the class related to what they were doing as with the actual outcomes in writing. And as with that class, the indications as to the kind of relation that they were

Products and relations 229

developing to working with poems were not all positive. Their own judgements on what they had written, delivered in private colloquy with me, were sometimes bleak. Charlotte had written on the Iron Man, and didn't care for the car-lights image she had used for his eyes. Russell, who had written about the *Marie Celeste* for some reason (probably thinking of it as myth, and finding pamphlets on the story in the room), didn't like his own idea of a giant squid 'making itself at home in the sails'. Neither Mary nor Janet liked what they had done, either. This seemed like a turn-around in their attitudes.

Such oscillations in the teacher's judgement often reflect the lack of an overall perspective. Perhaps I did not know the children well enough. But whatever the reason for such wavering, an uncertainty about the children's attitude is often enough to deter the teacher from adventurous ideas – like appealing to them to take an interest in a booklet of poems. And yet, a week or so later (two days after 'the most boring lesson this term', as I described it in exasperation to them, having tried to rouse interest in the writing of some dialogue based on remarks actually overheard) I noted that 'they obviously wanted to read their conversations out loud – persuading each other to read – had obviously read each others'' (before the lesson).

A first product

At this point, in a confident streak, I introduced them to the idea that they might like to make a collection of some of the term's work in a file, which we would add to over the rest of the year. A month or so before the end of term, then, their writing, or some of it, became recapitulatory. The consequences of this first attempt at a 'product' were encouraging. The children turned towards themselves and their own work to decide on the next step forward; I was freed from the kind of precarious initiating moves that involve speaking to the whole class, and could spend most of the time with individuals. At the same time much of the tension associated with routine classwork disappeared because the children were absorbed in their work, not more deeply than usual perhaps, but in a more private way.

In other words the children's relation to writing had changed in response to the idea of making a collection. They were no longer straining to produce new things, but reading back over what they had written; they were more reflective and less 'active', rewriting and redrafting. Perhaps returning in this way to 'old' work is a way of ascribing to it the value which is associated with permanence and survival; to the extent that the routine piece is treated as ephemeral, it lacks that dimension of value. Reconsidering writing, in conversation with friends and with the teacher, lends it a seriousness not visible previously. The objective solidity of carvings, pots, and paintings gives them a permanence which is enacted, one might even say, in their being taken away and relocated. The routine piece of writing, if it is never referred to again or transcribed, can easily lose any importance it had.

The 'files' sessions went on intermittently for the last three weeks of term, alongside other things. The change of atmosphere that comes over a classroom at such times is like a shift to 'workshop' conditions. A degree of agreeable anarchy – an absence of overt control but not an absence of order – arises from the fact that everyone is working more independently than usual.

In such an atmosphere it seemed easier, for instance, to suggest to Kate and Samantha that they should go outside to see whether 'crispy crunch' was really a good expression for the sound of leaves underfoot. It was possible to listen more to individual children; the round of conversations I had with them at this point was only the second opportunity of the term for that level of individual attention. Talking to Charlotte, for instance, who seemed diffident about her writing, I was able to discover something useful about her perceptions of it; she liked a group of lines in one poem and didn't care for one line in another; her views seemed perceptive, and henceforward I saw her diffidence as modesty more than uncertainty.

In such ways it seemed possible to notice more clearly what children were doing. The opportunity to take up a different, more serious relation to their writing was not being neglected. Matthew, for instance, who had started the year more uncertainly than anyone, was carefully transcribing his third attempt at a 'Minotaur' poem. Several children were not just reworking old poems, but starting new ones, sometimes on subjects we had tried out – like autumn – sometimes not. I noted that one child who had written enthusiastically earlier in the term 'seemed lost'

Products and relations 231

when the idea of redrafting something was suggested to her, but even she painstakingly rewrote a small number of pieces.

The need to design covers and add drawings and sometimes photocopies of pictures to their files also helps to alter the relation of children to writing. Drawing seems to induce a contemplative stance towards subjects. I value the concentration I see for its help in establishing a mood and a form of awareness. In another session at about this time, at the end of November, we simply read poems from *The Second Cadbury Book of Children's Poetry*.[1] Presumably because it is by children, the collection generates particular interest; on this occasion, perhaps because of the effort on the files, this was very marked. I read aloud their choices, and the children's response was frequently 'that's good', and so on. When I thought to let them read on their own for a while, I heard 'read another' instead. At the end of the session, I noticed that Russell, a new boy that term who had neither written very much nor seemed much interested in writing or reading, was clinging on to his book when someone was trying to collect them.

Through such perceptions, some apparently trivial, the lesson signalled something about the relation the class had begun to take up to the reading of poems: it perhaps also indicated that their own writing was being treated with less scepticism than I thought some had shown. No one expressed any sentiment that implied, 'I couldn't do that'. And my own message for them was that publication in books such as that was possible for them.

The idea of a booklet

My confidence in their ability to handle unusual topics and 'produce' their writing was thus built up out of their confidence. About a month into the spring term I decided to try the same work with this class that I had with another previously. This began with looking at video pictures I had taken of Chinese paintings and Japanese prints. I noted that this was done 'accidentally', and unplanned. I brought in a number of books of my own, with reproductions of great European painters, and made photocopies of pictures that children happened to take a particular interest in. The attempts subsequently made on set subjects – 'Head', 'Wave', 'Bridge', 'Wreck' – and on their own choices, from ideas given to them by the pictures, were their first poems of the term.

The results were encouraging, and I typed out for them a full set of first versions and, having spent some time reading out bits I liked, asked the class to work in small groups to talk about each others' poems and what they liked about them and how they might be improved. I also typed out a selection for everybody of some of the striking parts of their poems, as a kind of encouragement but also as a way of helping them to look for interesting things in each others' work. They were asked to write comments directly onto the typed pieces of paper.

King Philip's face – Janet

Once he was happy/but now/he is afraid of something, or deep/in thoughts/and worries./His lips are pursed, as if he knows something/that he mustn't tell, anyone

My town – Edward (from a Lowry painting)

Evening comes/In come the boats/Mothers come back/Boys eating their tea/Babies in bed/Empty playground/The last of the smoke/All quiet!

Portrait – Neil

A firm, determined man.
Going TOO well in the ways of the world.
Unhappy, maybe.

Buddha – Neil

Thoughts that seem to say
'Look what I've created'.

Buddha – Charlotte

Thinking thoughts of friends
  when they were his.
Wondering when he will be stared at
  and prayed at again.

Head – Marion

Examining something the old man is
Or looking severely at a child.

Bridge – Peter (from a Hokusai painting)

A wobbly thing it is,
It has a mind of its own.

Here's a bridge/A little ragged bridge – Greg

The exercise may seem elaborate, even a little excessive. Why do it? The typing was time-consuming, though not more so than marking a set of books. (The search for valuable material is itself a valuable form of 'marking'.) I would argue that it is occasionally very helpful to work in this way, not because it 'exercises children's critical faculties' but for a value nearer to hand, and implicit in the altered social relationships. As I suggested earlier (p.137), given the opportunity to talk about poems they have written, and to listen to friends' comments and suggestions, children are placed in a relation to their own and their friends' writing which is quite different from that they take up when they simply read the teacher's friendly or less friendly comments in the margin of their books. The altered relation to poems seems to me not to develop just as a later consequence of shuffling social arrangements around; it is rather that the altered learning relation changes at once with the altered social relation. Nor is it a piece of ideology, a cunning way of temporarily exiling the teacher and his chronic judgemental tendencies; it is a way of restructuring a social relationship so as to allow room for both pupil and teacher, rather than just the teacher, to have opinions on poems. And my reason for embarking on this restructuring was simply that it felt, in view of the children's developing confidence, particularly opportune. The comments they made on each others' writing seemed serious and intended to be helpful. For instance, Lucy about Gillian's 'Wave': 'I love the idea of the sea being dressed up in a blue coat and a white collar.' She suggested an improvement: 'Instead of "crash, crash, crash", "swisha, washa, sasa"', and even put two arrows indicating long and short 'a' sounds in the last word. Matthew, whose commitment I was at times anxious about, makes eight endorsing comments; he likes various bits, like 'going TOO well in the ways of the world'. About another piece he says: 'Good poem but hard to understand but good'. 'A weird good poem', someone commented of Marion's piece, 'The Triumph of Death', adding two suggested alterations; leave out the last verse, and change 'Not a dog but a skeleton' to 'A dog of a skeleton'. Marion wrote about a piece of Dawn's: 'Good lines – the cat lies in wait, It strains it's eyes in hate'. She suggested leaving out 'with birds above him, that fly within him' (perhaps an example of a child not seeing something unusually imaginative) and commented: 'Quite good, and very fun, but somthings shouldn't of been put in it. Some bits are really weird.'

Numerous other remarks suggested to me a genuine interest in each others' writing. About the two quotes from 'Bridge' poems, Edward wrote, 'I like this very much it sounds like a wooden wobely bridge', and, 'I like the word raggered because it is a nice word but not normally used to describe a bridge.' Others said they liked the word 'ragged'. Russell wrote of Edward's piece 'My Town': 'I like this because it has the same feeling as the machine gunners (all quiet as if theres an air raid).' Some extracts seemed to send readers back to the pictures; Charlotte said of Janet's 'King Philip's Face', 'I like that line because he does look like he has a secret or something.' Approval was in one instance expressed despite an uncertainty as to what prompted it; Neil said: 'I think this poem is nice, I don't know why.'

The usefulness of peers' comments, from the point of view of the children's developing relation to writing, seems undeniable. This might be seen particularly clearly by comparing my own written comment with a child's comment, on Lucy's 'Budha':

The Budha looks –
like an egyptian god –
The picture of wisdom
was in that face.

The Budha's eyes –
Have the sense of power –
But the sense of kindness
was in those eyes.

> The Budha's ears
> look like two ears.
> With 5 or 6 or 7 earings
> on those ears.
>
> The Budha sleeps
> with no gaurds
> No Hair Net
> On No Bed.

I wrote: 'Parts of it are interesting ("The picture of wisdom was in that face") but parts seem a bit "pointless" . . . ' Gillian picked out several good lines: 'Like an egyptian god', 'On No Bed', 'sense of kindness'; she suggested leaving out 'or 7' and altering 'No Hair Net' to 'With no pillow' – making the piece end very satisfactorily. So as well as a rather abrupt and judgemental teacher's comment, Lucy received pointed and appropriate critical encouragement from a friend. Her friend's comment was, ironically, more helpful as criticism, but it also seems clear that Lucy was likely to acknowledge the interest taken in the poem by friends as a different and more genuine kind of interest from the professional one taken by her teacher, who might be suspected of approving only 'because it's his job'.

Several children said that they found their friends' advice useful. Sandra wrote, 'If Kate wrote more about the actual face and discribed it.' Kate said, discussing the helpfulness of the comments in class, that Sandra had helped by saying that 'more description of thought' was needed, so that evidently the advice given in conversation was slightly more explicit. Kate said she had gone back to look at the Rembrandt head again.

I can imagine an impatience developing at the idea of so much to-ing and fro-ing, so much swirling of comment and talk and trying again. Why don't they just get on with it? To which I would say that the essential reason for handling classes in this way is to lift their writing to a level of social interest and importance that it does not have if the teacher alone has the right to speak about it. It thus elaborates into formal and often sensitive dialogue a process which would otherwise take place only fragmentarily, in casual comment back and forth. Placing 'criticism' at the centre of the children's own conversation, so to speak, becomes a way of altering their routine relation to writing, and of giving them – for pedagogic not ideological reasons – more control over the process of learning.

It was the quality of their relation with each other's work, as well of course as the perceptiveness of their pieces and their apparent interest in interpreting pictures, that prodded me towards taking further an idea that might normally at such a stage have been considered exhausted. It was at this point, then, that I introduced them – in the way I have described on p.226 – to the idea of making a booklet of their poems. The theme was still not decided on but I had already taken out several slide collections from a local library, including some Japanese prints. In the last forty-five minutes or so of the session in which they had looked at the photocopied sheet of 'good bits' from their poems, I showed them a few slides, some of pictures they had seen reproductions of, like a Rembrandt self-portrait, and Hokusai's famous 'Wave', and others that were new to them. They then looked at the slides in small groups, using six hand-viewers and two Diastars (small back-projecting viewers giving clear images in daylight and invaluable for classroom use).

This was in mid-March, towards the end of term. At this point it might be useful to have a recapitulatory sketch of the pace at which this small project developed, and of the class's relation to writing which – I am arguing – that project expressed. I said that I sensed in mid-November some 'general endorsement' of the idea of writing poetry and talking about it. The myth poems that were written then had been encouraging, despite my reservations about asking for them at that time. And yet there had also been less positive signs, especially in the marked scepticism some children felt about their writing. It was in December that they began collecting some of their best work in a file intended eventually to contain a selection of the year's work; I described the change that took place in the working atmosphere while they were engaged on this. A few weeks into the spring term there followed the videoed film of still pictures, and the writing of poems about pictures. The slides that later caught their enthusiasm, as I shall describe in a moment, were introduced to them in mid-March, along with the idea of the booklet of poems.

The development of the children's relation to writing to the point where it seemed legitimate to express it through that particular product was thus drawn out over two terms; the

Products and relations 237

booklet itself was produced at the end of the summer term. I would not wish, though, to say that the booklet 'took' a year, or that it was 'planned' that it should. Neither expression articulates what I am trying to say about the uncertain emergence of products through relations; both words imply the idea of products as distinct projects considered or prefigured separately from the children's developing relation to writing. That development, as I have tried to show, is unpredictable and slow, and the teacher's perception of it is slow too. Far from the product dictating its own temporal terms, it is dependent for its legitimacy on being an expression of the children's relation to their work. Thus for products to be genuinely expressive the teacher has to be aware of shifts in the way children relate to writing. Because of this there is always, it seems to me, an element of arbitrariness in the teacher's initial decisions about products. The teacher discovers what is possible – what expresses the children's relation to writing – in the process of attempting to develop a product. Whether a booklet, a tape, a file, a video, characteristically then 'takes' a week or a year, therefore, is not the issue; the teacher's concern is how to ensure that there is an expressive connection between the product and the relation of the children to it.

I felt that that the possibilities of the booklet became clear at the point I have just described above. I remember having a strong impression of the way enthusiasm was gathering round the idea of using the slides. In the lesson I referred to, one group was searching through the book of prints and the slide collection for pictures to write about under the 'Wave' heading I had given them. Edward and Peter, who would easily find their own forms of amusement during lessons, asked if they could come in at lunchtime to look at some slides. They came in and spent half an hour or so looking mainly at Japanese prints, two or three of samurai warriors and several of bridges from a famous series by Hokusai. Two days later, after half an hour or so spent by the class on the same work, the same two boys asked again if they could work through break. By this time they had gathered Russell into their group, and the three spent the whole of the break looking at slides, talking a great deal, and writing. I noted several remarks I overheard, all suggesting not just an involvement but an unusually serious one: from a straightforward 'Really nice' about a slide, to spontaneous talk about what they were writing; 'Ed, that's my poem', Peter said, handing one over, and Edward, comparing what he had said about the same picture, of a storm I believe, said to Peter and Russell, 'I said the heavens were opening up.' Towards the end of break, Edward started to draw from the book of Japanese prints I had brought in.

I had wondered over lunch, before the afternoon session with them, whether they ought yet again to carry on; it is not so much that teachers instinctively expect the bottom to fall out of the most propitious enterprises, but that they value such enthusiasm too much to want to see it declining to tolerant acquiescence. Some temperaments will give up a good thing sooner than they need, for this reason. On this occasion, though, the question was decided by their requests for slides and pictures as soon as they came into the room for the afternoon session. This purple patch of enthusiasm and commitment had lasted several days, however, and in the session after that afternoon one I left it for them to decide whether they carried on or moved on to something else. I asked only two boys to write, on the grounds, I said, that they hadn't yet done as much as they could have. In this otherwise free-choice time, several were writing, and one or two had gone back to the original pictures they had tried to write about.

Relation and product as overlapping objectives

Clearly, this is an account of one's work at its pleasurable best, a description of children relating to their work in a way that is unusually positive, autonomous, and sustained. All teachers will recognize these passages, which seem to stand out in disquieting contrast both to run-of-the-mill collaboration with one's aims or overt rejection of them. Yet despite its atypical character on one level, it seems to me that the modulations or routine versions of such successes, the less dramatic but none the less equally clear upturns in the graph of children's day-by-day commitment which hint at the developing relation, are the staple true 'results' of every teacher's teaching.

That is, there is a sense in which the relation I have tried to sketch out is for teachers a more pressingly mundane reality than anything more apparently 'objective'. It is for this reason that test and exam results, two-line profiles of assessment, and the rest, despite their apparent solidity, often seem to have a fatally nebulous character when set alongside the teacher's perception, for example, that a particular child has finally 'come round a bit' or 'is trying'. There is both a commonsense professional and a technical–professional language for describing achievement measured at a particular point, or between points, but there seems no equally firm way of taking hold of the notion of a developing relation to a particular discipline, particularly over time. Concepts like motivation may seem to help to some extent, but imply a kind of local urgency which may apparently be lacking in children about whom one perceives none the less a movement towards a general endorsement of an activity about which they had previously been sceptical, indifferent, passive, and so on. And the 'highly motivated' child may be motivated towards success at a level at which the long-term relation of pupils to what they are learning is not thought to be of consequence.

Such development, then, is far more important to the teacher than somehow the language he has to use allows him persuasively to say. I can here describe examples, and express my own feelings about them, but not much more. In the case of the class under consideration, for instance, I have hinted at some pleasant surprise at the way Edward and Peter 'came round', but it is difficult to formulate more closely what that means, despite believing that something important, though perhaps temporary, had taken place. One thing might be said, and that is that such shifts are often fortuitous; the teacher has to be alert for them, therefore. I recall a change at this point in Russell, for example, in whom I had discerned a worrying apathy, not just to work but more deeply to aspects of the self that surface in work. In the afternoon session described above he had started painstakingly to draw some Chinese-looking characters on the cover of the file he had started in November. Since he had also joined in with his friends looking at the slides one break, it seemed that this represented taking his first free steps of the year, so to speak.

I said to them again, at the start of the summer term, that in addition to their own personal files we would produce a booklet of poems, on a theme still to be decided. So we were aiming at two products for their writing, apart from the end-of-term project for the final three weeks. As an objective for the term, this had a certain clarity. It could not have become an authentic objective for the children without some perception on their part of the possibilities of implementing it. But they had seen what the personal files could become, and they had written plenty of poems that in general they thought well of; there were no children in the class, I judged, who hadn't done something they weren't pleased about.

The other half of the story, so to speak, is the way in which the product – once it is launched with the endorsement of the class – reflects back on their work and in turn affects that. The two boys who over the year had withheld their commitment longest – Russell and Mark – were both caught up about a month into the summer term in copying drawings from the books I brought in, and attempting their own. I had shown that class a booklet previously produced by another, and they saw at once the advantages of the drawings. Russell set to work on a cover and was pleased that his drawing was subsequently used, and Mark's drawings were so much praised that he became keen to write something to go with them.

Through the summer term, various opportunities arose to focus on these products without the work seeming to be distorted. The only new writing of poems that the class tried derived from three topics. With two topics the class wrote prose first, and poems arose afterwards. These two were television films, one about the first precarious year in the life of a buzzard, Mordicus, the other, *Truk,* a film showing how the submarine life of a Pacific atoll had taken over wrecked warships. After looking at these I suggested that the booklet we were going to do could contain poems about pictures, so that, finally, we now had a theme. The third source of poems, done after the suggestion of a theme, was a set of BBC Radiovision slides, about dragons in paintings at the National Gallery;[3] Edward and Neil had found these themselves, and asked if they could use them. I suggested that they might present some to the whole class, and they did. The slides appealed to all sensibilities, apparently, and there was at least one more session where small groups worked with the Diastars and hand-viewers thinking up new poems. Edward gave me a clue to their absorption here, when he was trying something about the *Truk* film; he didn't care for his Truk pieces, prose or poems: 'they aren't as good as the slide poems, where you could keep looking at the picture'.

A month or so before the end of term, I typed out a first draft of a booklet, with something in it from everyone in the class. This was passed round for everyone to read, and it was at this point that one or two decided that they could write something better than the piece that seemed likely to represent them. A number of quite new poems were written, and several more drawings were done, so that there were eventually twenty or so to choose from. The conversations I had with children were often of an 'editorial' kind; they were in some ways more interventionist than usual, but in some ways also particularly valuable as teaching moments, perhaps partly because the actuality of an editorial role allowed one to be more drastic and brisk than usual without the children's feeling squashed. For example I typed out Charlotte's 'Bridge' piece, on Peter's drawing, as an almost concrete poem, with the words falling down from the bridge as she envisaged the traveller doing. I did ask if she minded my having done this; it appeared not just that she did not, but that she was rather pleased by the whole idea and the appearance of her poem. Neil had written a poem of about 120 lines, which I asked him to shorten, and he did. I then altered what he had done somewhat, and asked him if my suggestions suited him; they seemed to. Zoe, five of whose short poems were included at first, chose to leave out two which seemed less good; similarly Peter and Neil, who had three each initially, chose in my view the appropriate ones to cut. Again, the talks I had with them about these decisions had a more real feel to them than some of the term's ordinary 'consultations', and I put it down as a valuable increment of awareness to the children that their writing could be talked about in that unusually purposeful way, preparatory to publication.

The children's relation to their writing was thus, even at the last minute, still being developed through the final shaping for publication of the poems they had written. The product that began as a notion made possible by a relation ends by ensuring the further development of that relation. In short, just as products depend on relations, so they become necessary to implement them and ensure their growth. When I had the final version photocopied, collated, and given out for the children to take home, Russell said, 'I didn't think it would work out so well.'

I started by suggesting that the teacher may need to envisage things that his class cannot, and that that is one aspect of his relationship with them; but that he cannot just propose, and assume that the implementation of his ideas is a matter of his own personal skill or commitment. The children, who do most of the disposing, are deeply involved at the level of the kind of genuine, natural pleasure – or lack of it – in what they are doing; and such an involvement was in this case something that built up pleasingly but unpredictably over a long period of time. What I have essentially tried to show is the futility of attempting to magic the product into existence by any of those traditional short-cuts that the display-conscious or product-conscious teacher has been encouraged to indulge in, often with the fatal approval of heads and advisers. The futility is to consider either the product or the child's relation to writing in isolation.

10
'But is it poetry?'

Reservations

From time to time the question of what a poem 'is' has appeared in the narratives I have offered – not surprisingly, since it would be hard to talk to children about poems without raising it. But I have not raised it with the reader; I have assumed throughout that the children have been writing 'poems', without pausing to confront any doubts as to whether their writings may legitimately be so described. For example, a 'real' poet might well say, 'The pieces they write are often interesting, fresh, and spontaneous, but not fully fledged crafted works of the kind that I write.' That seems a very plausible reservation, and I suspect something like it colours many a colleague's unspoken verdict on the value of encouraging children's poems; they look on it as a mildly delusive absorption in something not even quite real. The idea dies hard that this is what children 'waste their time' doing when more 'basic' things are neglected, and in moments of stress this uncomplicated prejudice resurfaces. If only for this reason, teachers often ask themselves 'But is it poetry? Is what I'm doing the real thing, and worthwhile, the way science and maths and computers are?' Clearly. I should say yes, but I wish to suggest a way in which teachers may handle their doubts so as to enable them to defend their own children's poetry. But it is an aggressive form of defence, and consists not in turning back to particular poems, to argue for their poeticality, but in asking the sceptical questioner what the question means.

There is a less predictable scepticism, which appears amongst those anxious to speak 'for' children's writing but concerned also not to endorse it too easily. They may be alarmed by 'the anarchic production of quantity in place of quality', as Sybil Marshall puts it.[1] In her book *Creative Writing*, alongside the strong encouragement given to the idea of the 'creative', there runs a worry lest writing does not reflect 'true' creativity. The 'quality' of the poems seems to be in doubt: 'To literature lovers, the word poetry implies organization, discipline and imagery beyond the range of children to achieve.'[2] This is true of the kind of poems children most often write: 'Free verse, to be worthy of the name of poetry, must show an attempt at the same subtle choice of word and phrase, and the same disciplined organization, as any other form of poetry.' Other writers who have appeared to wish to encourage children's writing have shown less than complete trust in the children's capacity to rise to the idea. Lane and Kemp, in their book *An Approach to Creative Writing in the Primary School*,[3] remark that 'Some children have a natural aptitude for writing verse. However, only a very small percentage of any class can just do this.' They stress the need for specific ideas to be given to the class, and suggest that 'the teacher should guide each line of the poem'.[4]

These emphases not only involve assuming, without real warrant for doing so, that the teacher knows what a poem is, but also amount to a presumption that children lack a kind of skill or expertise, which needs to be provided; their consequence for the teacher is the sense that for children to write poems involves reaching up to a preconceived technical threshold. They thus foster nervousness. So does any assumption that children have not or cannot do this or that. It is possible to assume a deficit in the imagination, as the behaviourist tradition does. It seems to me that Barry Maybury, the compiler of several excellent anthologies for children, implicitly does that in his *Creative Writing for Juniors*. He seems to propose a rather passive role for the pupil's imagination when he structures his suggestions round the basic and continuous need for 'stimuli': 'Spectacular lessons of this kind are a very good way of providing stimulus for creative writing; we want the imagination to be aroused, and there is nothing like the unexpected or unusual to stir it.'[5] The imagination is in need of something to get it going; the stimulus does this, and produces a need for words, and even here 'the kind of words one offers really depends on the degree of impoverishment of their vocabulary.'

The teacher may be thus disposed, by training, to see the writing of children as hampered by inadequate vocabulary, unroused imagination, inability to write 'verse', lack of technical skill, lack of organization and discipline, and so on. In contrast to this, the basic working assumption on which, I think, my own teaching role has been based in the foregoing narratives is that the positing in advance of an intrinsic lack of capacity is likely to create the problems it imagines. If it is presumed that children writing a poem about food will be hampered by inadequate vocabulary – delicious, mouth-watering, succulent – the teacher's projected poem will tend to be the kind of poem that children cannot yet write, the one crammed full of adequate vocabulary.

There is a fatal self-fulfilling dynamic about the teacher's presumption of deficit. The settled scepticism of the training-institution writer looking at children's poems from a professional role outside the classroom – when it is in the classroom that basic perspectives are shaped – becomes perhaps even more of a hindrance. The teacher's judgements, in theory, can be revised. Expressions of a transitory sense of defeat or failure, routine moments of exasperation are, as judgements, visible for the provisional perspectives that they are. The academic writer's scepticisms implicitly lay claim to a broader and more stable view, but the broad and generalizing tendencies of the language, as in the examples quoted just now, tend to efface details of the contexts they derive from, so that one encounters claims of deficit rather than evidence of it. Frequently the sceptical emphasis seems only to rearticulate in summary and persuasive form the routine frustrations of teachers, just as their deeper reservations may express broader cultural doubts. Thus, perhaps, the origin of the writer's views in personal experience, their embeddedness in a particular social context, comes to be disguised, and the routine personal impasse is thus interpreted in terms of its relation to some presumed invariant incapacities, in large, pessimistic terms. And because of the universalizing way these restrictive perspectives are presented, the teacher feels inclined to defer to them.

I have tried to demonstrate that the teacher's own work with children can make plain the inadequacy of assumptions of incapacity. Any narrative of some length starts to yield evidence of children doing things one expected them not to. It then becomes preferable to think of any children's 'lack' of imagination, technical skill, and so on, in the way I came to think of them in Chapter 2, as an absence of them from certain phases of a process, rather than an absence of them from children. Instead of saying 'They don't have the technical skill', one says, 'We are not at a point where their technical skill has emerged'. This becomes a comment on a procces, rather than a judgement on a child, and implies that whatever is missing may be generated in a later phase of that same process. This is not evading the issue of skill, imagination, and so on, but relocating it. I have offered several examples of children's 'capacity' emerging from their extended working in a particular area; of the children writing Chinese poems it would only be possible to say that the skill they demonstrated in imitating the models emerged during the work itself. It would have been odd to presume it was 'there' beforehand.

In short, the reservations I have referred to, which seem damaging to the integrity of a commitment to children's writing, are likely to predispose teachers to overlook some of the craft and imagination that children deploy. Some other basic outlook seems desirable, and there have always been others in much less doubt about whether a child's poetry is poetry. A Chinese poet, Bing Xin, writes simply: 'The child/is a great poet,/with an imperfect tongue/lisping perfect verses.'[6] Chukovsky described the child as a 'linguistic genius'. His remarkable *From Two to Five*, for all its seeming naivety and dated ideological underpinning, sees the child as a 'natural' poet who from an early age patterns language (with 'rhymed monologues' and 'jabber-rhymes')[7] and speaks in metaphor (mother's 'balloony' legs). His notion of some problems of 'craft' is not cluttered by anxiety: 'Children begin to understand and to use metrically correct rhythms in their poetry at about the age of 10.'[8] He has an interesting comment on the development of free verse (and of

'But is it poetry?' 247

course it is interesting that he sees it as a development): 'As the child grows older he is more likely to compose free verse, since clapping and chanting are now replaced by thought and introspection.'[9]

Acceptance

Such views avoid the problem of needing to disbar much that the child offers as a poem from qualifying as a poem through having set up a high 'threshold' of technical competence or awareness; I am drawn to them for that reason alone. It is worrying to the teacher if pieces of writing he thought of as poems threaten to become something else: 'prose broken up into short units and set out on the page to look like free verse', for example. Many of the 'poems' discussed and reproduced here might well be reconsidered, and verdicts of not-a-poem might well be passed on some of them, perhaps by critics who do not write anymore. How is one to respond to such a hypothetical but entirely probable verdict?

I shall suggest two responses. The first is to say that, as a matter of preference and convenience, because it is generally more appealing, the less mean-spirited view of the poem is that with which the teacher chooses to work. This is less frivolous than it sounds, for, quite obviously, it is much more useful for the teacher in the encouragement of writing than a conception of the poem which adds unnecessary metaphysical difficulties to an already objectively difficult endeavour. Any response which, without bringing about loss of conviction, broadens the category of what is accepted as a poem, seems useful. At the same time, this response may seem ultimately to be merely a preference unless it is reinforced by some plausible conception of the poem. A second response is therefore to say – as I shall try to suggest is reasonable – that the conception of the poetic that appears to inform some of the reservations I have noted is a great deal less plausible than that which informs a more 'tolerant' practice.

For the sake of an example I shall take Sybil Marshall's contention that 'poetry implies organization, discipline and imagery'.[10] This seems straightforward and unproblematic, until one asks whether the same predicate could not be annexed to 'prose'. That too implies organization, discipline, and imagery. The stress on 'organization' and so on contributes to building up in the reader's mind a conception of the poem which is unrealistically distinct from prose. And it is interesting to reflect that if one 'defined' prose in that way, there would presumably be frequent disputes as to whether a child's writing was 'really' prose or not.

Along with the taken-for-granted existence of a boundary between prose and poetry lies the conviction that the intrinsic attributes of 'the poem' are peculiarly evident and describable. 'Poetry is' statements suggest that a consensus exists; that we know, or agree, about what 'poetic language' is. But if one looks to 'theory' to authenticate a particular view of poetry, so as to have an agreed set of criteria to test poems against, one encounters just as much of a problem there as in the classroom; in a sense one finds the same problem, because for all the strenuous attempts made this century to isolate the poetic, by Russian Formalists and others after them, no satisfactory way of so definitively describing the poem seems to have been reached. Perhaps, as Auden suggested, while the 'distinction between verse and prose is self-evident', it is 'a sheer waste of time to look for a definition of the difference between poetry and prose.'[11]

It seems rather that it has proved so difficult that the attempt has apparently almost been abandoned, at least in the form of a search for intrinsic linguistic criteria. Shifting the focus of interest, speech-act theorists have noted features of social contexts, particular attitudes and expectations bound up with offering and receiving poems; it was a mistake, Mary Louise Pratt says, to posit 'a contrast based on intrinsic features of expressions'.[12] She suggests that because the roles of metrics, rhythm, metaphor, and so on, have been investigated in poetry (and called 'poetic devices'),[13] and their occurrence outside poetry has been less examined, the attempt to 'define' the poetic becomes circular and self-justifying. Her own solution locates 'the essence of... poeticality... in a particular disposition of speaker and audience with regard to the message.'[14] This helps me to understand why I am willing, socially, to handle 'as' poems pieces of writing that would not affect one as poems frequently do. It helps the teacher by seeing the primary 'disposition' of child and teacher towards messages as part of poeticality; this

'But is it poetry?' 249

immediately enlarges the sphere of one's concerns, from pieces of writing, to various features of the social situation in which these writings occur.

This should help the teacher, for if 'poeticality' starts with the 'disposition' of speakers and listeners in a speech situation, then some poeticality is achieved by setting up such a situation. Equally helpful is the theorist's uncertainty about the 'differences' between poetry and prose. The teacher's problem of deciding which is which is not so much shared as shelved. Without this uncertainty, teachers may work with markedly polarized notions of prose and poetry; these would entail confusingly imposing criteria on poetry which may be as applicable to prose but which are applied only to poetry. (The notion of 'rhythm', for instance, tends to be confined to discussions of poems.) They may also be applied more vigorously to children's poems than to others – because they can be more coercively deployed in the classroom than outside it. The consideration that there may be some necessary arbitrariness about deciding whether a piece is really a poem or not helps to resolve a familiar difficulty – the sense of often not having good grounds for deciding one way or the other – by suggesting that often there may not be.

I can imagine an impatience arising: why is theory needed to sort out a simple difficulty? Why is theorizing necessary at all, indeed, for a 'practising' teacher? The difficulty is that by teaching poetry and encouraging the writing of it, one continuously uses the words 'poetry' and 'poem', and in doing so deploys some theory or notion of what the poem is. In practice, 'practising' means 'theorizing'. The theory is quite likely to be implicit rather then explicit, but it is there, and there is a danger, if it is inexplicit, that is may be so because it is unformulated; that is, one does not know oneself, which sufficient clarity, what one is asking children to do, or why.

Furthermore, children are expected to 'theorize' in their own way. They have thrust on them the need to make decisions about whether to present something as a poem or as something else; they have continously to ask, in effect, 'Is this a poem?', 'Is this what he thinks a poem is?', 'Is this alright to go in a poem?', and so on . Children need to know if their teacher takes 'rhythm' to mean 'scanning', or agrees with the quip that free verse is 'like playing tennis without a net'; and so on. The meaning of the word 'poem' is negotiated in the classroom, over and over again, each time children and teachers collaborate on anything that relates to poetry, so that the child's idea of a poem is the outcome of a series of such negotiations. And clearly, if different teachers emphasize different aspects of poems (that is, have different theories about them), children have to understand what each teacher wants; that is, they have to grasp something of each person's theory in order to write.

Receiving the ambiguous

The teacher receiving a poem from a child greets it with a felt response, and often with the feeling 'But is it a poem?' The 'but' is illuminating; it suggests the same ambiguous uncertainty that Sklovskij, the Russian Formalist, (quoted by Mary Louise Pratt) noted in 1917: 'A work can be (1) intended as prosaic and accepted as poetic, or (2) intended as poetic and accepted as prosaic.'[15] This often-noted paradox or complication is exactly the dilemma that confronts teachers every day when they are handed 'my poem', and they immediately feel 'But this isn't really a poem', and feel further inclined to say so. What other response is appropriate for 'the work that may be intended as poetic and accepted as prosaic'? Yet it uncomfortably attempts to deny the intention of the writer to offer it as one thing not another. Something of the difficulty seems to be circumvented however if we accept, with Mary Lousie Pratt, that 'poeticality' resides in 'a particular disposition of speaker and audience with regard to the message'. We may then accept not just that the intention of the writer to offer a poem puts the reader under some sort of obligation to receive it as a poem, but that it takes part in 'poeticality' by being so offered. The poetic 'speech act' initiated by the pupil's offer need not terminate in the teacher's disposition to say 'but this is not a poem'; recognizing that there is more to poeticality than the intrinsic features of particular poems, the teacher will contribute to the 'speech act' initiated, not completed, by the pupil.

In other words, the arbitrariness that Sklovskij noted, far from puzzling the teacher further, should allow him to recognize that the real problem is not delivering unassailable verdicts on the poeticality of particular poems, but coming to some way of agreeing in practice with children as to what a 'poem' should be. 'Defining' the poem comes to be a social activity, and the poem what the teacher and children agree to treat as a poem. Any such extension of the scope of definition beyond intrinsic attributes to social agreement (the partners in which still have 'intrinsic' criteria as well) will make sense of a number of situations that can puzzle the teacher – certain 'mistakes', for example. I read some lines in Dawn's book that I took to be a poem about a magician. She had not intended a poem, but had merely listed some attributes that the magician in the story would have; I had made that suggestion, and forgotten about it.

> Helix the wizard
> Hair like a ghost.
> Long bushy eye brows
> Which cover his evil eyes
> Wrinkles spreading along his forhead
> A black evil cloak spreading far
> and long pointed shoes

For the reader 'misreading' the list it was a poem; for the writer it was not. Whether it 'was' a poem then depends on whether it continued to be treated as one. Once I understood Dawn's intentions – and remembered what I had asked – I was prepared to reread it as a list. Equally, she was prepared to reread it as a poem. It was finally a list, by mutual agreement. (For Dawn it might by now have become a poem.)

The notion of social agreement helps the teacher to make sense of the familiar experience of the 'poetic received as prosaic'. One sometimes feels that 'cheating' is involved in the presentation as poems of language which might be recast as prose without loss of conviction. More often, teachers may sense an arbitrariness about pupils' decisions to present writing as poems. Kim, aged 9, wrote this after seeing the film *White Stallion*:

> The only sounds were the reeds in the wind,
> And the fish jumping in the water.
> The boy felt a magical feel,
> As if he was in a wonderful place
> Where no man had stood.

This could be two sentences of prose: 'The only sounds were the reeds in the wind, and the fish jumping in the water. The boy felt a magical feel, as if he was in a wonderful place, where no man had stood.' But instead of wrestling with what is essentially poetic about the language itself, it seems to clarify matters to accept that for the time being at least Kim is offering it as a poem; and that it is receivable as a poem. What it is 'really' is not the point so much as what it is 'actually'. It is a poem.

The same notion also sheds light perhaps on another kind of writing about which it often feels appropriate to ask 'Is it a poem?', namely the prose that seems poetic, 'the work . . . intended as prosaic and received as poetic.' For example, in another piece of prose written at the same time in the same class, Rachel's idea about how the film might end included these lines, in which the boy who captures the stallion is speaking:

> The heavenly feel of wind and the salty smell of the sea rushing at me at once. I felt as if something had burst inside me and trickled into all the parts of my body, like a firework going off and sparks sprinkling everywhere.

This may be read as poetic language; the metaphor is worked out with a rather conscious sense of its appropriateness, and an ear for the duration of the firework going off 'and sparks sprinkling everywhere.' And if the reader finds 'prose rhythms' in this, it is arguable that 'verse rhythms' are there too:

> I felt as if something
> had burst inside me,
> and trickled
> into all the parts of my body,
> like a firework going off,
> and sparks sprinkling everywhere.

The same uncertainty may often strike the teacher reading. Rachel also wrote some while later a piece about a balloon which has poetic immediacy: 'A bright green rubbery balloon grows bigger and bigger as I blow. Soon it reaches the height of its expansion, it is not rubbery now, it is hard and almost transparent. Then I let it go and it deflates slowly, gradually growing darker, softer and smaller, while making a small pffing sound.

'But is it poetry?'

Now it's the same old balloon, bright green, rubbery, and small.'
There is no problem, I imagine, with one's response to this, until what one says or does involves acknowledging – in a way that communicates itself to pupils – the relation of its poetic character to its other character as prose. In other words, what does one say?

I should answer that these are offered as not-poems, so (at this point at least) that is what they are. Their having been offered as 'story' is something to do, presumably, with the definition that has been constructed. But occasionally something about a piece of prose tips one towards suggesting to a child that it might be relined as verse. This piece, for instance, by Anna, a girl of 10:

The Pheasant

> He looks round him. Every move he makes. He looks as though he has metal clogs in all his joints, which need oiling. His red neck looks so, hot and bright. He takes his steps cautiously. His tail feathers trail long the ground like a cloak. Then he suddenly boosts up into the air with a hollow clucking sound that seems to echo. The leaves on the trees rustle, he is gone.

This was not offered as a poem, but was received as intensely poetic. However, the manner was in certain respects that which we had together distinguished from the manner of poems. At this point with this class, I was speaking in terms of a story/poem distinction, with intrinsic criteria for the poem like a tendency to prefer short phrases to sentences, and a tendency to use separate lines for distinct phrases. So that the enacted definition of the poem seemed to bind the reader to seeing it as not a poem. There were also, though, occasions on which we had experimented with lining out prose as poems, and vice versa, so that our definition of the poem included some recognition of the arbitrariness or ambiguity of deciding. This legitimated, it seemed to me, an intervention to suggest to Anna that she could try lining it out as a poem to see what it looked like.

Noticing what they are doing

In one sense the question 'Is it poetry?' is about products, and that is the sense it would most often carry, not least when the questioner is a teacher confronted by children's poems. My suggestion has been that these come to be called poems in the way that other poems come to be called poems, by writers and readers handling them as such and in the process acknowledging certain intrinsically poetic things about them. I have not tried to 'prove' the essential poeticality of particular examples, arguing instead that since 'poeticality' seems a thorny and unresolved issue, it would be better for the teacher to recognize that fact, and for an awareness of the difficulties associated with it to inform the setting up with the children of a working notion of the poem. This means first that when a child says 'this is a poem' there is a sense it which it already is, since the child has been involved in deciding what to call a poem, and is therefore only exercising the power of definition that has been offered. The teacher is thereby freed from a kind of adjudication that often involves rejection.

Second, and in particular, the puzzle of an apparently arbitrary middle ground or overlap between prose and poetry becomes more of an opportunity than a problem; once the teacher notes the extent to which it really still is a problem for others, whether or not certain pieces are poems or prose becomes a matter that is 'decided' primarily by the writer's opting to offer them as one or the other, and then by the teacher-reader's simply acceding to that or engaging in some intervention to look again at the piece in the light of the 'definition' that has been set up. This is clearly another argument for a flexible view of the poem, and pushes further into the background any concern with registering which poems 'pass' and which do not.

I wish in this section, however, to look at the question in a different way, taking the word 'poetry' as denoting a group of activities that add up to the practice of poetry in general – writing, reading, talking, criticizing, recommending, publishing, and so on. 'Is it poetry?' then means something like, 'Have these activities resembled the practice of poetry in this wide sense? Have they been a nourishing milieu for the poem itself?' I have tried to describe the child's poem as embedded in and emerging from a social milieu that enriches its extra-literary value and contributes to its literary value, and in terms of which it is to some extent at least explicable. 'Is it poetry?' then addresses not just the products but the process as well. The teacher asks: was the process 'poetry'? Were the children engaged with their poetry in the way that poets are with theirs?

I have tried to suggest that they were. The examples of children rewriting their work, discussing with each other how to improve their writing, saying what they like and why, collaborating on booklets, and so on, have been offered as illustrations of activities which in their most interrelated and active phases form a kind of eco-system, a lively social milieu for writing, that adds up to 'poetry' in this second sense. I should say therefore that what they have been doing 'is poetry' in this second sense too. And it is worth pointing out that it is possible to see this 'poetry', the activity of a serious and complete engagement, as intellectually more demanding than is often presumed. Louis Arnaud Reid remarks that 'The idea that the making and appreciation of art is a unique kind of insight and discovery, certainly not (pursued seriously) inferior to science, or history or moral judgement – is not only alien to the minds of many teachers; it is an idea of which there is little clear or explicit recognition anywhere.'[16] Even more alien might be the notion that children of 9 to 13 are so engaged. But that would be my interpretation of what, for a final example of such activity, I describe immediately below – some responses of the class mentioned immediately above to their viewing of the film *White Stallion*, some notes in preparation for writing, and some opinions of each others' work, all occurring during one brief part of a session. What they are doing is 'making and appreciating' in Reid's sense, and they seem to generate as much 'insight and discovery' as they could in any part of the curriculum. The recorded interchanges occurred in a fairly informal part of the session, when most of the class were trying to turn their notes into a first-draft poem.

In response to my suggestion, Rachel read out her notes about the moment when the boy and the old man are asleep and the boy dreams of Crin Blanc: 'His noble head/Turned towards the men, as if to say/Here we go again', she read. 'Like a poem,' someone said – articulating a view of the poem, and in 'criticism'. She had in fact lined out her pencil notes as if they were a first draft, moving on, without invitation, to a stage beyond 'notes'. So had James. He said, 'I'm writing lines, like a poem', and his neighbour Kim said, 'Sir, James has done a poem!' Several children at least were, as I saw it, placing what they had written against the idea of the poem that had been built up during the year. The way they speak suggests children's need continually to redefine what poems are as part of writing them, and in order to write them.

I wondered, I said, what the old man was dreaming, and asked if it seemed that he had always lived there. No, and yes. Kim said that he dreamed quietly; he probably always had lived there, 'the way he does things so easily, the nets'. The observation was his own; he had looked hard at the old man and seen – with 'insight' – beyond the old man's gestures and physical movements to something else. This perception immediately seemed to lead him further; he said that he was 'quiet and knowledgeable, like a prophet'. An interpretive 'discovery', then, an apprehension of wisdom and personal quiet. We focused on the stallion's head for a few moments, and his facial expression. Someone asked if the expression was 'sympathetic', 'ashamed', or what. Rachel said 'You can make it what you like... your imagination.' This again, was a perceptive and wholly artistic insight into the possibilities of working outwards creatively from the film rather than attempting to do a literal 'translation' into another medium. There were comments in the same conversation about the music. Christine said 'Music makes the film', a lovely insight into the artistic wholeness of the film, a 'discovery' of it as a single unified symbol rather than a set of symbols, to use Suzanne Langer's terminology.[17] Gareth then noted how 'The music changes from violent to calm.' In general, their collaborative 'appreciation' of the film seemed intellectually impressive; they went beneath the visual surfaces of what was depicted, interpreting the events as carrying meanings that were hidden in what was given, or seeing the possibility of further reinterpretation of what confronted them.

It might be objected that there is nothing remarkable about this; children talk like this all the time about films and stories. I should agree with the second statement, but not the first. About that I suggest that what is truly remarkable is that such activity is not seen as remarkable. Teachers are readily impressed, even bemused, by the speed and precocity of children's understanding of computers, for instance. In other less novel fields the perception of the remarkable may be dulled by familiarity, or it may simply not be seen because, as Reid suggests, there is a predisposition to interpret 'making and appreciation' as an

'But is it poetry?' 257

inferior, 'easier' kind of intellectual activity, so that its surface is taken note of, but not its meaning.

The discussion I have described was for me 'poetry', since poetry is the practice of poetry. Ultimately the most devitalizing perspectives are those that fail to acknowledge, continuously, this ecological dimension. The basic difficulty with objections such as Sybil Marshall's plausible-looking reservations about free verse, for example, which must show 'the same subtle choice of word and phrase, and the same disciplined organization, as any other form of poetry',[18] is that they implicitly invite attention only to the product. The appropriate appraisal would be of the overall context of production, and would invite the teacher to attend to the process of the poem's construction, the significance for the writer of what has been written, the interventionist dilemmas of the teacher as reader, editor, publisher, and so on. Nor does the narrowing of appraisal to judgements on poems take into account the fact that the most committed attempts to produce poems can end in sterility – as any poet knows. It is a narrowly literary–critical perspective in a context where a far broader pedagogic one is needed. To put it plainly, even if one cannot find anything good to say about a poem, some demonstration of faith is needed in any commitment that has gone into it; that seems pedagogically and socially preferable to the stance that says: this isn't poetry; poetry is subtle word choice, discipline, good images, and so on.

It also seems more more honestly consistent. The encouragement – even faith – that is implicit in saying 'I want you to look for good metaphors and write a poem using them' is denied in the gesture which answers merely, 'You haven't found any good ones – this isn't really a poem.' The pupil may well have been engaged on precisely that activity which one had asked of him or her; he or she has searched for metaphors but not found any. As so often, it is the word 'poem' that is the problem. It might be better to take the emphasis on poetry as activity one stage further and think of 'poem' as a verb masquerading as a noun. The pupil has, perhaps, been poeming, but hasn't discovered the things that one looks for when one goes poeming, just as one can 'go mushrooming' without finding a mushroom. It would be offensive to say to the empty-handed mushroomer that he has not in fact been mushrooming because there is no product; the empty hand isn't a mushroom. The empty lines where the poem might have been invite awareness that the writer may have been looking in the wrong places, or in the wrong way. 'This isn't a poem' asserts baldly that there has been no journey, no visit.

Philip Larkin remarked that 'Most of the time one is engaged in doing, or trying to do, something of which the value is doubtful and the mode of operation unclear... Yet writing a poem is not an act of the will... the poems that get written may seem trivial and unedifying, compared with those that don't.'[19] About the subject choices even of his maturity, he says, 'one can still make enormously time-wasting mistakes'. The teacher ought more often perhaps to admit these dimensions of possibility into the classroom; time ought to be wasted; the trivial and valueless ought to be allowed for and expected, as testimony to the truth of writing.

Notes

Preface

1 James Britton (1983) *Prospect and Retrospect – Selected Essays*, ed. Gordon M. Pradl, New Jersey: Boynton Cook, 214.
2 ibid.
3 Mary Jane Drummond, quoted in *The Times Educational Supplement*, 11 October 1985.
4 ibid.
5 Marjorie L. Hourd and Gertrude E. Cooper (1971) *Coming into Their Own*, London: Heinemann.
6 Britton, op. cit., 197.
7 ibid., 198.

1 'How do I get them to write poems?'

1 Answer: A Christmas cracker.
2 André Obey (1969) *Noah*, London: Heinemann.
3 Geoffrey Summerfield (ed.) (1971) *Creatures Moving*, Harmondsworth: Penguin.
4 Theodore Roethke (1985) *Collected Poems*, London: Faber & Faber.

2 A new class

1. Helen Cresswell (1985) 'Particle Goes Green', in Sara and Stephen Corrin (eds) *Stories for Nine-Year-Olds*, Harmondsworth: Puffin, 17.
2. Sara and Stephen Corrin (1985) *Stories for Tens and Over*, Harmondsworth: Puffin.
3. Bill Naughton (1968) *The Goalkeeper's Revenge and Other Stories*, Harmondsworth: Puffin.
4. Ian Seraillier (1984) *The Labours of Heracles*, London: Heinemann Educational.
5. (1984) *The Second Cadbury Book of Children's Poetry*, London: Beaver.
6. Myra Cohn Livingstone (1984) *The Child as Poet: Myth or Reality*, New York: Horn Books.
7. Ted Hughes, (1967) *Poetry in the Making*, London: Faber & Faber, 56.
8. Ted Hughes (1976) *Season Songs*, London: Faber & Faber, 63, 41.
9. Beatrice Furner (1975), in Richard L. Larson (ed.) *Children and Writing in the Elementary School*, Oxford: Oxford University Press, 162.
10. Robert Witkin (1974) *The Intelligence of Feeling*, London: Heinemann Educational, 170.

3 New subjects

1. Ian Seraillier (1984) *The Labours of Heracles*, London: Heinemann Educational.
2. Rex Warner (1950) *Men and Gods*, London: Heinemann Educational, 35, 125.

4 Children's autonomy

1. Ted Hughes (1970) *The Coming of the Kings*, London: Faber & Faber.
2. Peter Abbs (1982) *English Within the Arts*, London: Hodder & Stoughton.
3. Rex Warner (1950) *Men and Gods*, London: Heinemann Educational, 141.
4. Wallace Stevens, Letter 505, quoted in Frank Doggatt (1980) *Wallace Stevens, The Making of the Poem*, Baltimore: Johns Hopkins University Press, 9.

5 Wallace Stevens, Letter 274, quoted in Doggatt, op. cit., 18.
6 Donald Graves (1983) *Writing: Teachers and Children at Work*, London: Heinemann Educational, 78.

5 Intervention

1 Ted Hughes (1967) *Poetry in the Making*, London: Faber & Faber, 100.
2 Marie Peel (1968) *Seeing to the Heart*, London, Chatto & Windus, 15.
3 A.A. Milne (1927) *Now We Are Six*, London: Methuen.
4 Valerie Eliot (ed.) (1971) *The Waste Land — Facsimile and transcript of original, including annotations by Pound*, London: Faber & Faber.
5 I.V. Hansen (1970) *The Year's Turning*, London: Edward Arnold, 5.
6 Donald Graves (1983) *Writing: Teachers and Children at Work*, London: Heinemann Educational.

6 Literary models

1 Ted Hughes (1970) *The Coming of the Kings*, London: Faber & Faber, 31.
2 Anna Akhmatova, quoted in Amanda Haight (1976) *A Poetic Pilgrimage*, Oxford: Oxford University Press, 179.
3 Seamus Heaney and Ted Hughes (eds) (1982) *The Rattle Bag*, London: Faber & Faber.
4 James Liu, *Art of Chinese Poetry*, quoted in G.D. Martin (1975) *Language, Truth and Poetry*, Edinburgh: Edinburgh University Press, 211.
5 A.R. Davis (ed.) (1962) *The Penguin Book of Chinese Verse*, Harmondsworth: Penguin.
6 Arthur Waley (1961) *Chinese Poems*, London: Unwin Books.
7 Robert Payne (ed.) (1947) *The White Pony*, New York: Mentor.
8 ibid., xiii.
9 ibid., 112.
10 ibid., 271.
11 A. R. Davis, op. cit., 13.

7 The world out there

1. George Saunders (ed.) (1970) *I Took My Mind A Walk*, Harmondsworth: Penguin.
2. Norman MacCaig (1971) *Surroundings*, London: Chatto & Windus.
3. W. Hart-Smith (1985) *Selected Poems 1936–1984*, London: Angus & Robertson.
4. Martin Buber (1970) 'Between man and man', *Education* 3: 90.
5. Liam Hudson (1972) *Contrary Imaginations*, Harmondsworth: Penguin, 136.
6. David Holbrook (1979) *English for Meaning*, Windsor: NFER.

8 Other contexts

1. Siegfried Kracauer (1965) *Theory of Film*, Oxford: Oxford University Press, *passim*.
2. Miroslav Holub (1967) *Selected Poems*, Harmondsworth: Penguin.

9 Products and relations

1. (1984) *The Second Cadbury Book of Children's Poetry*, London: Beaver.
2. Robert Westall (1984) *The Machine Gunners*, Harmondsworth: Puffin.
3. (1983) *Dragons*, Harlow: Longman.

10 'But is it poetry?'

1. Sybil Marshall (1976) *Creative Writing*, London: Macmillan Education, 16.
2. ibid., 16.
3. S.M. Lane and J. Kemp (1967) *An Approach to Creative Writing in the Primary School*, Glasgow: Blackie, 35.
4. ibid., 40.
5. Barry Maybury (1967) *Creative Writing for Juniors*, London: Batsford, 57.
6. Bing Xin, from 'A maze of stars', quoted in *Agenda* 20, no. 3/4 (Autumn 1982): 78.

7 K. Chukovsky (1963) *From Two to Five*, trans. Norton, Los Angeles: California University Press, 2.
8 ibid., 71.
9 ibid., 70.
10 Sybil Marshall, op. cit., 16.
11 W.H. Auden (1963) *The Dyer's Hand*, London: Faber & Faber, 23.
12 Mary Louise Pratt (1977) *Towards a Speech Act Theory of Literary Discourse*, Bloomington: Indiana University Press, 129.
13 ibid., 5.
14 ibid., 87.
15 Slovskij, quoted in Mary Louise Pratt, op. cit., 88.
16 Louis Arnaud Reid (1969) *Meaning in the Arts*, London: Allen & Unwin, 270.
17 Suzanne Langer (1984) *Mind, An Essay on Human Feeling*, Baltimore: Johns Hopkins University Press, 84.
18 Sybil Marshall, op. cit., 16.
19 Philip Larkin (1983) *Required Writing*, London: Faber & Faber, 83–4.

Index

Abbs, P. 103
academic writing ix, 5–6, 245;
 see also creativity, teaching
Akhamatova, A. 143
anxiety, teacher's 16–18, 27, 208;
 see also new class
Auden, W. H. 248
autonomy, children's 9–11, 13,
 36, 50, 81–114; and dependency
 104–6; and routine 99; *see also*
 revisions, group criticism

Bing Xin 246
Britton, J. vii
Buber, M. 179

Chukovsky, K. 246
classrooms, neglect of ix, 103
communal writing: beginnings
 52–8, 59–62, 125–7; choices
 60–1; and group talk 129–33;
 see also group criticism
consultations 117–19, 121–5
creativity: block to 79–83;
 claims of 30; and gestation
 74, 107–8; and intervention
 69–70; models of 47–51, 103–4;
 neglect of 222–3; teacher's 116,
 119–21; and work 106–8; *see
 also* imitation

Drummond, M. J. vii

evaluation x; pupils' 184–6, 210
expectations, teachers' 33, 36,
 39, 46, 63, 95, 154, 245–6
experience, children's 176,
 198–201, 217–19

failure, teacher's sense of 17–20,
 27, 49–50; *see also* new class
film: cinema 187–97; visual
 poetry of 190–2
film: video 33, 42, 77, 151,
 202–3, 214, 231
finding one's place 28, 35–8,
 41–6
Furner, B. 47

Graves, D. 108
group criticism
 160–2, 232–5

Hansen, I. 119
Hart-Smith, W. H. 169
Holbrook, D. 186
Holub, M. 202
Hourd, M. x
Hudson, L. 186
Hughes, T. 98, 115, 140

imitation, of literary models
 140–66; and creativity 143–6;
 and emulation 142–3; not
 parody 140–1; and tradition
 155–6
interdisciplinary work 212–20
interventions, teacher's 12, 13,
 115–37, 162, 226; and
 interference 83, 119–20,
 179–80; and 'teaching' 126–7

Kracauer, S. 188

Lane, S. M. and Kemp, J. 244
Langer, S. 256
Larkin, P. 258
Liu, J. 147
Livingstone, M. C. 30

MacCaig, N. 169
Marshall, S. 244
Maybury, B. 244
misreadings 28–9, 251
myth 52–3, 197–201; and
 personal experience 200

new class 16–50; *see also*
 anxiety, expectations, failure,
 relation, teaching
new topics, unpredictability of
 51–2

observation 42, 167–86;
 'framing' of 170–2, 174–5; and
 metaphor 175

openness 21; offers of 22–3, 50; *see also* new class

Payne, R. 147
Peel, M. 116
Penguin English Project 9, 169
Picture Box 33, 48
pleasure, children's in writing xi, 50, 136–7, 242
poems: children's responses to 147–51; idea of 54, 243, 247–50; and 'notes' 33, 77, 203, 207–8; and 'phrases' 53–4; and 'poetic' subjects 40; process of 2; and prose 25, 247–53; and rhyme 31, 37; and science 172–4 (*see also* science); and skill 244–6; uncertain origins of 2–6
poetry, practice of 254–8; *see also* poems
Pratt, M. L. 248
products 162, 222–42; *see also* relation
putting work to one side 73, 159

reappraisal, teacher's 20–31, 43–4; and detachment 26
Reid, L. A. 256
relation, of children to writing 50, 64, 74, 222–42; 'authentic' 89; and group talk 136–7; indications of 227; of individuals 41–6, 109–14, 227–8; relationship, of teacher and children 23, 26, 34–5; and unfamiliarity 26

revisions, children's of their own writing 44, 66–7, 89–92, 92–8, 98–102, 129–33, 133–8, 163–6, 219
routine busy-ness 212
routine judgements 28–9, 58–9, 93, revision of 28–30, 153–4

science 201–12
Serraillier, I. 26
Slovskij 250
Stevens, W. 107
stimulus 47–8, 102–4, 244–5

teaching: and accountability xi; complexity of 27; emotionality of 46; and institutional pressure 30–1; knowledge about 6; and listening 85; mechanistic model of 47–51; in 1980s vii; 'results' of 11, 35, 39, 50, 123–4, 185–6, 238; routine images of 75–6; strategies 6; theory of ix, 5, 76; *see also* autonomy, interventions, new class

uncertainty, teacher's 17, 63; *see also* new class

waiting, teacher's 35–41; *see also* new class
Witkin, R. 47

For Product Safety Concerns and Information please contact our EU representative GPSR@taylorandfrancis.com
Taylor & Francis Verlag GmbH, Kaufingerstraße 24, 80331 München, Germany

www.ingramcontent.com/pod-product-compliance
Lightning Source LLC
Chambersburg PA
CBHW060557230426
43670CB00011B/1854